PEARSON

Supplement for Calculus for the Life Sciences

Custom Edition for Penn State University

Taken from:
Calculus: Early Transcendentals, Second Edition
by William Briggs, Lyle Cochran, Bernard Gillett, and Eric Schulz

Finite Mathematics and Calculus with Applications, Tenth Edition
by Margaret L. Lial, Raymond N. Greenwell, and Nathan P. Ritchey

Additional Topics for Calculus for Life Sciences, Second Edition
by Raymond N. Greenwell, Nathan P. Ritchey, and Margaret L. Lial

Thomas' Calculus, Thirteenth Edition
by George B. Thomas, Jr., Maurice D. Weir, Joel Hass, and Christopher Heil

Cover Art: Courtesy of PhotoDisc and Getty Images

Taken from:

Calculus: Early Transcendentals, Second Edition
by William Briggs, Lyle Cochran, Bernard Gillett, and Eric Schulz
Copyright © 2015, 2011 by Pearson Education, Inc.
New York, New York 10013

Finite Mathematics and Calculus with Applications, Tenth Edition
by Margaret L. Lial, Raymond N. Greenwell, and Nathan P. Ritchey
Copyright © 2016 by Pearson Education, Inc.
New York, New York 10013

Additional Topics for Calculus for Life Sciences, Second Edition
by Raymond N. Greenwell, Nathan P. Ritchey, and Margaret L. Lial
Copyright © 2015 by Pearson Education, Inc.
New York, New York 10013

Thomas' Calculus, Thirteenth Edition
by George B. Thomas, Jr., Maurice D. Weir, Joel Hass, and Christopher Heil
Copyright © 2014, 2010, 2008 by Pearson Education, Inc.
New York, New York 10013

This special edition published in cooperation with Pearson Learning Solutions.

All trademarks, service marks, registered trademarks, and registered service marks are the property of their respective owners and are used herein for identification purposes only.

Pearson Learning Solutions, 501 Boylston Street, Suite 900, Boston, MA 02116
A Pearson Education Company
www.pearsoned.com

Printed in the United States of America

1 2 3 4 5 6 7 8 9 10 V092 18 17 16 15

000200010271966624

TG

ISBN 10: 1-323-14205-3
ISBN 13: 978-1-323-14205-9

Contents

The Intermediate Value Theorem

Suppose that during a road trip, we travel by car at speeds that range from 0 mph to 65 mph. The speed of a car moving along the highway is a continuous function and we can conclude that somewhere during the trip, we were driving exactly 40 mph. For that matter, there is at least one point in the trip that we were driving every speed between 0 mph and 65 mph.

This is an example of the *Intermediate Value Theorem*. Geometrically, the Intermediate Value Theorem states that if f is continuous on the Interval $[a, b]$ and k is a number between $f(a)$ and $f(b)$, then the graph of f intersects the line $y = k$ at least once, as shown in Figure 1.

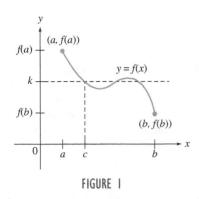

FIGURE 1

For a function f that is continuous on $[a, b]$, there is at least one intermediate value, such as c, for which the graph of f intersects the line $y = k$.

THEOREM 1: The Intermediate Value Theorem

Suppose f is a function that is continuous on the interval $[a, b]$ and k is any number between $f(a)$ and $f(b)$. Then there is at least one number c between a and b with $f(c) = k$.

Figure 1 shows that more than one intersection can occur. The Intermediate Value Theorem guarantees that there is *at least* one.

The proof of this theorem uses the Completeness Property of the real numbers and will have to wait for a more advanced course.

EXAMPLE 1   Using the Intermediate Value Theorem

Let $f(x) = x^3 - 2x - 5$. Use the Intermediate Value Theorem to show that there is a number c such that $f(c) = 0$.

SOLUTION

Since f is a polynomial function, f is continuous at each real number. Also, $f(1) = -6$ and $f(3) = 16$, so $f(1) < 0 < f(3)$, as illustrated in Figure 2 generated by a graphing calculator. The Intermediate Value theorem ensures that there is a number c in $(1, 3)$ with $f(c) = 0$.

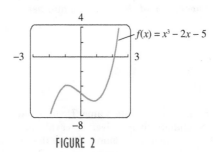

FIGURE 2

The Intermediate Value Theorem guarantees $f(c) = 0$ for some c.

By successively applying the Intermediate Value Theorem, it is possible to determine an approximate value of c for which $f(c) = 0$. For the function described in Example 1. Figure 3 indicates that $f(2) < 0 < f(2.2)$. By the Intermediate Value Theorem, there exists a number c in $(2, 2.2)$ such that $f(c) = 0$. By "zooming-in" further, Figure 4 indicates that

$f(2.05) < 0 < f(2.15)$. The Intermediate Value Theorem implies that there exists a number c in (2.05, 2.15) such that $f(c) = 0$. As the figure suggests, a reasonable estimate for c is $c \approx 2.09$. In fact, $f(2.09) = -0.05$. Further applications of the Intermediate Value Theorem can produce an even better approximation for c.

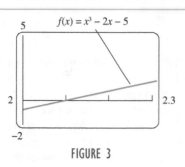

FIGURE 3

Zooming in on c in Figure 2

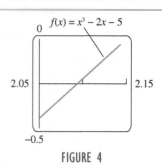

FIGURE 4

Zooming in still Further in Figure 3

The Intermediate Value Theorem requires that the function be continuous on the interval [a, b]. If a function is *not* continuous, then it may *not* be possible to satisfy the conclusions of the theorem. For example, in Figure 5, no input value c exists for which $f(c) = 1.5$ on [0, 2].

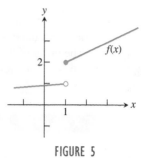

FIGURE 5

Since f is not continuous, the Intermediate Value Theorem does not apply.

EXERCISES

In Exercises 1–4, a function f, an interval [a, b] and a number k between $f(a)$ and $f(b)$ are given. Verify that the conclusion of the Intermediate Value Theorem holds by finding a number c in (a, b) with $f(c) = k$.

1. $f(x) = 7x - 4$, [1, 3], $k = 15$

2. $f(x) = x^2 - 1$, [−1, 2], $k = 2$

3. $f(x) = x^3 + 1$, [−2, 3], $k = 9$

4. $f(x) = x^2 + 5x + 3$, [−3, 1], $k = 1$

In Exercise 5–10, (a) use the Intermediate Value Theorem to show that $f(x) = 0$ has a solution on the given interval, and (b) use technology to determine an approximate solution that is accurate to within 10^{-1}.

5. $f(x) = x^3 - 2x^2 - 5$, [2, 3]

6. $f(x) = x^3 - x - 1$, [1, 2]

7. $f(x) = x^3 - 9x^2 + 12$, [−2, 0]

8. $f(x) = x^3 - 9x^2 + 12$, [8, 9]

9. $f(x) = \cos x - x$, [0, $\pi/2$]

10. $f(x) = x - 0.2 \sin x - 0.8$, [0, $\pi/2$]

11. *Soda Pop* A machine that fills two-liter bottles of soda dispenses $p(t) = 0.1t^2 + 2t$ liters of soda in t seconds. *Source: Chris Boucher.*

a. How long does it take the machine to fill a two-liter bottle?

b. The machine is programmed to dispense soda for 0.954 seconds into each bottle, but it is an old machine and sometimes its timing mechanism is off by as much as 0.1 second. If the plastic bottles used in the process hold 2.04 liters of soda before overflowing, will there be soda on the floor at the end of the day?

c. If the plant wants to be sure that each bottle contains between 1.96 and 2.04 liters of soda, how accurate must the time on the machine be?

d. Suppose the dispensing function p turned out to be

$$p(t) = \begin{cases} 0.1t^2 + 2t, & \text{if } 0 \le t \le 0.954. \\ 0.1t^2 + 2t + 0.1, & \text{if } t > 0.954. \end{cases}$$

What difficulty will the plant have?

12. *Construction* A box is to be constructed from six square pieces of plywood, each 0.5 inches thick. The volume of the box must be within 1 cubic inch of 125 cubic inches. How accurately must the six pieces of plywood be measured? ***Source: Chris Boucher.***

13. *Chemistry** Fahrenheit and Celsius temperatures are related by the equation $C = \dfrac{5}{9}(F - 32)$. If a chemistry experiment must be performed at 30°C with an error of no more than 2°C, how accurate must your Fahrenheit thermometer be to effectively carry out the experiment? ***Source: Chris Boucher.***

14. Suppose that a wildlife biologist is walking along a path to a research station. The biologist starts her three hour hike at 8 am and continues to walk non stop toward her destination. Once she reaches her destination she spends the rest of the day collecting samples. The next morning, at 8 am, she begins her journey back along the same path to the spot where her journey began. Use the Intermediate Value Theorem to argue that there is place on the path where the biologist will cross at the same time of day on both days.

15. Suppose that a bike enthusiast decides to take a Rails to Trails path on a six hour bike ride from one town to another. The biker begins the trip at 6 am, completes the trip non stop, and then spends the rest of the day and night at his destination. The very next morning, at 6 am, he rides his bike back along the same trail to his point of departure. Use the Intermediate Value Theorem to argue that there is point on the trail where the biker will cross at the same time of day on both days.

*Contributed by Chris Boucher

3.1 Extension B

Sequences and Limits

The previous section sets the stage for an in-depth investigation of sequences and infinite series. This section is devoted to sequences, and the remainder of the chapter deals with series.

Limit of a Sequence and Limit Laws

A fundamental question about sequences concerns the behavior of the terms as we go out farther and farther in the sequence. For example, in the sequence

$$\{a_n\}_{n=0}^{\infty} = \left\{\frac{1}{n^2 + 1}\right\}_{n=0}^{\infty} = \left\{1, \frac{1}{2}, \frac{1}{5}, \frac{1}{10}, \dots\right\},$$

the terms remain positive and decrease to 0. We say that this sequence converges and its limit is 0, written $\lim\limits_{n\to\infty} a_n = 0$. Similarly, the terms of the sequence

$$\{b_n\}_{n=1}^{\infty} = \left\{(-1)^n \frac{n(n + 1)}{2}\right\}_{n=1}^{\infty} = \{-1, 3, -6, 10, \dots\}$$

increase in magnitude and do not approach a unique value as n increases. In this case, we say that the sequence diverges.

Limits of sequences are really no different from limits at infinity of functions except that the variable n assumes only integer values as $n \to \infty$. This idea works as follows.

Given a sequence $\{a_n\}$, we define a function f such that $f(n) = a_n$ for all indices n. For example, if $a_n = n/(n + 1)$, then we let $f(x) = x/(x + 1)$. We know that $\lim\limits_{x\to\infty} f(x) = 1$; because the terms of the sequence lie on the graph of f, it follows that $\lim\limits_{n\to\infty} a_n = 1$ (Figure 1). This reasoning is the basis of the following theorem.

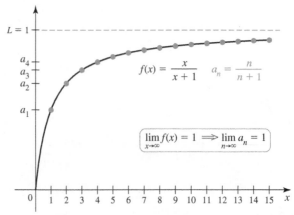

Figure 1

▶ The converse of Theorem 2 is not true. For example, if $a_n = \cos 2\pi n$, then $\lim\limits_{n\to\infty} a_n = 1$, but $\lim\limits_{x\to\infty} \cos 2\pi x$ does not exist.

> **THEOREM 1   Limits of Sequences from Limits of Functions**
> Suppose f is a function such that $f(n) = a_n$ for all positive integers n. If $\lim\limits_{x\to\infty} f(x) = L$, then the limit of the sequence $\{a_n\}$ is also L.

Because of the correspondence between limits of sequences and limits of functions at infinity, we have the following properties that are analogous to those for functions.

▶ The limit of a sequence $\{a_n\}$ is determined by the terms in the *tail* of the sequence—the terms with large values of n. If the sequences $\{a_n\}$ and $\{b_n\}$ differ in their first 100 terms but have identical terms for $n > 100$, then they have the same limit. For this reason, the initial index of a sequence (for example, $n = 0$ or $n = 1$) is often not specified.

> **THEOREM 2   Limit Laws for Sequences**
> Assume that the sequences $\{a_n\}$ and $\{b_n\}$ have limits A and B, respectively. Then
>
> **1.** $\lim\limits_{n\to\infty} (a_n \pm b_n) = A \pm B$
>
> **2.** $\lim\limits_{n\to\infty} ca_n = cA$, where c is a real number
>
> **3.** $\lim\limits_{n\to\infty} a_n b_n = AB$
>
> **4.** $\lim\limits_{n\to\infty} \dfrac{a_n}{b_n} = \dfrac{A}{B}$, provided $B \neq 0$.

EXAMPLE 1   Limits of sequences Determine the limits of the following sequences.

a. $a_n = \dfrac{3n^3}{n^3 + 1}$ **b.** $b_n = \left(\dfrac{n + 5}{n}\right)^n$ **c.** $c_n = n^{1/n}$

SOLUTION

a. A function with the property that $f(n) = a_n$ is $f(x) = \dfrac{3x^3}{x^3 + 1}$. Dividing numerator and denominator by x^3, we find that $\lim\limits_{x\to\infty} f(x) = 3$. (Alternatively, we can apply l'Hôpital's Rule and obtain the same result.) We conclude that $\lim\limits_{n\to\infty} a_n = 3$.

b. The limit

$$\lim_{n\to\infty} b_n = \lim_{n\to\infty} \left(\frac{n + 5}{n}\right)^n = \lim_{n\to\infty} \left(1 + \frac{5}{n}\right)^n$$

has the indeterminate form 1^∞. Recall that for this limit, we first evaluate

$$L = \lim_{n\to\infty} \ln\left(1 + \frac{5}{n}\right)^n = \lim_{n\to\infty} n \ln\left(1 + \frac{5}{n}\right),$$

▶ When using l'Hôpital's Rule, it is customary to treat n as a continuous variable and differentiate with respect to n, rather than write the sequence as a function of x, as was done in Example 1a.

and then, if L exists, $\lim\limits_{n\to\infty} b_n = e^L$. Using l'Hôpital's Rule for the indeterminate form $0/0$, we have

$$L = \lim_{n\to\infty} n \ln\left(1 + \frac{5}{n}\right) = \lim_{n\to\infty} \frac{\ln\left(1 + (5/n)\right)}{1/n} \quad \text{Indeterminate form } 0/0$$

$$= \lim_{n\to\infty} \frac{\dfrac{1}{1 + (5/n)}\left(-\dfrac{5}{n^2}\right)}{-1/n^2} \quad \text{L'Hôpital's Rule}$$

$$= \lim_{n\to\infty} \frac{5}{1 + (5/n)} = 5. \quad \text{Simplify; } 5/n \to 0 \text{ as } n \to \infty.$$

▶ For a review of l'Hôpital's Rule, we showed that $\lim\limits_{x\to\infty} \left(1 + \dfrac{a}{x}\right)^x = e^a$.

Because $\lim\limits_{n\to\infty} b_n = e^L = e^5$, we have $\lim\limits_{n\to\infty} \left(\dfrac{5 + n}{n}\right)^n = e^5$.

c. The limit has the indeterminate form ∞^0, so we first evaluate $L = \lim\limits_{n\to\infty} \ln n^{1/n} = \lim\limits_{n\to\infty} \dfrac{\ln n}{n}$; if L exists, then $\lim\limits_{n\to\infty} c_n = e^L$. Using either l'Hôpital's Rule or the relative growth rates, we find that $L = 0$. Therefore, $\lim\limits_{n\to\infty} c_n = e^0 = 1$.

Related Exercises 9–34 ◄

Terminology for Sequences

We now introduce some terminology for sequences that is similar to that used for functions. The following terms are used to describe sequences $\{a_n\}$.

> **DEFINITIONS Terminology for Sequences**
>
> $\{a_n\}$ is **increasing** if $a_{n+1} > a_n$; for example, $\{0, 1, 2, 3, \ldots\}$.
>
> $\{a_n\}$ is **nondecreasing** if $a_{n+1} \geq a_n$; for example, $\{1, 1, 2, 2, 3, 3, \ldots\}$.
>
> $\{a_n\}$ is **decreasing** if $a_{n+1} < a_n$; for example, $\{2, 1, 0, -1, \ldots\}$.
>
> $\{a_n\}$ is **nonincreasing** if $a_{n+1} \leq a_n$; for example, $\{0, -1, -1, -2, -2, -3, -3, \ldots\}$.
>
> $\{a_n\}$ is **monotonic** if it is either nonincreasing or nondecreasing (it moves in one direction).
>
> $\{a_n\}$ is **bounded** if there is number M such that $|a_n| \leq M$, for all relevant values of n.

> ➤ Because an increasing sequence is, by definition, nondecreasing, it is also monotonic. Similarly, a decreasing sequence is monotonic.

For example, the sequence

$$\{a_n\} = \left\{ 1 - \frac{1}{n} \right\}_{n=1}^{\infty} = \left\{ 0, \frac{1}{2}, \frac{2}{3}, \frac{3}{4}, \ldots \right\}$$

satisfies $|a_n| \leq 1$, for $n \geq 1$, and its terms are increasing in size. Therefore, the sequence is bounded and increasing; it is also monotonic (Figure 2). The sequence

$$\{a_n\} = \left\{ 1 + \frac{1}{n} \right\}_{n=1}^{\infty} = \left\{ 2, \frac{3}{2}, \frac{4}{3}, \frac{5}{4}, \ldots \right\}$$

satisfies $|a_n| \leq 2$, for $n \geq 1$, and its terms are decreasing in size. Therefore, the sequence is bounded and decreasing; it is also monotonic (Figure 2).

QUICK CHECK 1 Classify the following sequences as bounded, monotonic, or neither.

a. $\left\{ \frac{1}{2}, \frac{3}{4}, \frac{7}{8}, \frac{15}{16}, \ldots \right\}$

b. $\left\{ 1, -\frac{1}{2}, \frac{1}{4}, -\frac{1}{8}, \frac{1}{16}, \ldots \right\}$

c. $\{ 1, -2, 3, -4, 5, \ldots \}$

d. $\{ 1, 1, 1, 1, \ldots \}$ ◄

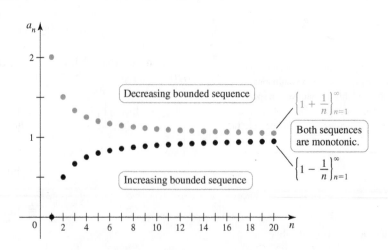

Figure 2

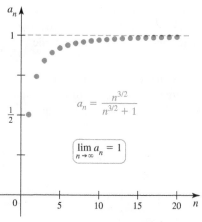

Figure 3

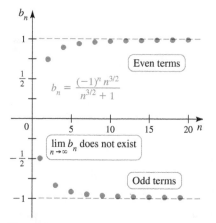

Figure 4

EXAMPLE 2 Limits of sequences and graphing Compare and contrast the behavior of $\{a_n\}$ and $\{b_n\}$ as $n \to \infty$.

a. $a_n = \dfrac{n^{3/2}}{n^{3/2} + 1}$ **b.** $b_n = \dfrac{(-1)^n \, n^{3/2}}{n^{3/2} + 1}$

SOLUTION

a. The terms of $\{a_n\}$ are positive, increasing, and bounded (Figure 3). Dividing the numerator and denominator of a_n by $n^{3/2}$, we see that

$$\lim_{n \to \infty} a_n = \lim_{n \to \infty} \frac{n^{3/2}}{n^{3/2} + 1} = \lim_{n \to \infty} \frac{1}{1 + \underbrace{\frac{1}{n^{3/2}}}_{\text{approaches 0 as } n \to \infty}} = 1.$$

b. The terms of the bounded sequence $\{b_n\}$ alternate in sign. Using the result of part (a), it follows that the even terms form an increasing sequence that approaches 1 and the odd terms form a decreasing sequence that approaches -1 (Figure 4). Therefore, the sequence diverges, illustrating the fact that the presence of $(-1)^n$ may significantly alter the behavior of a sequence.

Related Exercises 35–44 ◄

Geometric Sequences

Geometric sequences have the property that each term is obtained by multiplying the previous term by a fixed constant, called the **ratio**. They have the form $\{r^n\}$ or $\{ar^n\}$, where the ratio r and $a \neq 0$ are real numbers.

EXAMPLE 3   Geometric sequences Graph the following sequences and discuss their behavior.

a. $\{0.75^n\}$ **b.** $\{(-0.75)^n\}$ **c.** $\{1.15^n\}$ **d.** $\{(-1.15)^n\}$

SOLUTION

a. When a number less than 1 in magnitude is raised to increasing powers, the resulting numbers decrease to zero. The sequence $\{0.75^n\}$ converges to zero and is monotonic (Figure 5).

b. Note that $\{(-0.75)^n\} = \{(-1)^n 0.75^n\}$. Observe also that the factor $(-1)^n$ oscillates between 1 and -1, while 0.75^n decreases to zero as n increases. Therefore, the sequence oscillates and converges to zero (Figure 6).

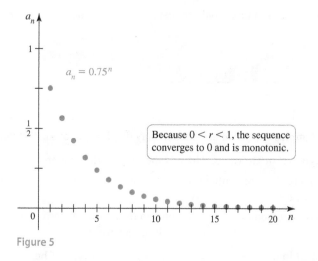

Figure 5

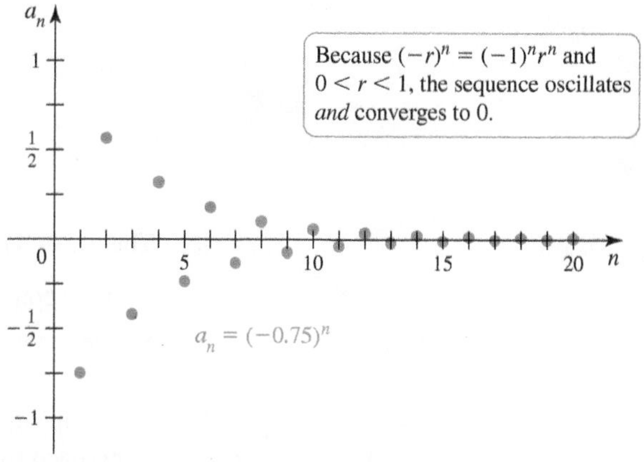

Figure 6

c. When a number greater than 1 in magnitude is raised to increasing powers, the resulting numbers increase in magnitude. The terms of the sequence $\{1.15^n\}$ are positive and increase without bound. In this case, the sequence diverges and is monotonic (Figure 7).

d. We write $\{(-1.15)^n\} = \{(-1)^n \, 1.15^n\}$ and observe that $(-1)^n$ oscillates between 1 and -1, while 1.15^n increases without bound as n increases. The terms of the sequence increase in magnitude without bound and alternate in sign. In this case, the sequence oscillates and diverges (Figure 8).

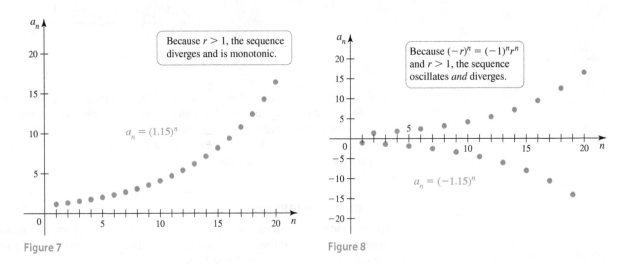

Because $r > 1$, the sequence diverges and is monotonic.

$a_n = (1.15)^n$

Figure 7

Because $(-r)^n = (-1)^n r^n$ and $r > 1$, the sequence oscillates *and* diverges.

$a_n = (-1.15)^n$

Figure 8

Related Exercises 45–52 ◀

QUICK CHECK 2 Describe the behavior of $\{r^n\}$ in the cases $r = -1$ and $r = 1$. ◀

The results of Example 3 and Quick Check 2 are summarized in the following theorem.

THEOREM 3 Geometric Sequences
Let r be a real number. Then

$$\lim_{n \to \infty} r^n = \begin{cases} 0 & \text{if } |r| < 1 \\ 1 & \text{if } r = 1 \\ \text{does not exist} & \text{if } r \le -1 \text{ or } r > 1. \end{cases}$$

If $r > 0$, then $\{r^n\}$ is a monotonic sequence. If $r < 0$, then $\{r^n\}$ oscillates.

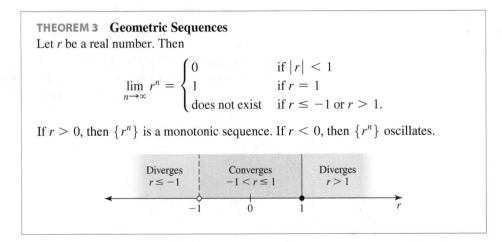

The previous examples show that a sequence may display any of the following behaviors:

• It may converge to a single value, which is the limit of the sequence.

• Its terms may increase in magnitude without bound (either with one sign or with mixed signs), in which case the sequence diverges.

• Its terms may remain bounded but settle into an oscillating pattern in which the terms approach two or more values; in this case, the sequence diverges.

Not illustrated in the preceding examples is one other type of behavior: The terms of a sequence may remain bounded, but wander chaotically forever without a pattern. In this case, the sequence also diverges (see the Guided Project *Chaos!*)

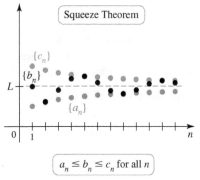

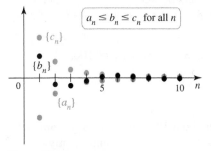

Figure 9

Figure 10

The Squeeze Theorem

We cite two theorems that are used to evaluate limits and to establish that limits exist. The first theorem is a direct analog of the Squeeze Theorem.

> **THEOREM 4   Squeeze Theorem for Sequences**
> Let $\{a_n\}$, $\{b_n\}$, and $\{c_n\}$ be sequences with $a_n \le b_n \le c_n$ for all integers n greater than some index N. If $\lim\limits_{n \to \infty} a_n = \lim\limits_{n \to \infty} c_n = L$, then $\lim\limits_{n \to \infty} b_n = L$ (Figure 9).

EXAMPLE 4   Squeeze Theorem Find the limit of the sequence $b_n = \dfrac{\cos n}{n^2 + 1}$.

SOLUTION The goal is to find two sequences $\{a_n\}$ and $\{c_n\}$ whose terms lie below and above the terms of the given sequence $\{b_n\}$. Note that $-1 \le \cos n \le 1$, for all n. Therefore,

$$\underbrace{-\frac{1}{n^2 + 1}}_{a_n} \le \underbrace{\frac{\cos n}{n^2 + 1}}_{b_n} \le \underbrace{\frac{1}{n^2 + 1}}_{c_n}.$$

Letting $a_n = -\dfrac{1}{n^2 + 1}$ and $c_n = \dfrac{1}{n^2 + 1}$, we have $a_n \le b_n \le c_n$, for $n \ge 1$. Furthermore, $\lim\limits_{n \to \infty} a_n = \lim\limits_{n \to \infty} c_n = 0$. By the Squeeze Theorem, $\lim\limits_{n \to \infty} b_n = 0$ (Figure 10).

Related Exercises 53–58 ◄

Bounded Monotonic Sequence Theorem

Suppose you pour a cup of hot coffee and put it on your desk to cool. Assume that every minute you measure the temperature of the coffee to create a sequence of temperature readings $\{T_1, T_2, T_3, \dots \}$. This sequence has two notable properties: First, the terms of the sequence are decreasing (because the coffee is cooling); and second, the sequence is bounded below (because the temperature of the coffee cannot be less than the temperature of the surrounding room). In fact, if the measurements continue indefinitely, the sequence of temperatures converges to the temperature of the room. This example illustrates an important theorem that characterizes convergent sequences in terms of boundedness and monotonicity. The theorem is easy to believe, but its proof is beyond the scope of this text.

> **THEOREM 5   Bounded Monotonic Sequences**
> A bounded monotonic sequence converges.

► **Some optional terminology** M is called an *upper bound* of the first sequence in Figure 11a, and N is a *lower bound* of the second sequence in Figure 11b. The number M^* is the *least upper bound* of a sequence (or a set) if it is the smallest of all the upper bounds. It is a fundamental property of the real numbers that if a sequence (or a nonempty set) is bounded above, then it has a least upper bound. It can be shown that an increasing sequence that is bounded above converges to its least upper bound. Similarly, a decreasing sequence that is bounded below converges to its greatest lower bound.

Figure 11 shows the two cases of this theorem. In the first case, we see a nondecreasing sequence, all of whose terms are less than M. It must converge to a limit less than or equal to M. Similarly, a nonincreasing sequence, all of whose terms are greater than N, must converge to a limit greater than or equal to N.

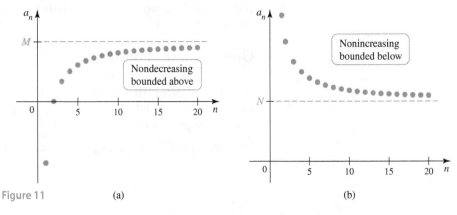

Figure 11   (a)   (b)

An Application: Recurrence Relations

▶ Most drugs decay exponentially in the bloodstream and have a characteristic half-life assuming that the drug absorbs quickly into the blood.

EXAMPLE 5   Sequences for drug doses Suppose your doctor prescribes a 100-mg dose of an antibiotic to be taken every 12 hours. Furthermore, the drug is known to have a half-life of 12 hours; that is, every 12 hours half of the drug in your blood is eliminated.

a. Find the sequence that gives the amount of drug in your blood immediately after each dose.

b. Use a graph to propose the limit of this sequence; that is, in the long run, how much drug do you have in your blood?

c. Find the limit of the sequence directly.

SOLUTION

a. Let d_n be the amount of drug in the blood immediately following the nth dose, where $n = 1, 2, 3, \ldots$ and $d_1 = 100$ mg. We want to write a recurrence relation that gives the amount of drug in the blood after the $(n + 1)$st dose (d_{n+1}) in terms of the amount of drug after the nth dose (d_n). In the 12 hours between the nth dose and the $(n + 1)$st dose, half of the drug in the blood is eliminated *and* another 100 mg of drug is added. So we have

$$d_{n+1} = 0.5\, d_n + 100, \qquad \text{for } n = 1, 2, 3, \ldots, \text{ with } d_1 = 100,$$

which is the recurrence relation for the sequence $\{d_n\}$.

b. We see from Figure 12 that after about 10 doses (5 days) the amount of antibiotic in the blood is close to 200 mg, and—importantly for your body—it never exceeds 200 mg.

c. The graph of part (b) gives evidence that the terms of the sequence are increasing and bounded (Exercise 96). By the Bounded Monotonic Sequence Theorem, the sequence has a limit; therefore, $\lim\limits_{n \to \infty} d_n = L$ and $\lim\limits_{n \to \infty} d_{n+1} = L$. We now take the limit of both sides of the recurrence relation:

$$d_{n+1} = 0.5\, d_n + 100 \qquad \text{Recurrence relation}$$

$$\underbrace{\lim_{n \to \infty} d_{n+1}}_{L} = 0.5 \underbrace{\lim_{n \to \infty} d_n}_{L} + \lim_{n \to \infty} 100 \quad \text{Limits of both sides}$$

$$L = 0.5L + 100. \qquad \text{Substitute } L.$$

Solving for L, the steady-state drug level is $L = 200$.

Related Exercises 59–62 ◀

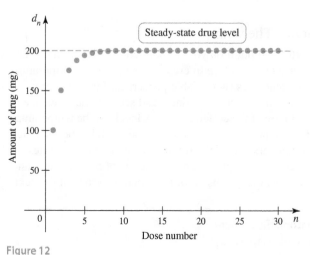

Figure 12

QUICK CHECK 3 If a drug has the same half-life as in Example 5, (i) how would the steady-state level of drug in the blood change if the regular dose were 150 mg instead of 100 mg? (ii) How would the steady-state level change if the dosing interval were 6 hr instead of 12 hr? ◀

Growth Rates of Sequences

All the hard work we did to establish the relative growth rates of functions is now applied to sequences. Here is the question: Given two nondecreasing sequences of positive terms $\{a_n\}$ and $\{b_n\}$, which sequence grows faster as $n \to \infty$? As with functions, to compare growth rates, we evaluate $\lim\limits_{n \to \infty} a_n/b_n$. If $\lim\limits_{n \to \infty} a_n/b_n = 0$, then $\{b_n\}$ grows faster than $\{a_n\}$. If $\lim\limits_{n \to \infty} a_n/b_n = \infty$, then $\{a_n\}$ grows faster than $\{b_n\}$.

Using earlier results, we immediately arrive at the following ranking of growth rates of sequences as $n \to \infty$, with positive real numbers p, q, r, s, and $b > 1$:

$$\{\ln^q n\} \ll \{n^p\} \ll \{n^p \ln^r n\} \ll \{n^{p+s}\} \ll \{b^n\} \ll \{n^n\}.$$

As before, the notation $\{a_n\} \ll \{b_n\}$ means $\{b_n\}$ *grows faster than* $\{a_n\}$ as $n \to \infty$. Another important sequence that should be added to the list is the **factorial sequence** $\{n!\}$, where $n! = n(n-1)(n-2) \cdots 2 \cdot 1$. Where does the factorial sequence $\{n!\}$ appear in the list? The following argument provides some intuition. Notice that

$$n^n = \underbrace{n \cdot n \cdot n \cdots n}_{n \text{ factors}}, \qquad \text{whereas}$$

$$n! = \underbrace{n \cdot (n-1) \cdot (n-2) \cdots 2 \cdot 1}_{n \text{ factors}}.$$

The nth term of both sequences involves the product of n factors; however, the factors of $n!$ decrease, while the factors of n^n are the same. Based on this observation, we claim that $\{n^n\}$ grows faster than $\{n!\}$, and we have the ordering $\{n!\} \ll \{n^n\}$. But where does $\{n!\}$ appear in the list relative to $\{b^n\}$? Again, some intuition is gained by noting that

$$b^n = \underbrace{b \cdot b \cdot b \cdots b}_{n \text{ factors}}, \qquad \text{whereas}$$

$$n! = \underbrace{n \cdot (n-1) \cdot (n-2) \cdots 2 \cdot 1}_{n \text{ factors}}.$$

The nth term of both sequences involves a product of n factors; however, the factors of b^n remain constant as n increases, while the factors of $n!$ increase with n. So we claim that $\{n!\}$ grows faster than $\{b^n\}$. This conjecture is supported by computation, although the outcome of the race may not be immediately evident if b is large.

> ► $0! = 1$ (by definition)
>
> $1! = 1$
>
> $2! = 2 \cdot 1! = 2$
>
> $3! = 3 \cdot 2! = 6$
>
> $4! = 4 \cdot 3! = 24$
>
> $5! = 5 \cdot 4! = 120$
>
> $6! = 6 \cdot 5! = 720$

THEOREM 6   Growth Rates of Sequences

The following sequences are ordered according to increasing growth rates as $n \to \infty$; that is, if $\{a_n\}$ appears before $\{b_n\}$ in the list, then $\displaystyle\lim_{n \to \infty} \frac{a_n}{b_n} = 0$ and

$$\lim_{n \to \infty} \frac{b_n}{a_n} = \infty:$$

$$\{\ln^q n\} \ll \{n^p\} \ll \{n^p \ln^r n\} \ll \{n^{p+s}\} \ll \{b^n\} \ll \{n!\} \ll \{n^n\}.$$

The ordering applies for positive real numbers p, q, r, s, and $b > 1$.

QUICK CHECK 4 Which sequence grows faster: $\{\ln n\}$ or $\{n^{1.1}\}$? What is

$$\lim_{n \to \infty} \frac{n^{1,000,000}}{e^n}? \quad ◄$$

It is worth noting that the rankings in Theorem 6 do not change if a sequence is multiplied by a positive constant.

EXAMPLE 6   Convergence and growth rates Compare growth rates of sequences to determine whether the following sequences converge.

a. $\left\{ \dfrac{\ln n^{10}}{0.00001n} \right\}$ **b.** $\left\{ \dfrac{n^8 \ln n}{n^{8.001}} \right\}$ **c.** $\left\{ \dfrac{n!}{10^n} \right\}$

SOLUTION

a. Because $\ln n^{10} = 10 \ln n$, the sequence in the numerator is a constant multiple of the sequence $\{\ln n\}$. Similarly, the sequence in the denominator is a constant multiple of the sequence $\{n\}$. By Theorem 6, $\{n\}$ grows faster than $\{\ln n\}$ as $n \to \infty$; therefore, the sequence $\left\{ \dfrac{\ln n^{10}}{0.00001n} \right\}$ converges to zero.

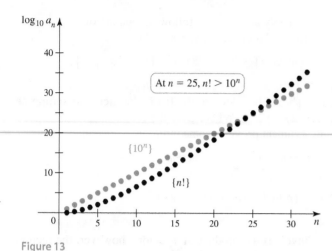

At $n = 25$, $n! > 10^n$

$\{10^n\}$

$\{n!\}$

Figure 13

b. The sequence in the numerator is $\{n^p \ln^r n\}$ of Theorem 6 with $p = 8$ and $r = 1$. The sequence in the denominator is $\{n^{p+s}\}$ of Theorem 8.6 with $p = 8$ and $s = 0.001$. Because $\{n^{p+s}\}$ grows faster than $\{n^p \ln^r n\}$ as $n \to \infty$, we conclude that $\left\{\dfrac{n^8 \ln n}{n^{8.001}}\right\}$ converges to zero.

c. Using Theorem 3.6, we see that $n!$ grows faster than any exponential function as $n \to \infty$. Therefore, $\lim\limits_{n \to \infty} \dfrac{n!}{10^n} = \infty$, and the sequence diverges. Figure 13 gives a visual comparison of the growth rates of $\{n!\}$ and $\{10^n\}$. Because these sequences grow so quickly, we plot the logarithm of the terms. The exponential sequence $\{10^n\}$ dominates the factorial sequence $\{n!\}$ until $n = 25$ terms. At that point, the factorial sequence overtakes the exponential sequence.

Related Exercises 63–68 ◄

Formal Definition of a Limit of a Sequence

As with limits of functions, there is a formal definition of the limit of a sequence.

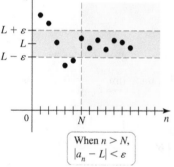

When $n > N$,
$|a_n - L| < \varepsilon$

Figure 14

> **DEFINITION Limit of a Sequence**
>
> The sequence $\{a_n\}$ converges to L provided the terms of a_n can be made arbitrarily close to L by taking n sufficiently large. More precisely, $\{a_n\}$ has the unique limit L if given any $\varepsilon > 0$, it is possible to find a positive integer N (depending only on ε) such that
>
> $$|a_n - L| < \varepsilon \qquad \text{whenever } n > N.$$
>
> If the **limit of a sequence** is L, we say the sequence **converges** to L, written
>
> $$\lim_{n \to \infty} a_n = L.$$
>
> A sequence that does not converge is said to **diverge**.

The formal definition of the limit of a convergent sequence is interpreted in much the same way as the limit at infinity of a function. Given a small tolerance $\varepsilon > 0$, how far out in the sequence must you go so that all succeeding terms are within ε of the limit L (Figure 14)? Given *any* value of $\varepsilon > 0$ (no matter how small), you must find a value of N such that all terms beyond a_N are within ε of L.

EXAMPLE 7 Limits using the formal definition Consider the claim that
$$\lim_{n \to \infty} a_n = \lim_{n \to \infty} \frac{n}{n-1} = 1.$$

a. Given $\varepsilon = 0.01$, find a value of N that satisfies the conditions of the limit definition.

b. Prove that $\lim\limits_{n \to \infty} a_n = 1$.

SOLUTION

a. We must find an integer N such that $|a_n - 1| < \varepsilon = 0.01$ whenever $n > N$. This condition can be written

$$|a_n - 1| = \left|\frac{n}{n-1} - 1\right| = \left|\frac{1}{n-1}\right| < 0.01.$$

Noting that $n > 1$, the absolute value can be removed. The condition on n becomes $n - 1 > 1/0.01 = 100$, or $n > 101$. Therefore, we take $N = 101$ or any larger number. This means that $|a_n - 1| < 0.01$ whenever $n > 101$.

b. Given *any* $\varepsilon > 0$, we must find a value of N (depending on ε) that guarantees

$$|a_n - 1| = \left|\frac{n}{n-1} - 1\right| < \varepsilon \text{ whenever } n > N. \text{ For } n > 1, \text{ the inequality}$$

$$\left|\frac{n}{n-1} - 1\right| < \varepsilon \text{ implies that}$$

$$\left|\frac{n}{n-1} - 1\right| = \frac{1}{n-1} < \varepsilon.$$

Solving for n, we find that $\dfrac{1}{n-1} < \varepsilon$ or $n - 1 > \dfrac{1}{\varepsilon}$ or $n > \dfrac{1}{\varepsilon} + 1$. Therefore, given a tolerance $\varepsilon > 0$, we must look beyond a_N in the sequence, where $N \geq \dfrac{1}{\varepsilon} + 1$, to be

sure that the terms of the sequence are within ε of the limit 1. Because we can provide a value of N for *any* $\varepsilon > 0$, the limit exists and equals 1.

> In general, $1/\varepsilon + 1$ is not an integer, so N should be the least integer greater than $1/\varepsilon + 1$ or any larger integer.

Related Exercises 69–74 ◄

3.1 EXTENSION B EXERCISES

Review Questions

1. Give an example of a nonincreasing sequence with a limit.

2. Give an example of a nondecreasing sequence without a limit.

3. Give an example of a bounded sequence that has a limit.

4. Give an example of a bounded sequence without a limit.

5. For what values of r does the sequence $\{r^n\}$ converge? Diverge?

6. Explain how the methods used to find the limit of a function as $x \to \infty$ are used to find the limit of a sequence.

7. Compare the growth rates of $\{n^{100}\}$ and $\{e^{n/100}\}$ as $n \to \infty$.

8. Explain how two sequences that differ only in their first ten terms can have the same limit.

Basic Skills

9–34. Limits of sequences *Find the limit of the following sequences or determine that the limit does not exist.*

9. $\left\{\dfrac{n^3}{n^4 + 1}\right\}$ **10.** $\left\{\dfrac{n^{12}}{3n^{12} + 4}\right\}$ **11.** $\left\{\dfrac{3n^3 - 1}{2n^3 + 1}\right\}$

12. $\left\{\dfrac{2e^n + 1}{e^n}\right\}$ **13.** $\left\{\dfrac{3^{n+1} + 3}{3^n}\right\}$ **14.** $\left\{\dfrac{k}{\sqrt{9k^2 + 1}}\right\}$

15. $\{\tan^{-1} n\}$ **16.** $\{\sqrt{n^2 + 1} - n\}$ **17.** $\left\{\dfrac{\tan^{-1} n}{n}\right\}$

18. $\{n^{2/n}\}$ **19.** $\left\{\left(1 + \dfrac{2}{n}\right)^n\right\}$ **20.** $\left\{\left(\dfrac{n}{n+5}\right)^n\right\}$

21. $\left\{\sqrt{\left(1 + \dfrac{1}{2n}\right)^n}\right\}$ **22.** $\left\{\left(1 + \dfrac{4}{n}\right)^{3n}\right\}$ **23.** $\left\{\dfrac{n}{e^n + 3n}\right\}$

24. $\left\{\dfrac{\ln(1/n)}{n}\right\}$ **25.** $\left\{\left(\dfrac{1}{n}\right)^{1/n}\right\}$ **26.** $\left\{\left(1 - \dfrac{4}{n}\right)^n\right\}$

27. $\{b_n\}$, where $b_n = \begin{cases} n/(n+1) & \text{if } n \leq 5000 \\ ne^{-n} & \text{if } n > 5000 \end{cases}$

28. $\{\ln(n^3 + 1) - \ln(3n^3 + 10n)\}$

29. $\{\ln \sin(1/n) + \ln n\}$ **30.** $\{n(1 - \cos(1/n))\}$

31. $\left\{n \sin \dfrac{6}{n}\right\}$ **32.** $\left\{\dfrac{(-1)^n}{n}\right\}$

33. $\left\{\dfrac{(-1)^n n}{n + 1}\right\}$ **34.** $\left\{\dfrac{(-1)^{n+1} n^2}{2n^3 + n}\right\}$

T **35–44. Limits of sequences and graphing** *Find the limit of the following sequences or determine that the limit does not exist. Verify your result with a graphing utility.*

35. $a_n = \sin \dfrac{n\pi}{2}$ **36.** $a_n = \dfrac{(-1)^n n}{n + 1}$

37. $a_n = \dfrac{\sin(n\pi/3)}{\sqrt{n}}$ **38.** $a_n = \dfrac{3^n}{3^n + 4^n}$

39. $a_n = 1 + \cos \dfrac{1}{n}$ **40.** $a_n = \dfrac{e^{-n}}{2\sin(e^{-n})}$

41. $a_n = e^{-n} \cos n$ **42.** $a_n = \dfrac{\ln n}{n^{1.1}}$

43. $a_n = (-1)^n \sqrt[n]{n}$ **44.** $a_n = \cot\left(\dfrac{n\pi}{2n + 2}\right)$

45–52. Geometric sequences *Determine whether the following sequences converge or diverge, and state whether they are monotonic or whether they oscillate. Give the limit when the sequence converges.*

45. $\{0.2^n\}$ **46.** $\{1.2^n\}$ **47.** $\{(-0.7)^n\}$

48. $\{5(-1.01)^n\}$ **49.** $\{1.00001^n\}$ **50.** $\{2^{n+1} 3^{-n}\}$

51. $\{(-2.5)^n\}$ **52.** $\{100(-0.003)^n\}$

53–58. Squeeze Theorem *Find the limit of the following sequences or state that they diverge.*

53. $\left\{\dfrac{\cos n}{n}\right\}$ **54.** $\left\{\dfrac{\sin 6n}{5n}\right\}$ **55.** $\left\{\dfrac{\sin n}{2^n}\right\}$

56. $\left\{\dfrac{\cos(n\pi/2)}{\sqrt{n}}\right\}$ **57.** $\left\{\dfrac{2\tan^{-1} n}{n^3 + 4}\right\}$ **58.** $\left\{\dfrac{n \sin^3(n\pi/2)}{n + 1}\right\}$

T **59. Periodic dosing** Many people take aspirin on a regular basis as a preventive measure for heart disease. Suppose a person takes 80 mg of aspirin every 24 hours. Assume also that aspirin has a half-life of 24 hours; that is, every 24 hours, half of the drug in the blood is eliminated.

a. Find a recurrence relation for the sequence $\{d_n\}$ that gives the amount of drug in the blood after the nth dose, where $d_1 = 80$.

b. Using a calculator, determine the limit of the sequence. In the long run, how much drug is in the person's blood?

c. Confirm the result of part (b) by finding the limit of $\{d_n\}$ directly.

60. A car loan Marie takes out a $20,000 loan for a new car. The loan has an annual interest rate of 6% or, equivalently, a monthly interest rate of 0.5%. Each month, the bank adds interest to the loan balance (the interest is always 0.5% of the current balance), and then Marie makes a $200 payment to reduce the loan balance. Let B_n be the loan balance immediately after the nth payment, where $B_0 = \$20,000$.

a. Write the first five terms of the sequence $\{B_n\}$.

b. Find a recurrence relation that generates the sequence $\{B_n\}$.

c. Determine how many months are needed to reduce the loan balance to zero.

61. A savings plan James begins a savings plan in which he deposits $100 at the beginning of each month into an account that earns 9% interest annually or, equivalently, 0.75% per month. To be clear, on the first day of each month, the bank adds 0.75% of the current balance as interest, and then James deposits $100. Let B_n be the balance in the account after the nth deposit, where $B_0 = \$0$.

a. Write the first five terms of the sequence $\{B_n\}$.

b. Find a recurrence relation that generates the sequence $\{B_n\}$.

c. How many months are needed to reach a balance of $5000?

62. Diluting a solution A tank is filled with 100 L of a 40% alcohol solution (by volume). You repeatedly perform the following operation: Remove 2 L of the solution from the tank and replace them with 2 L of 10% alcohol solution.

a. Let C_n be the concentration of the solution in the tank after the nth replacement, where $C_0 = 40\%$. Write the first five terms of the sequence $\{C_n\}$.

b. After how many replacements does the alcohol concentration reach 15%?

c. Determine the limiting (steady-state) concentration of the solution that is approached after many replacements.

63–68. Growth rates of sequences *Use Theorem 8.6 to find the limit of the following sequences or state that they diverge.*

63. $\left\{\dfrac{n!}{n^n}\right\}$

64. $\left\{\dfrac{3^n}{n!}\right\}$

65. $\left\{\dfrac{n^{10}}{\ln^{20} n}\right\}$

66. $\left\{\dfrac{n^{10}}{\ln^{1000} n}\right\}$

67. $\left\{\dfrac{n^{1000}}{2^n}\right\}$

68. $\left\{\dfrac{e^{n/10}}{2^n}\right\}$

69–74. Formal proofs of limits *Use the formal definition of the limit of a sequence to prove the following limits.*

69. $\lim\limits_{n\to\infty} \dfrac{1}{n} = 0$

70. $\lim\limits_{n\to\infty} \dfrac{1}{n^2} = 0$

71. $\lim\limits_{n\to\infty} \dfrac{3n^2}{4n^2 + 1} = \dfrac{3}{4}$

72. $\lim\limits_{n\to\infty} b^{-n} = 0$, for $b > 1$

73. $\lim\limits_{n\to\infty} \dfrac{cn}{bn + 1} = \dfrac{c}{b}$, for real numbers $b > 0$ and $c > 0$

74. $\lim\limits_{n\to\infty} \dfrac{n}{n^2 + 1} = 0$

Further Explorations

75. Explain why or why not Determine whether the following statements are true and give an explanation or counterexample.

a. If $\lim\limits_{n\to\infty} a_n = 1$ and $\lim\limits_{n\to\infty} b_n = 3$, then $\lim\limits_{n\to\infty} \dfrac{b_n}{a_n} = 3$.

b. If $\lim\limits_{n\to\infty} a_n = 0$ and $\lim\limits_{n\to\infty} b_n = \infty$, then $\lim\limits_{n\to\infty} a_n b_n = 0$.

c. The convergent sequences $\{a_n\}$ and $\{b_n\}$ differ in their first 100 terms, but $a_n = b_n$, for $n > 100$. It follows that $\lim\limits_{n\to\infty} a_n = \lim\limits_{n\to\infty} b_n$.

d. If $\{a_n\} = \left\{1, \frac{1}{2}, \frac{1}{3}, \frac{1}{4}, \frac{1}{5}, \ldots\right\}$ and $\{b_n\} = \left\{1, 0, \frac{1}{2}, 0, \frac{1}{3}, 0, \frac{1}{4}, 0, \ldots\right\}$, then $\lim\limits_{n\to\infty} a_n = \lim\limits_{n\to\infty} b_n$.

e. If the sequence $\{a_n\}$ converges, then the sequence $\{(-1)^n a_n\}$ converges.

f. If the sequence $\{a_n\}$ diverges, then the sequence $\{0.000001 \, a_n\}$ diverges.

76–77. Reindexing *Express each sequence $\{a_n\}_{n=1}^{\infty}$ as an equivalent sequence of the form $\{b_n\}_{n=3}^{\infty}$.*

76. $\{2n + 1\}_{n=1}^{\infty}$

77. $\{n^2 + 6n - 9\}_{n=1}^{\infty}$

78–85. More sequences *Evaluate the limit of the following sequences or state that the limit does not exist.*

78. $a_n = \displaystyle\int_1^n x^{-2}\, dx$

79. $a_n = \dfrac{75^{n-1}}{99^n} + \dfrac{5^n \sin n}{8^n}$

80. $a_n = \tan^{-1}\left(\dfrac{10n}{10n + 4}\right)$

81. $a_n = \cos(0.99^n) + \dfrac{7^n + 9^n}{63^n}$

82. $a_n = \dfrac{4^n + 5n!}{n! + 2^n}$

83. $a_n = \dfrac{6^n + 3^n}{6^n + n^{100}}$

84. $a_n = \dfrac{n^8 + n^7}{n^7 + n^8 \ln n}$

85. $a_n = \dfrac{7^n}{n^7 5^n}$

86–90. Sequences by recurrence relations *Consider the following sequences defined by a recurrence relation. Use a calculator, analytical methods, and/or graphing to make a conjecture about the limit of the sequence or state that the sequence diverges.*

86. $a_{n+1} = \frac{1}{2}a_n + 2$; $a_0 = 5$

87. $a_{n+1} = 2a_n(1 - a_n)$; $a_0 = 0.3$

88. $a_{n+1} = \frac{1}{2}(a_n + 2/a_n)$; $a_0 = 2$

89. $a_{n+1} = 4a_n(1 - a_n)$; $a_0 = 0.5$

90. $a_{n+1} = \sqrt{2 + a_n}$; $a_0 = 1$

91. Crossover point The sequence $\{n!\}$ ultimately grows faster than the sequence $\{b^n\}$, for any $b > 1$, as $n \to \infty$. However, b^n is generally greater than $n!$ for small values of n. Use a calculator to determine the smallest value of n such that $n! > b^n$ for each of the cases $b = 2$, $b = e$, and $b = 10$.

Applications

92. Fish harvesting A fishery manager knows that her fish population naturally increases at a rate of 1.5% per month, while 80 fish are harvested each month. Let F_n be the fish population after the nth month, where $F_0 = 4000$ fish.

a. Write out the first five terms of the sequence $\{F_n\}$.

b. Find a recurrence relation that generates the sequence $\{F_n\}$.

c. Does the fish population decrease or increase in the long run?

d. Determine whether the fish population decreases or increases in the long run if the initial population is 5500 fish.

e. Determine the initial fish population F_0 below which the population decreases.

93. The hungry heifer A heifer weighing 200 lb today gains 5 lb per day with a food cost of 45¢/day. The price for heifers is 65¢/lb today but is falling 1¢/day.

a. Let h_n be the profit in selling the heifer on the nth day, where $h_0 = (200\text{ lb}) \cdot (\$0.65/\text{lb}) = \$130$. Write out the first 10 terms of the sequence $\{h_n\}$.

b. How many days after today should the heifer be sold to maximize the profit?

94. Sleep model After many nights of observation, you notice that if you oversleep one night, you tend to undersleep the following night, and vice versa. This pattern of compensation is described by the relationship

$$x_{n+1} = \frac{1}{2}(x_n + x_{n-1}), \quad \text{for } n = 1, 2, 3, \ldots,$$

where x_n is the number of hours of sleep you get on the nth night and $x_0 = 7$ and $x_1 = 6$ are the number of hours of sleep on the first two nights, respectively.

a. Write out the first six terms of the sequence $\{x_n\}$ and confirm that the terms alternately increase and decrease.

b. Show that the explicit formula

$$x_n = \frac{19}{3} + \frac{2}{3}\left(-\frac{1}{2}\right)^n, \text{ for } n \geq 0,$$

generates the terms of the sequence in part (a).

c. What is the limit of the sequence?

95. Calculator algorithm The CORDIC (COordinate Rotation DIgital Calculation) algorithm is used by most calculators to evaluate trigonometric and logarithmic functions. An important number in the CORDIC algorithm, called the *aggregate constant*, is given by the infinite product $\prod_{n=0}^{\infty} \dfrac{2^n}{\sqrt{1 + 2^{2n}}}$, where $\prod_{n=0}^{N} a_n$ represents the product $a_0 \cdot a_1 \cdots a_N$.

This infinite product is the limit of the sequence

$$\left\{ \prod_{n=0}^{0} \frac{2^n}{\sqrt{1 + 2^{2n}}}, \prod_{n=0}^{1} \frac{2^n}{\sqrt{1 + 2^{2n}}}, \prod_{n=0}^{2} \frac{2^n}{\sqrt{1 + 2^{2n}}}, \ldots \right\}.$$

Estimate the value of the aggregate constant. (See the Guided Project *CORDIC algorithms: How your calculator works*.)

Additional Exercises

96. Bounded monotonic proof Use mathematical induction to prove that the drug dose sequence in Example 5,

$$d_{n+1} = 0.5d_n + 100, d_1 = 100, \quad \text{for } n = 1, 2, 3, \ldots,$$

is bounded and monotonic.

97. Repeated square roots Consider the expression

$$\sqrt{1 + \sqrt{1 + \sqrt{1 + \sqrt{1 + \cdots}}}}, \text{ where the process continues indefinitely.}$$

a. Show that this expression can be built in steps using the recurrence relation $a_0 = 1, a_{n+1} = \sqrt{1 + a_n}$, for $n = 0, 1, 2, 3, \ldots$. Explain why the value of the expression can be interpreted as $\lim_{n \to \infty} a_n$, provided the limit exists.

b. Evaluate the first five terms of the sequence $\{a_n\}$.

c. Estimate the limit of the sequence. Compare your estimate with $(1 + \sqrt{5})/2$, a number known as the *golden mean*.

d. Assuming the limit exists, use the method of Example 5 to determine the limit exactly.

e. Repeat the preceding analysis for the expression

$$\sqrt{p + \sqrt{p + \sqrt{p + \sqrt{p + \cdots}}}}, \text{ where } p > 0. \text{ Make a}$$

table showing the approximate value of this expression for various values of p. Does the expression seem to have a limit for all positive values of p?

98. A sequence of products Find the limit of the sequence

$$\{a_n\}_{n=2}^{\infty} = \left\{ \left(1 - \frac{1}{2}\right)\left(1 - \frac{1}{3}\right) \cdots \left(1 - \frac{1}{n}\right) \right\}_{n=2}^{\infty}.$$

99. Continued fractions The expression

$$1 + \cfrac{1}{1 + \cfrac{1}{1 + \cfrac{1}{1 + \cfrac{1}{1 + \ddots}}}},$$

where the process continues indefinitely, is called a *continued fraction*.

a. Show that this expression can be built in steps using the recurrence relation $a_0 = 1, a_{n+1} = 1 + 1/a_n$, for $n = 0, 1, 2, 3, \ldots$. Explain why the value of the expression can be interpreted as $\lim_{n \to \infty} a_n$, provided the limit exists.

b. Evaluate the first five terms of the sequence $\{a_n\}$.

c. Using computation and/or graphing, estimate the limit of the sequence.

d. Assuming the limit exists, use the method of Example 5 to determine the limit exactly. Compare your estimate with $(1 + \sqrt{5})/2$, a number known as the *golden mean*.

e. Assuming the limit exists, use the same ideas to determine the value of

$$a + \cfrac{b}{a + \cfrac{b}{a + \cfrac{b}{a + \cfrac{b}{a + \ddots}}}},$$

where a and b are positive real numbers.

100. Tower of powers For a positive real number p, the tower of exponents p^{p^p} continues indefinitely and the expression is ambiguous. The tower could be built from the top as the limit of the sequence $\{p^p, (p^p)^p, ((p^p)^p)^p, \ldots\}$, in which case the sequence is defined recursively as

$$a_{n+1} = a_n^p \text{ (building from the top)}, \tag{1}$$

where $a_1 = p^p$. The tower could also be built from the bottom as the limit of the sequence $\{p^p, p^{(p^p)}, p^{(p^{(p^p)})}, \ldots\}$, in which case the sequence is defined recursively as

$$a_{n+1} = p^{a_n} \text{ (building from the bottom)}, \qquad (2)$$

where again $a_1 = p^p$.

a. Estimate the value of the tower with $p = 0.5$ by building from the top. That is, use tables to estimate the limit of the sequence defined recursively by (1) with $p = 0.5$. Estimate the maximum value of $p > 0$ for which the sequence has a limit.

b. Estimate the value of the tower with $p = 1.2$ by building from the bottom. That is, use tables to estimate the limit of the sequence defined recursively by (2) with $p = 1.2$. Estimate the maximum value of $p > 1$ for which the sequence has a limit.

T 101. Fibonacci sequence The famous Fibonacci sequence was proposed by Leonardo Pisano, also known as Fibonacci, in about A.D. 1200 as a model for the growth of rabbit populations. It is given by the recurrence relation $f_{n+1} = f_n + f_{n-1}$, for $n = 1, 2, 3, \ldots$, where $f_0 = 1$, $f_1 = 1$. Each term of the sequence is the sum of its two predecessors.

a. Write out the first ten terms of the sequence.
b. Is the sequence bounded?
c. Estimate or determine $\varphi = \lim\limits_{n \to \infty} \dfrac{f_{n+1}}{f_n}$, the ratio of the successive terms of the sequence. Provide evidence that $\varphi = (1 + \sqrt{5})/2$, a number known as the *golden mean*.
d. Use induction to verify the remarkable result that

$$f_n = \frac{1}{\sqrt{5}} \left(\varphi^n - (-1)^n \varphi^{-n} \right).$$

102. Arithmetic-geometric mean Pick two positive numbers a_0 and b_0 with $a_0 > b_0$, and write out the first few terms of the two sequences $\{a_n\}$ and $\{b_n\}$:

$$a_{n+1} = \frac{a_n + b_n}{2}, \qquad b_{n+1} = \sqrt{a_n b_n}, \qquad \text{for } n = 0, 1, 2, \ldots.$$

(Recall that the arithmetic mean $A = (p + q)/2$ and the geometric mean $G = \sqrt{pq}$ of two positive numbers p and q satisfy $A \geq G$.)

a. Show that $a_n > b_n$ for all n.
b. Show that $\{a_n\}$ is a decreasing sequence and $\{b_n\}$ is an increasing sequence.
c. Conclude that $\{a_n\}$ and $\{b_n\}$ converge.
d. Show that $a_{n+1} - b_{n+1} < (a_n - b_n)/2$ and conclude that $\lim\limits_{n \to \infty} a_n = \lim\limits_{n \to \infty} b_n$. The common value of these limits is called the arithmetic-geometric mean of a_0 and b_0, denoted $\mathrm{AGM}(a_0, b_0)$.
e. Estimate $\mathrm{AGM}(12, 20)$. Estimate Gauss' constant $1/\mathrm{AGM}(1, \sqrt{2})$.

103. The hailstone sequence Here is a fascinating (unsolved) problem known as the hailstone problem (or the Ulam Conjecture or the Collatz Conjecture). It involves sequences in two different ways. First, choose a positive integer N and call it a_0. This is the *seed* of a sequence. The rest of the sequence is generated as follows: For $n = 0, 1, 2, \ldots$

$$a_{n+1} = \begin{cases} a_n/2 & \text{if } a_n \text{ is even} \\ 3a_n + 1 & \text{if } a_n \text{ is odd.} \end{cases}$$

However, if $a_n = 1$ for any n, then the sequence terminates.

a. Compute the sequence that results from the seeds $N = 2, 3, 4, \ldots, 10$. You should verify that in all these cases, the sequence eventually terminates. The hailstone conjecture (still unproved) states that for all positive integers N, the sequence terminates after a finite number of terms.

b. Now define the hailstone sequence $\{H_k\}$, which is the number of terms needed for the sequence $\{a_n\}$ to terminate starting with a seed of k. Verify that $H_2 = 1$, $H_3 = 7$, and $H_4 = 2$.

c. Plot as many terms of the hailstone sequence as is feasible. How did the sequence get its name? Does the conjecture appear to be true?

104. Prove that if $\{a_n\} \ll \{b_n\}$ (as used in Theorem 8.6), then $\{ca_n\} \ll \{db_n\}$, where c and d are positive real numbers.

105. Convergence proof Consider the sequence defined by

$$a_{n+1} = \sqrt{3a_n}, a_1 = \sqrt{3}, \text{ for } n \geq 1.$$

a. Show that $\{a_n\}$ is increasing.
b. Show that $\{a_n\}$ is bounded between 0 and 3.
c. Explain why $\lim\limits_{n \to \infty} a_n$ exists.
d. Find $\lim\limits_{n \to \infty} a_n$.

T 106–110. Comparing sequences *In the following exercises, two sequences are given, one of which initially has smaller values, but eventually "overtakes" the other sequence. Find the sequence with the larger growth rate and the value of n at which it overtakes the other sequence.*

106. $a_n = \sqrt{n}$ and $b_n = 2 \ln n, n \geq 3$

107. $a_n = e^{n/2}$ and $b_n = n^5, n \geq 2$

108. $a_n = n^{1.001}$ and $b_n = \ln n^{10}, n \geq 1$

109. $a_n = n!$ and $b_n = n^{0.7n}, n \geq 2$

110. $a_n = n^{10}$ and $b_n = n^9 \ln^3 n, n \geq 7$

T 111. Comparing sequences with a parameter For what values of a does the sequence $\{n!\}$ grow faster than the sequence $\{n^{an}\}$?

(*Hint:* Stirling's formula is useful: $n! \approx \sqrt{2\pi n} \, n^n e^{-n}$, for large values of n.)

QUICK CHECK ANSWERS

1. a. Bounded, monotonic;   **b.** Bounded, not monotonic; **c.** Not bounded, not monotonic;   **d.** Bounded, monotonic (both nonincreasing and nondecreasing)   **2.** If $r = -1$, the sequence is $\{-1, 1, -1, 1, \ldots\}$, the terms alternate in sign, and the sequence diverges. If $r = 1$, the sequence is $\{1, 1, 1, 1, \ldots\}$, the terms are constant, and the sequence converges to 1.   **3.** Both changes would increase the steady-state level of drug.   **4.** $\{n^{1.1}\}$ grows faster; the limit is 0. ◄

4.6
Extension

Inverse Trigonometric Functions

APPLY IT How far back should you stand from a painting to get the best view?
In Exercise 16 in this section, we will use trigonometry to answer this question.

To solve the equation $y = e^x$ for x, we introduced a new function, the logarithmic function. Similarly, we introduce the *inverse sine* function in order to solve the equation $y = \sin x$ for x. The inverse sine function determines an angle from the sine of the angle. For example, since $\sin(\pi/2) = 1$, the inverse sine function must start with 1 and produce the result $\pi/2$. One difficulty is that there are many values of x such that $\sin x = 1$; $\pi/2$ is one, as are $5\pi/2$, $9\pi/2$, and $13\pi/2$. To be sure that the inverse sine produces only one answer, it is necessary to restrict the range of the inverse sine function. The range is commonly restricted to the interval $[-\pi/2, \pi/2]$. With this restriction, the inverse sine function is defined as follows.

INVERSE SINE

Let $x = \sin y$, for y in $[-\pi/2, \pi/2]$. Then
$$y = \sin^{-1} x.$$

EXAMPLE 1   Inverse Sine

Find each of the following
(a) $\sin^{-1}(1/2)$.

SOLUTION   Let $y = \sin^{-1}(1/2)$. Then, by the definition of the inverse sine function, $\sin y = 1/2$. Since $\sin(\pi/6) = 1/2$, and $\pi/6$ is in $[-\pi/2, \pi/2]$.

$$\sin^{-1} \frac{1}{2} = \frac{\pi}{6}.$$

(b) $\sin^{-1}\left(-\frac{\sqrt{3}}{2}\right) = -\frac{\pi}{3}$

(c) $\sin^{-1} 1 = \frac{\pi}{2}$

A graph of $y = \sin^{-1} x$ is shown in Figure 1. (Sometimes the notation $y = \arcsin x$ is used for $y = \sin^{-1} x$.)

For each of the other trigonometric functions, an inverse function can be defined by putting a suitable restriction on the range of the inverse function. The three most commonly used **inverse trigonometric functions** and their ranges are listed below.

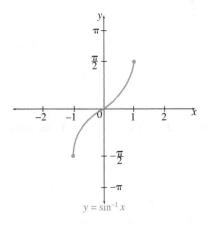

$y = \sin^{-1} x$

FIGURE 1

INVERSE TRIGONOMETRIC FUNCTIONS

$$y = \sin^{-1} x, \quad -\frac{\pi}{2} \leq y \leq \frac{\pi}{2}$$

$$y = \cos^{-1} x, \quad 0 \leq y \leq \pi$$

$$y = \tan^{-1} x, \quad -\frac{\pi}{2} < y < \frac{\pi}{2}$$

Graphs of $y = \cos^{-1} x$ and $y = \tan^{-1} x$ are shown in Figures 2 and 3, respectively.

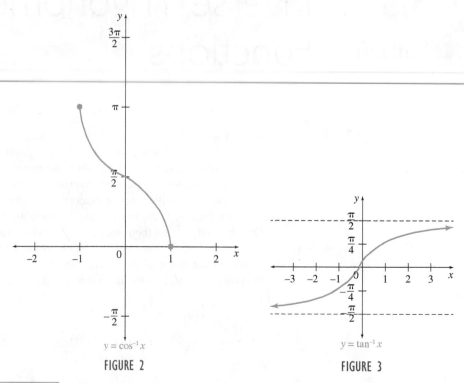

FIGURE 2   FIGURE 3

CAUTION   Even though $\sin^2 x = (\sin x)^2$, $\sin^{-1} x$ is *not* the same as $(\sin x)^{-1} = 1/\sin x = \csc x$.

EXAMPLE 2   Inverse cosine

Find $\cos^{-1}\left(-\sqrt{2}/2\right)$.

SOLUTION   The value of $\cos^{-1} x$ are in quadrants I and II, according to the definition given above. Since $-\sqrt{2}/2$ is negative, $\cos^{-1}(-\sqrt{2}/2)$ is restricted to quadrant II. Let $y = \cos^{-1}(-\sqrt{2}/2)$. Then $\cos y = -\sqrt{2}/2$. In quadrant II, $\cos(3\pi/4) = -\sqrt{2}/2$, so

$$\cos^{-1}\left(-\frac{\sqrt{2}}{2}\right) = \frac{3\pi}{4}.$$

EXAMPLE 3   Inverse Tangent

Find each of the following.

(a) $\tan^{-1} 1$

SOLUTION   We look for an angle y between $-\pi/2$ and $\pi/2$ such that $\tan y = 1$. Because $y = \pi/4$ satisfies these conditions,

$$\tan^{-1} 1 = \frac{\pi}{4}.$$

(b) $\tan^{-1}\left(-\sqrt{3}\right)$

SOLUTION   The angle must be in quadrant IV, where the tangent is negative. Recall from the 30°-60°-90° triangle that the side opposite 60°, or $\pi/3$, is $\sqrt{3}$, and the side adjacent is 1. Therefore,

$$\tan^{-1}\left(-\sqrt{3}\right) = -\frac{\pi}{3}.$$

Derivatives of Inverse Trigonometric Functions

We found that the derivatives of the trigonometric functions were themselves trigonometric functions. The derivatives of the inverse trigonometric function, however, are *algebraic functions*. To find the derivative of $y = \sin^{-1} x$, use the definition of $y = \sin^{-1} x$ to write

$$x = \sin y.$$

Use implicit differentiation to find $D_x y$. Taking the derivative with respect to x on both sides of $x = \sin y$ gives

$$D_x(x) = (\cos y)\, D_x y.$$

Since $D_x(x) = 1$,

$$1 = (\cos y)\, D_x y$$

or

$$D_x y = \frac{1}{\cos y}.$$

Since $\sin^2 y + \cos^2 y = 1$, $\cos y = \pm\sqrt{1 - \sin^2 y}$, and

$$D_x y = \frac{1}{\pm\sqrt{1 - \sin^2 y}}.$$

Choose the positive square root, since $\cos y > 0$ for y in $[-\pi/2,\ \pi/2]$. Replace $\sin y$ with x to get

$$D_x y = \frac{1}{\sqrt{1 - x^2}}.$$

This result is summarized below.

DERIVATIVE OF $\sin^{-1} x$

$$D_x(\sin^{-1} x) = \frac{1}{\sqrt{1 - x^2}}$$

EXAMPLE 4   Derivative of $\sin^{-1} x$

Find each derivative

(a) $y = \sin^{-1} 9x$

SOLUTION   Use the above formula with the chain rule to get

$$D_x(\sin^{-1} 9x) = \frac{1}{\sqrt{1 - (9x)^2}}\, D_x(9x) = \frac{9}{\sqrt{1 - 81x^2}}.$$

(b) $D_x\left[\sin^{-1}(5x^2 + 1)\right] = \frac{1}{\sqrt{1 - (5x^2 + 1)^2}}\, D_x(5x^2 + 1)$

$$= \frac{10x}{\sqrt{1 - (5x^2 + 1)^2}}$$

Starting with $y = \cos^{-1} x$ and $y = \tan^{-1} x$ and again using implicit differentiation gives the following derivatives.

DERIVATIVES OF $\cos^{-1} x$ AND $\tan^{-1} x$

$$D_x(\cos^{-1} x) = \frac{-1}{\sqrt{1 - x^2}}$$

$$D_x(\tan^{-1} x) = \frac{1}{1 + x^2}$$

EXAMPLE 5   Derivative of $\cos^{-1} x$ and $\sin^{-1} x$

Find each derivative

(a) $y = \cos^{-1}(3x^2)$

SOLUTION   Using the formula for the derivative of inverse cosine, together with the chain rule, gives

$$D_x\left[\cos^{-1}(3x^2)\right] = \frac{-1}{\sqrt{1-(3x^2)^2}}(6x) = \frac{-6x}{\sqrt{1-9x^4}}.$$

(b) $D_x\left[\tan^{-1}(8x^2)\right] = \dfrac{1}{1+(8x^2)^2}D_x(8x^2) = \dfrac{16x}{1+64x^4}$

(c) $D_x\left[\tan^{-1}(e^{2x})\right] = \dfrac{1}{1+(e^{2x})^2}D_x(e^{2x}) = \dfrac{2e^{2x}}{1+e^{4x}}$

EXERCISES

Give the value of y in radians.

1. $y = \sin^{-1}(-\sqrt{3}/2)$
2. $y = \cos^{-1}(\sqrt{3}/2)$
3. $y = \tan^{-1} 1$
4. $y = \tan^{-1}(-1)$
5. $y = \sin^{-1}(-1)$
6. $y = \cos^{-1}(-1)$
7. $y = \cos^{-1}(1/2)$
8. $y = \sin^{-1}(-\sqrt{2}/2)$
9. $y = \cos^{-1}(-\sqrt{2}/2)$
10. $y = \tan^{-1}(\sqrt{3}/3)$
11. $y = \tan^{-1}(-\sqrt{3})$
12. $y = \cos^{-1}(-1/2)$

Use a calculator to give each value in degrees.

13. $\sin^{-1}(-0.1392)$
14. $\cos^{-1}(-0.1392)$
15. $\cos^{-1}(-0.8988)$
16. $\sin^{-1} 0.7880$
17. $\cos^{-1} 0.9272$
18. $\tan^{-1} 1.7321$

19. $\tan^{-1} 1.111$
20. $\sin^{-1} 0.8192$
21. $\tan^{-1}(-0.9004)$
22. $\tan^{-1}(-0.2867)$
23. $\sin^{-1} 0.9272$
24. $\cos^{-1} 0.4384$

Find the derivative of each inverse trigonometric function.

25. $y = \sin^{-1} 12x$
26. $y = \cos^{-1} 10x$
27. $y = \tan^{-1} 3x$
28. $y = \sin^{-1}(1/x)$
29. $y = \cos^{-1}(-2/x)$
30. $y = \cos^{-1}\sqrt{x}$
31. $y = \tan^{-1}(\ln|7x|)$
32. $y = \tan^{-1}(\ln|x+2|)$
33. $y = \ln|\tan^{-1}(x+1)|$
34. $y = \ln|\tan^{-1}(3x-5)|$
35. Verify the formulas for the derivatives of $\cos^{-1} x$ and $\tan^{-1} x$ by implicitly differentiating $x = \cos y$ and $x = \tan y$.

ANSWERS

1. $-\pi/3$
2. $\pi/6$
3. $\pi/4$
4. $-\pi/4$
5. $-\pi/2$
6. π
7. $\pi/3$
8. $-\pi/4$
9. $3\pi/4$
10. $\pi/6$
11. $-\pi/3$
12. $2\pi/3$
13. $-8°$
14. $98°$
15. $154°$
16. $52°$
17. $22°$
18. $60°$
19. $48°$
20. $55°$
21. $-42°$
22. $-16°$
23. $68°$
24. $64°$
25. $dy/dx = 12/\sqrt{1-144x^2}$
26. $dy/dx = -10/\sqrt{1-100x^2}$

27. $dy/dx = 3/(1+9x^2)$
28. $dy/dx = -1/(|x|\sqrt{x^2-1})$
29. $dy/dx = -2/(|x|\sqrt{x^2-4})$
30. $dy/dx = -1/(2x^{1/2}\sqrt{1-x})$
31. $dy/dx = 1/[x(1+[\ln|7x|]^2)]$
32. $dy/dx = 1/[(x+2)(1+[\ln|x+2|]^2)]$
33. $dy/dx = 1/[(1+[x+1]^2)\tan^{-1}(x+1)]$
34. $dy/dx = 3/[(1+[3x-5]^2)\tan^{-1}(3x-5)]$

6.3

Extension

Logarithmic Differentiation

Additional material to supplement section 6.3 p.340 of *Calculus for the Life Sciences*.

Logarithmic differentiation is a method for taking the derivative of complicated functions involving products, quotients, and powers. It is also useful for differentiating functions of the form $y = f(x)^{g(x)}$.

In logarithmic differentiation, follow these steps.

1. Take the natural logarithm of both sides of the equation.

2. Simplify using properties of logarithms.

3. Take the derivative of both sides using implicit differentiation.

4. Solve for dy/dx, writing the final answer in terms of x.

The following examples illustrate the process.

EXAMPLE 1   Logarithmic Differentiation

Find the derivative of the function

$$y = \frac{(3x + 2)^4(x^3 + 8)^2}{(x^2 + 1)^3}.$$

SOLUTION   We could take the derivative using the product, quotient, and chain rules, but this would be tedious. To use logarithmic differentiation, take the natural logarithm of both sides and simplify.

$$
\begin{aligned}
\ln y &= \ln\left[\frac{(3x + 2)^4(x^3 + 8)^2}{(x^2 + 1)^3}\right] \\
&= \ln\left[(3x + 2)^4(x^3 + 8)^2\right] - \ln(x^2 + 1)^3 && \ln u/v = \ln u - \ln v \\
&= \ln(3x + 2)^4 + \ln(x^3 + 8)^2 - \ln(x^2 + 1)^3 && \ln uv = \ln u + \ln v \\
&= 4\ln(3x + 2) + 2\ln(x^3 + 8) - 3\ln(x^2 + 1) && \ln u^v = v\ln u
\end{aligned}
$$

Now differentiate implicitly, remembering to use the chain rule.

$$
\begin{aligned}
\frac{1}{y}\cdot\frac{dy}{dx} &= \frac{4}{3x + 2}\cdot 3 + \frac{2}{x^3 + 8}\cdot 3x^2 - \frac{3}{x^2 + 1}\cdot 2x \\
&= \frac{12}{3x + 2} + \frac{6x^2}{x^3 + 8} - \frac{6x}{x^2 + 1}
\end{aligned}
$$

Finally, multiply both sides by y to get dy/dx, and substitute the original expression for y.

$$
\begin{aligned}
\frac{dy}{dx} &= y\left(\frac{12}{3x + 2} + \frac{6x^2}{x^3 + 8} - \frac{6x}{x^2 + 1}\right) \\
&= \frac{(3x + 2)^4(x^3 + 8)^2}{(x^2 + 1)^3}\left(\frac{12}{3x + 2} + \frac{6x^2}{x^3 + 8} - \frac{6x}{x^2 + 1}\right)
\end{aligned}
$$

If you have any doubts of the value of logarithmic differentiation, try taking the derivative of the original function without logarithmic differentiation, using the product, quotient, and chain rules.

EXAMPLE 2   Logarithmic Differentiation

Find the derivative of the function

$$y = \sin x^{\cos x}.$$

SOLUTION   It would be a blunder to use the rule $D_x(x^n) = nx^{n-1}$ plus the chain rule to get $dy/dx = \cos x(\sin x)^{\cos x - 1}(\cos x)$. The power rule applies only when n is a constant. Similarly, it would be a blunder to use the rule $D_x(a^x) = (\ln a) a^x$ plus the chain rule to get $dy/dx = (\ln (\sin x))(\sin x)^{\cos x}(-\sin x)$. The rule for differentiating a^x applies only when a is a constant.

So what are we to do? Use logarithmic differentiation. As before, take the natural logarithm of both sides and simplify.

$$\ln y = \ln (\sin x^{\cos x})$$
$$= \cos x \cdot \ln (\sin x) \qquad \ln u^v = v \ln u$$

Now differentiate implicitly, remembering to use the chain rule.

$$\frac{1}{y} \cdot \frac{dy}{dx} = \cos x \cdot \frac{1}{\sin x} \cdot \cos x + \ln (\sin x) \cdot (-\sin x)$$
$$= \frac{\cos^2 x}{\sin x} - \sin x \cdot \ln(\sin x)$$

Finally, multiply both sides by y to get dy/dx, and substitute the original expression for y.

$$\frac{dy}{dx} = y \left(\frac{\cos^2 x}{\sin x} - \sin x \cdot \ln (\sin x) \right)$$
$$= \sin x^{\cos x} \left(\frac{\cos^2 x}{\sin x} - \sin x \cdot \ln (\sin x) \right)$$

It is interesting to note that if the two wrong answers discussed in the first paragraph of this solution are added together, they give the correct answer. (Verify this!) This is not a coincidence; it follows from the multivariable chain rule. For more details, see *Thomas' Calculus* by George B. Thomas, Jr. Maurice D. Weir, and Joel Hass, 12th ed., Pearson, 2010, Section 14.4.

EXERCISES

Use logarithmic differentiation to find the derivative of each of the following functions.

1. $y = \dfrac{(2x + 5)^3(3x + 8)^4}{(7x + 1)^5}$

2. $y = \dfrac{(3x - 2)^5}{(4x + 9)^{3/2}(2x + 1)^4}$

3. $y = \dfrac{(x^3 + 4)^2(x^2 + 4)^3}{\sqrt{x^6 + 1}}$

4. $y = \dfrac{(6x^3 + 5)^{1/3}}{(4x^2 + 7)^3\sqrt{8x^2 + 1}}$

Find the derivative of each of the following functions.

5. $y = x^x$

6. $y = x^{6x}$

7. $y = x^{\ln x}$

8. $y = (\ln x)^x$

9. $y = (\cos x)^{\tan x}$

10. $y = (\tan x)^{\sin x}$

ANSWERS

1. $dy/dx = (2x + 5)^3(3x + 8)^4/(7x + 1)^5[6/(2x + 5) + 12/(3x + 8) - 35/(7x + 1)]$

2. $dy/dx = (3x - 2)^5/[(4x + 9)^{3/2}(2x + 1)^4][15/(3x - 2) - 6/(4x + 9) - 8/(2x + 1)]$

3. $dy/dx = (x^3 + 4)^2(x^2 + 4)^3[6x^2/(x^3 + 4) + 6x/(x^2 + 4) - 3x^5/(x^6 + 1)]/\sqrt{x^6 + 1}$

4. $dy/dx = (6x^3 + 5)^{1/3}[6x^2/(6x^3 + 5) - 24x/(4x^2 + 7) - 8x/(8x^2 + 1)]/[(4x^2 + 7)^3\sqrt{8x^2 + 1}]$

5. $dy/dx = x^x(1 + \ln x)$

6. $dy/dx = x^{6x}(6 + 6\ln x)$

7. $dy/dx = x^{\ln x}(2\ln x)/x$

8. $dy/dx = (\ln x)^x(1/\ln x + \ln \ln x)$

9. $dy/dx = (\cos x)^{\tan x}(\sec^2 x \ln \cos x - \tan^2 x)$

10. $dy/dx = (\tan x)^{\sin x}(\sin x \sec^2 x/\tan x + \sec^2 x \ln \cos x)$

Integrals of Inverse Trigonometric Functions

Integrals The three derivatives of inverse trigonometric functions found earlier lead to the following integrals.

$$\int \frac{1}{\sqrt{1-x^2}}\,dx = \sin^{-1}x + C$$

$$\int \frac{-1}{\sqrt{1-x^2}}\,dx = \cos^{-1}x + C$$

$$\int \frac{1}{1+x^2}\,dx = \tan^{-1}x + C$$

The second integral is seldom used, since we could just as well have written the antiderivative as $-\sin^{-1}x + C$.

EXAMPLE 1 Integrals Involving Inverse Trigonometric Functions

Find each integral.

(a) $\displaystyle\int \frac{2x}{\sqrt{1-x^4}}\,dx$

SOLUTION Let $u = x^2$ to get $du = 2x\,dx$, so that

$$\int \frac{2x}{\sqrt{1-x^4}}\,dx = \int \frac{2x\,dx}{\sqrt{1-(x^2)^2}}$$
$$= \int \frac{du}{\sqrt{1-u^2}}$$
$$= \sin^{-1}u + C$$
$$= \sin^{-1}(x^2) + C.$$

(b) $\displaystyle\int \frac{e^x}{1+e^{2x}}\,dx$

SOLUTION Let $u = e^x$, with $du = e^x\,dx$. Then

$$\int \frac{e^x}{1+e^{2x}}\,dx = \int \frac{e^x\,dx}{1+(e^x)^2}$$
$$= \int \frac{du}{1+u^2}$$
$$= \tan^{-1}u + C$$
$$= \tan^{-1}e^x + C.$$

EXERCISES

Find each integral.

1. $\displaystyle\int \frac{x^3}{1 + x^8}\,dx$

2. $\displaystyle\int \frac{x^2}{\sqrt{1 - x^6}}\,dx$

3. $\displaystyle\int \frac{e^x}{\sqrt{1 - e^{2x}}}\,dx$

4. $\displaystyle\int \frac{-e^{2x}}{1 + e^{4x}}\,dx$

5. $\displaystyle\int \frac{4}{\sqrt{1 - 9x^2}}\,dx$

6. $\displaystyle\int \frac{\cos x}{1 + \sin^2 x}\,dx$

7. $\displaystyle\int \frac{1/x}{1 + (\ln x)^2}\,dx$

8. $\displaystyle\int \frac{1}{\sqrt{25 - x^2}}\,dx$

9. $\displaystyle\int_0^1 \frac{1}{1 + x^2}\,dx$

10. $\displaystyle\int_0^5 \frac{1}{\sqrt{1 - x^2}}\,dx$

11. $\displaystyle\int_0^2 \frac{1}{\sqrt{16 - x^2}}\,dx$

12. $\displaystyle\int_0^1 \frac{x^{1/3}}{1 + x^{8/3}}\,dx$

13. $\displaystyle\int_0^x \frac{1}{1 + x^2}\,dx$

APPLICATIONS

General Interest

Viewing Art   *While visiting a museum, Patricia Vidrine Quinlan views a painting that is 3 ft high and hanging 6 ft above the ground. (See the figure.) Assume Patricia's eyes are 5 ft above the ground, and let x be the distance from the spot where Patricia is standing to the wall displaying the painting.*

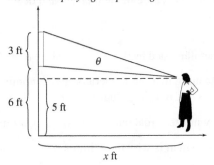

14. Show that θ, the viewing angle subtended by the painting, is given by
$$\theta = \tan^{-1}\frac{4}{x} - \tan^{-1}\frac{1}{x}.$$
(*Hint:* $\tan^{-1}\dfrac{4}{x}$ is an angle whose tangent is 4/x.)

15. Find the value of θ for each of the following values of x. Round to the nearest degree.

   a. 1   **b.** 2   **c.** 3   **d.** 4

APPLY IT

16. Find how far Patricia should stand from the wall to maximize θ, which should give her the best view of the painting.

17. Later Patricia views a painting that is 4 feet high and hanging 7 feet above the ground. How far should she stand from the wall to get the best view of this painting?

ANSWERS

Find each integral.

1. $(1/4)\tan^{-1} x^4 + C$

2. $(1/3)\sin^{-1} x^3 + C$

3. $\sin^{-1} e^x + C$

4. $(-1/2)\tan^{-1} e^{2x} + C$

5. $(4/3)\sin^{-1} 3x + C$

6. $\tan^{-1}\sin x + C$

7. $\tan^{-1}\ln |x| + C$

8. $\sin^{-1} x/5 + C$

9. $\pi/4$

10. $\pi/6$

11. $\pi/6$

12. $3\pi/16$

13. $\pi/2$

15. a. $31°$ **b.** $37°$ **c.** $35°$ **d.** $31°$

16. 2 ft

17. $2\sqrt{3}$ ft ≈ 3.46 ft

8 Extension

L'Hôpital's Rule

The study of limits was thorough but not exhaustive. Some limits, called *indeterminate forms*, cannot generally be evaluated. These limits tend to be the more interesting limits that arise in practice. A powerful result called *l'Hôpital's Rule* enables us to evaluate such limits with relative ease.

Here is how indeterminate forms arise. If f is a *continuous* function at a point a, then we know that $\lim_{x \to a} f(x) = f(a)$, allowing the limit to be evaluated by computing $f(a)$. But there are many limits that cannot be evaluated by substitution. In fact, we encountered such a limit in Section 3.4:

$$\lim_{x \to 0} \frac{\sin x}{x} = 1.$$

If we attempt to substitute $x = 0$ into $(\sin x)/x$, we get $0/0$, which has no meaning. Yet we proved that $(\sin x)/x$ has the limit 1 at $x = 0$. This limit is an example of an *indeterminate form*; specifically, $\lim_{x \to 0} \dfrac{\sin x}{x}$ has the form $0/0$ because the numerator and denominator both approach 0 as $x \to 0$.

The meaning of an *indeterminate form* is further illustrated by $\lim_{x \to \infty} \dfrac{ax}{x + 1}$, where $a \neq 0$. This limit has the indeterminate form ∞ / ∞ (meaning that the numerator and denominator become arbitrarily large in magnitude as $x \to \infty$), but the actual value of the limit is

$$\lim_{x \to \infty} \frac{ax}{x + 1} = a \lim_{x \to \infty} \frac{x}{x + 1} = a,$$

where a is any nonzero real number. In general, a limit with the form ∞ / ∞ or $0/0$ can have *any* value—which is why these limits must be handled carefully.

L'Hôpital's Rule for the Form 0/0

Consider a function of the form $f(x)/g(x)$ and assume that $\lim_{x \to a} f(x) = \lim_{x \to a} g(x) = 0$.

Then the limit $\lim_{x \to a} \dfrac{f(x)}{g(x)}$ has the indeterminate form $0/0$. We first state l'Hôpital's Rule and then prove a special case.

> Guillaume François l'Hôpital (lo-pee-tal) (1661–1704) is credited with writing the first calculus textbook. Much of the material in his book, including l'Hôpital's Rule, was provided by the Swiss mathematician Johann Bernoulli (1667–1748).

THEOREM 1 L'Hôpital's Rule

Suppose f and g are differentiable on an open interval I containing a with $g'(x) \neq 0$ on I when $x \neq a$. If $\lim\limits_{x \to a} f(x) = \lim\limits_{x \to a} g(x) = 0$, then

$$\lim_{x \to a} \frac{f(x)}{g(x)} = \lim_{x \to a} \frac{f'(x)}{g'(x)},$$

provided the limit on the right exists (or is $\pm \infty$). The rule also applies if $x \to a$ is replaced with $x \to \pm \infty$, $x \to a^+$, or $x \to a^-$.

Proof (special case): The proof of this theorem relies on the Generalized Mean Value Theorem. We prove a special case of the theorem in which we assume that f' and g' are continuous at a, $f(a) = g(a) = 0$, and $g'(a) \neq 0$. We have

$$\lim_{x \to a} \frac{f'(x)}{g'(x)} = \frac{f'(a)}{g'(a)} \qquad \text{Continuity of } f' \text{ and } g'$$

$$= \frac{\lim\limits_{x \to a} \dfrac{f(x) - f(a)}{x - a}}{\lim\limits_{x \to a} \dfrac{g(x) - g(a)}{x - a}} \qquad \text{Definition of } f'(a) \text{ and } g'(a)$$

$$= \lim_{x \to a} \frac{\dfrac{f(x) - f(a)}{x - a}}{\dfrac{g(x) - g(a)}{x - a}} \qquad \text{Limit of a quotient, } g'(a) \neq 0$$

$$= \lim_{x \to a} \frac{f(x) - f(a)}{g(x) - g(a)} \qquad \text{Cancel } x - a.$$

$$= \lim_{x \to a} \frac{f(x)}{g(x)}. \qquad f(a) = g(a) = 0 \qquad \blacktriangleleft$$

> The definition of the derivative provides an example of an indeterminate form. Assuming f is differentiable at x,
>
> $$f'(x) = \lim_{h \to 0} \frac{f(x + h) - f(x)}{h}$$
>
> has the form $0/0$.

The geometry of l'Hôpital's Rule offers some insight. First consider two *linear* functions, f and g, whose graphs both pass through the point $(a, 0)$ with slopes 4 and 2, respectively; this means that

$$f(x) = 4(x - a) \quad \text{and} \quad g(x) = 2(x - a).$$

Furthermore, $f(a) = g(a) = 0, f'(x) = 4$, and $g'(x) = 2$ (Figure 1).

Looking at the quotient f/g, we see that

$$\frac{f(x)}{g(x)} = \frac{4(x - a)}{2(x - a)} = \frac{4}{2} = \frac{f'(x)}{g'(x)}. \qquad \text{Exactly}$$

This argument may be generalized, and we find that for any linear functions f and g with $f(a) = g(a) = 0$,

$$\lim_{x \to a} \frac{f(x)}{g(x)} = \lim_{x \to a} \frac{f'(x)}{g'(x)},$$

provided $g'(a) \neq 0$.

If f and g are not linear functions, we replace them with their linear approximations at a (Figure 2). Zooming in on the point a, the curves are close to their respective tangent lines $y = f'(a)(x - a)$ and $y = g'(a)(x - a)$, which have slopes $f'(a)$ and $g'(a) \neq 0$, respectively. Near $x = a$, we have

$$\frac{f(x)}{g(x)} \approx \frac{f'(a)(x - a)}{g'(a)(x - a)} = \frac{f'(a)}{g'(a)}.$$

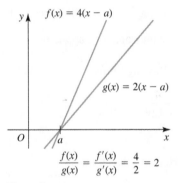

$f(x) = 4(x - a)$

$g(x) = 2(x - a)$

$$\frac{f(x)}{g(x)} = \frac{f'(x)}{g'(x)} = \frac{4}{2} = 2$$

Figure 1

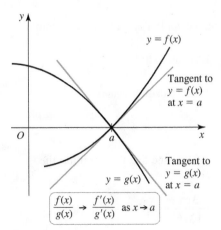

$y = f(x)$

Tangent to $y = f(x)$ at $x = a$

$y = g(x)$

Tangent to $y = g(x)$ at $x = a$

$$\frac{f(x)}{g(x)} \to \frac{f'(x)}{g'(x)} \quad \text{as } x \to a$$

Figure 2

QUICK CHECK 1 Which of the following functions lead to an indeterminate form as $x \to 0$: $f(x) = x^2/(x + 2)$, $g(x) = (\tan 3x)/x$, or $h(x) = (1 - \cos x)/x^2$? ◄

Therefore, the ratio of the functions is well approximated by the ratio of the derivatives. In the limit as $x \to a$, we again have

$$\lim_{x \to a} \frac{f(x)}{g(x)} = \lim_{x \to a} \frac{f'(x)}{g'(x)}.$$

EXAMPLE 1   Using l'Hôpital's Rule Evaluate the following limits.

a. $\lim\limits_{x \to 1} \dfrac{x^3 + x^2 - 2x}{x - 1}$ **b.** $\lim\limits_{x \to 0} \dfrac{\sqrt{9 + 3x} - 3}{x}$

SOLUTION

➤ The limit in part (a) can also be evaluated by factoring the numerator and canceling $(x - 1)$:

$$\lim_{x \to 1} \frac{x^3 + x^2 - 2x}{x - 1}$$
$$= \lim_{x \to 1} \frac{x(x - 1)(x + 2)}{x - 1}$$
$$= \lim_{x \to 1} x(x + 2) = 3.$$

a. Direct substitution of $x = 1$ into $\dfrac{x^3 + x^2 - 2x}{x - 1}$ produces the indeterminate form $0/0$. Applying l'Hôpital's Rule with $f(x) = x^3 + x^2 - 2x$ and $g(x) = x - 1$ gives

$$\lim_{x \to 1} \frac{x^3 + x^2 - 2x}{x - 1} = \lim_{x \to 1} \frac{f'(x)}{g'(x)} = \lim_{x \to 1} \frac{3x^2 + 2x - 2}{1} = 3.$$

b. Substituting $x = 0$ into this function produces the indeterminate form $0/0$. Let $f(x) = \sqrt{9 + 3x} - 3$ and $g(x) = x$, and note that $f'(x) = \dfrac{3}{2\sqrt{9 + 3x}}$ and $g'(x) = 1$. Applying l'Hôpital's Rule, we have

$$\lim_{x \to 0} \underbrace{\frac{\sqrt{9 + 3x} - 3}{x}}_{f/g} = \lim_{x \to 0} \underbrace{\frac{\dfrac{3}{2\sqrt{9 + 3x}}}{1}}_{f'/g'} = \frac{1}{2}.$$

Related Exercises 13–22 ◄

L'Hôpital's Rule requires evaluating $\lim\limits_{x \to a} f'(x)/g'(x)$. It may happen that this second limit is another indeterminate form to which l'Hôpital's Rule may again be applied.

EXAMPLE 2   L'Hôpital's Rule repeated Evaluate the following limits.

a. $\lim\limits_{x \to 0} \dfrac{e^x - x - 1}{x^2}$ **b.** $\lim\limits_{x \to 2} \dfrac{x^3 - 3x^2 + 4}{x^4 - 4x^3 + 7x^2 - 12x + 12}$

SOLUTION

a. This limit has the indeterminate form $0/0$. Applying l'Hôpital's Rule, we have

$$\lim_{x \to 0} \frac{e^x - x - 1}{x^2} = \lim_{x \to 0} \frac{e^x - 1}{2x},$$

which is another limit of the form $0/0$. Therefore, we apply l'Hôpital's Rule again:

$$\lim_{x \to 0} \frac{e^x - x - 1}{x^2} = \lim_{x \to 0} \frac{e^x - 1}{2x} \qquad \text{L'Hôpital's Rule}$$
$$= \lim_{x \to 0} \frac{e^x}{2} \qquad \text{L'Hôpital's Rule again}$$
$$= \frac{1}{2}. \qquad \text{Evaluate limit.}$$

b. Evaluating the numerator and denominator at $x = 2$, we see that this limit has the form $0/0$. Applying l'Hôpital's Rule twice, we have

$$\lim_{x \to 2} \frac{x^3 - 3x^2 + 4}{x^4 - 4x^3 + 7x^2 - 12x + 12} = \lim_{x \to 2} \underbrace{\frac{3x^2 - 6x}{4x^3 - 12x^2 + 14x - 12}}_{\text{limit of the form } 0/0} \qquad \text{L'Hôpital's Rule}$$

$$= \lim_{x \to 2} \frac{6x - 6}{12x^2 - 24x + 14} \qquad \text{L'Hôpital's Rule again}$$

$$= \frac{3}{7}. \qquad \text{Evaluate limit.}$$

It is easy to overlook a crucial step in this computation: After applying l'Hôpital's Rule the first time, you *must* establish that the new limit is an indeterminate form before applying l'Hôpital's Rule a second time.

Related Exercises 23–36 ◄

Indeterminate Form ∞/∞

L'Hôpital's Rule also applies directly to limits of the form $\lim_{x \to a} f(x)/g(x)$, where $\lim_{x \to a} f(x) = \pm \infty$ and $\lim_{x \to a} g(x) = \pm \infty$; this indeterminate form is denoted ∞ / ∞. The proof of this result is found in advanced books.

THEOREM 2   L'Hôpital's Rule (∞ / ∞)

Suppose that f and g are differentiable on an open interval I containing a, with $g'(x) \neq 0$ on I when $x \neq a$. If $\lim_{x \to a} f(x) = \pm \infty$ and $\lim_{x \to a} g(x) = \pm \infty$, then

$$\lim_{x \to a} \frac{f(x)}{g(x)} = \lim_{x \to a} \frac{f'(x)}{g'(x)},$$

provided the limit on the right exists (or is $\pm \infty$). The rule also applies for $x \to \pm \infty$, $x \to a^+$, or $x \to a^-$.

QUICK CHECK 2 Which of the following functions lead to an indeterminate form as $x \to \infty$: $f(x) = \sin x / x$, $g(x) = 2^x / x^2$, or $h(x) = (3x^2 + 4)/x^2$? ◄

EXAMPLE 3   L'Hôpital's Rule for ∞ / ∞ Evaluate the following limits.

a. $\lim_{x \to \infty} \dfrac{4x^3 - 6x^2 + 1}{2x^3 - 10x + 3}$ **b.** $\lim_{x \to \pi/2^-} \dfrac{1 + \tan x}{\sec x}$

SOLUTION

> The limit in Example 3a could also be evaluated by first dividing the numerator and denominator by x^3.

a. This limit has the indeterminate form ∞ / ∞ because both the numerator and the denominator approach ∞ as $x \to \infty$. Applying l'Hôpital's Rule three times, we have

$$\lim_{x \to \infty} \underbrace{\frac{4x^3 - 6x^2 + 1}{2x^3 - 10x + 3}}_{\infty/\infty} = \lim_{x \to \infty} \underbrace{\frac{12x^2 - 12x}{6x^2 - 10}}_{\infty/\infty} = \lim_{x \to \infty} \underbrace{\frac{24x - 12}{12x}}_{\infty/\infty} = \lim_{x \to \infty} \frac{24}{12} = 2.$$

b. In this limit, both the numerator and denominator approach ∞ as $x \to \pi/2^-$. L'Hôpital's Rule gives us

> In Exercise 3b, notice that we simplify $\sec^2 x / (\sec x \tan x)$ before taking the final limit. This step is important.

$$\lim_{x \to \pi/2^-} \frac{1 + \tan x}{\sec x} = \lim_{x \to \pi/2^-} \frac{\sec^2 x}{\sec x \tan x} \qquad \text{L'Hôpital's Rule}$$

$$= \lim_{x \to \pi/2^-} \frac{1}{\sin x} \qquad \text{Simplify.}$$

$$= 1. \qquad \text{Evaluate limit.}$$

Related Exercises 37–44 ◄

Related Indeterminate Forms: $0 \cdot \infty$ and $\infty - \infty$

We now consider limits of the form $\lim\limits_{x \to a} f(x)g(x)$, where $\lim\limits_{x \to a} f(x) = 0$ and $\lim\limits_{x \to a} g(x) = \pm\infty$; such limits are denoted $0 \cdot \infty$. *L'Hôpital's Rule cannot be directly applied to limits of this form.* Furthermore, it's risky to jump to conclusions about such limits. Suppose $f(x) = x$ and $g(x) = \dfrac{1}{x^2}$, in which case $\lim\limits_{x \to 0} f(x) = 0$, $\lim\limits_{x \to 0} g(x) = \infty$, and

$\lim\limits_{x \to 0} f(x)g(x) = \lim\limits_{x \to 0} \dfrac{1}{x}$ does not exist. On the other hand, if $f(x) = x$ and $g(x) = \dfrac{1}{\sqrt{x}}$, we have $\lim\limits_{x \to 0^+} f(x) = 0$, $\lim\limits_{x \to 0^+} g(x) = \infty$, and $\lim\limits_{x \to 0^+} f(x)g(x) = \lim\limits_{x \to 0^+} \sqrt{x} = 0$. So a limit of the form $0 \cdot \infty$, in which the two functions compete with each other, may have any value or may not exist. The following example illustrates how this indeterminate form can be recast in the form $0/0$ or ∞/∞.

EXAMPLE 4   L'Hôpital's Rule for $0 \cdot \infty$ Evaluate $\lim\limits_{x \to \infty} x^2 \sin\left(\dfrac{1}{4x^2}\right)$.

SOLUTION This limit has the form $0 \cdot \infty$. A common technique that converts this form to either $0/0$ or ∞/∞ is to *divide by the reciprocal*. We rewrite the limit and apply l'Hôpital's Rule:

$$\underbrace{\lim\limits_{x \to \infty} x^2 \sin\left(\dfrac{1}{4x^2}\right)}_{0 \cdot \infty \text{ form}} = \underbrace{\lim\limits_{x \to \infty} \dfrac{\sin\left(\dfrac{1}{4x^2}\right)}{\dfrac{1}{x^2}}}_{\text{recast in } 0/0 \text{ form}} \qquad x^2 = \dfrac{1}{1/x^2}$$

$$= \lim\limits_{x \to \infty} \dfrac{\cos\left(\dfrac{1}{4x^2}\right)\dfrac{1}{4}(-2x^{-3})}{-2x^{-3}} \qquad \text{L'Hôpital's Rule}$$

$$= \dfrac{1}{4} \lim\limits_{x \to \infty} \cos\left(\dfrac{1}{4x^2}\right) \qquad \text{Simplify.}$$

$$= \dfrac{1}{4}. \qquad\qquad \dfrac{1}{4x^2} \to 0, \cos 0 = 1$$

Related Exercises 45–50 ◄

QUICK CHECK 3 What is the form of the limit $\lim\limits_{x \to \pi/2^-} (x - \pi/2)(\tan x)$? Write it in the form $0/0$. ◄

Limits of the form $\lim\limits_{x \to a} (f(x) - g(x))$, where $\lim\limits_{x \to a} f(x) = \infty$ and $\lim\limits_{x \to a} g(x) = \infty$, are indeterminate forms that we denote $\infty - \infty$. L'Hôpital's Rule cannot be applied directly to an $\infty - \infty$ form. It must first be expressed in the form $0/0$ or ∞/∞. With the $\infty - \infty$ form, it is easy to reach erroneous conclusions. For example, if $f(x) = 3x + 5$ and $g(x) = 3x$, then

$$\lim\limits_{x \to \infty} ((3x + 5) - (3x)) = 5.$$

However, if $f(x) = 3x$ and $g(x) = 2x$, then

$$\lim\limits_{x \to \infty} (3x - 2x) = \lim\limits_{x \to \infty} x = \infty.$$

These examples show again why indeterminate forms are deceptive. Before proceeding, we introduce another useful technique.

Occasionally, it helps to convert a limit as $x \to \infty$ to a limit as $t \to 0^+$ (or vice versa) by a *change of variables*. To evaluate $\lim\limits_{x \to \infty} f(x)$, we define $t = 1/x$ and note that as $x \to \infty$, $t \to 0^+$. Then

$$\lim_{x \to \infty} f(x) = \lim_{t \to 0^+} f\left(\frac{1}{t}\right).$$

This idea is illustrated in the next example.

EXAMPLE 5   L'Hôpital's Rule for $\infty - \infty$ Evaluate $\lim\limits_{x \to \infty} (x - \sqrt{x^2 - 3x})$.

SOLUTION As $x \to \infty$, both terms in the difference $x - \sqrt{x^2 - 3x}$ approach ∞ and this limit has the form $\infty - \infty$. We first factor x from the expression and form a quotient:

$$\lim_{x \to \infty} (x - \sqrt{x^2 - 3x}) = \lim_{x \to \infty} (x - \sqrt{x^2(1 - 3/x)} \qquad \text{Factor } x^2 \text{ under square root.}$$

$$= \lim_{x \to \infty} x(1 - \sqrt{1 - 3/x}) \qquad x > 0, \text{ so } \sqrt{x^2} = x$$

$$= \lim_{x \to \infty} \frac{1 - \sqrt{1 - 3/x}}{1/x}. \qquad \begin{array}{l} \text{Write } 0 \cdot \infty \text{ form as } 0/0 \\ \text{form; } x = \dfrac{1}{1/x}. \end{array}$$

This new limit has the form $0/0$, and l'Hôpital's Rule may be applied. One way to proceed is to use the change of variables $t = 1/x$:

$$\lim_{x \to \infty} \frac{1 - \sqrt{1 - 3/x}}{1/x} = \lim_{t \to 0^+} \frac{1 - \sqrt{1 - 3t}}{t} \qquad \text{Let } t = 1/x; \text{ replace } \lim_{x \to \infty} \text{ with } \lim_{t \to 0^+}.$$

$$= \lim_{t \to 0^+} \frac{\dfrac{3}{2\sqrt{1 - 3t}}}{1} \qquad \text{L'Hôpital's Rule}$$

$$= \frac{3}{2}. \qquad \text{Evaluate limit.}$$

Related Exercises 51–54 ◀

Indeterminate Forms 1^∞, 0^0, and ∞^0

The indeterminate forms 1^∞, 0^0, and ∞^0 all arise in limits of the form $\lim\limits_{x \to a} f(x)^{g(x)}$, where $x \to a$ could be replaced with $x \to a^\pm$ or $x \to \pm\infty$. L'Hôpital's Rule cannot be applied directly to the indeterminate forms 1^∞, 0^0, and ∞^0. They must first be expressed in the form $0/0$ or ∞/∞. Here is how we proceed.

The inverse relationship between $\ln x$ and e^x says that $f^g = e^{g \ln f}$, so we first write

$$\lim_{x \to a} f(x)^{g(x)} = \lim_{x \to a} e^{g(x) \ln f(x)}.$$

By the continuity of the exponential function, we switch the order of the limit and the exponential function; therefore,

$$\lim_{x \to a} f(x)^{g(x)} = \lim_{x \to a} e^{g(x) \ln f(x)} = e^{\lim_{x \to a} g(x) \ln f(x)},$$

provided $\lim\limits_{x \to a} g(x) \ln f(x)$ exists. Therefore, $\lim\limits_{x \to a} f(x)^{g(x)}$ is evaluated using the following two steps.

PROCEDURE   Indeterminate forms 1^∞, 0^0, and ∞^0

Assume $\lim\limits_{x \to a} f(x)^{g(x)}$ has the indeterminate form 1^∞, 0^0, or ∞^0.

1. Analyze $L = \lim\limits_{x \to a} g(x) \ln f(x)$. This limit can be put in the form $0/0$ or ∞/∞, both of which are handled by l'Hôpital's Rule.

▶ Notice the following:
- For 1^∞, L has the form $\infty \cdot \ln 1 = \infty \cdot 0$.
- For 0^0, L has the form $0 \cdot \ln 0 = 0 \cdot -\infty$.
- For ∞^0, L has the form $0 \cdot \ln \infty = 0 \cdot \infty$.

2. When L is finite, $\lim\limits_{x \to a} f(x)^{g(x)} = e^L$. If $L = \infty$ or $-\infty$, then $\lim\limits_{x \to a} f(x)^{g(x)} = \infty$

or $\lim\limits_{x \to a} f(x)^{g(x)} = 0$, respectively.

QUICK CHECK 4 Explain why a limit of the form 0^∞ is not an indeterminate form. ◄

EXAMPLE 6   Indeterminate forms 0^0 and 1^∞ Evaluate the following limits.

a. $\lim\limits_{x \to 0^+} x^x$ **b.** $\lim\limits_{x \to \infty} \left(1 + \dfrac{1}{x} \right)^x$

SOLUTION

a. This limit has the form 0^0. Using the given two-step procedure, we note that $x^x = e^{x \ln x}$ and first evaluate

$$L = \lim_{x \to 0^+} x \ln x.$$

This limit has the form $0 \cdot \infty$, which may be put in the form ∞ / ∞ so that l'Hôpital's Rule can be applied:

$$L = \lim_{x \to 0^+} x \ln x = \lim_{x \to 0^+} \frac{\ln x}{1/x} \qquad x = \frac{1}{1/x}$$

$$= \lim_{x \to 0^+} \frac{1/x}{-1/x^2} \qquad \text{L'Hôpital's Rule for } \infty / \infty \text{ form}$$

$$= \lim_{x \to 0^+} (-x) = 0. \qquad \text{Simplify and evaluate the limit.}$$

The second step is to exponentiate the limit:

$$\lim_{x \to 0^+} x^x = e^L = e^0 = 1.$$

We conclude that $\lim\limits_{x \to 0^+} x^x = 1$ (Figure 3).

b. This limit has the form 1^∞. Noting that $(1 + 1/x)^x = e^{x \ln (1 + 1/x)}$, the first step is to evaluate

$$L = \lim_{x \to \infty} x \ln \left(1 + \frac{1}{x} \right),$$

which has the form $0 \cdot \infty$. Proceeding as in part (a), we have

$$L = \lim_{x \to \infty} x \ln \left(1 + \frac{1}{x} \right) = \lim_{x \to \infty} \frac{\ln (1 + 1/x)}{1/x} \qquad x = \frac{1}{1/x}$$

$$= \lim_{x \to \infty} \frac{\dfrac{1}{1 + 1/x} \cdot \left(-\dfrac{1}{x^2} \right)}{\left(-\dfrac{1}{x^2} \right)} \qquad \text{L'Hôpital's Rule for 0/0 form}$$

$$= \lim_{x \to \infty} \frac{1}{1 + 1/x} = 1. \qquad \text{Simplify and evaluate.}$$

The second step is to exponentiate the limit:

$$\lim_{x \to \infty} \left(1 + \frac{1}{x} \right)^x = e^L = e^1 = e.$$

The function $y = (1 + 1/x)^x$ (Figure 4) has a horizontal asymptote $y = e \approx 2.71828$.

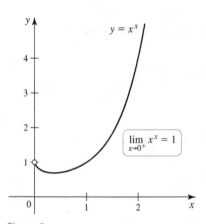

Figure 3

▶ The limit in Example 6b is often given as a definition of e. It is a special case of the more general limit

$$\lim_{x \to \infty} \left(1 + \frac{a}{x} \right)^x = e^a.$$

See Exercise 119.

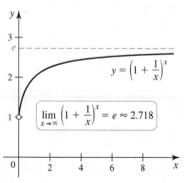

Figure 4

Related Exercises 55–68 ◄

Growth Rates of Functions

An important use of l'Hôpital's Rule is to compare the growth rates of functions. Here are two questions—one practical and one theoretical—that demonstrate the importance of comparative growth rates of functions.

> Models of epidemics produce more complicated functions than the one given here, but they have the same general features.

- A particular theory for modeling the spread of an epidemic predicts that the number of infected people t days after the start of the epidemic is given by the function

$$N(t) = 2.5t^2 e^{-0.01t} = 2.5 \frac{t^2}{e^{0.01t}}.$$

Question: In the long run (as $t \to \infty$), does the epidemic spread or does it die out?

> The Prime Number Theorem was proved simultaneously (two different proofs) in 1896 by Jacques Hadamard and Charles de la Vallée Poussin, relying on fundamental ideas contributed by Riemann.

- A prime number is an integer $p \geq 2$ that has only two divisors, 1 and itself. The first few prime numbers are 2, 3, 5, 7, and 11. A celebrated theorem states that the number of prime numbers less than x is approximately

$$P(x) = \frac{x}{\ln x}, \quad \text{for large values of } x.$$

Question: According to this theorem, is the number of prime numbers infinite?

These two questions involve a comparison of two functions. In the first question, if t^2 grows faster than $e^{0.01t}$ as $t \to \infty$, then $\lim_{t \to \infty} N(t) = \infty$ and the epidemic grows. If $e^{0.01t}$ grows faster than t^2 as $t \to \infty$, then $\lim_{t \to \infty} N(t) = 0$ and the epidemic dies out. We will explain what is meant by *grows faster than* in a moment.

In the second question, the comparison is between x and $\ln x$. If x grows faster than $\ln x$ as $x \to \infty$, then $\lim_{x \to \infty} P(x) = \infty$ and the number of prime numbers is infinite.

Our goal is to obtain a ranking of the following families of functions based on their growth rates:

> Another function with a large growth rate is the factorial function, defined for integers as $f(n) = n! = n(n-1) \cdots 2 \cdot 1$. See Exercise 116.

- mx, where $m > 0$ (represents linear functions)
- x^p, where $p > 0$ (represents polynomials and algebraic functions)
- x^x (sometimes called a *superexponential* or *tower function*)
- $\ln x$ (represents logarithmic functions)
- $\ln^q x$, where $q > 0$ (represents powers of logarithmic functions)
- $x^p \ln x$, where $p > 0$ (a combination of powers and logarithms)
- e^x (represents exponential functions).

QUICK CHECK 5 Before proceeding, use your intuition and rank these classes of functions in order of their growth rates. ◄

We need to be precise about growth rates and what it means for f to grow faster than g as $x \to \infty$. We work with the following definitions.

DEFINITION Growth Rates of Functions (as $x \to \infty$)

Suppose f and g are functions with $\lim_{x \to \infty} f(x) = \lim_{x \to \infty} g(x) = \infty$. Then **$f$ grows faster than g** as $x \to \infty$ if

$$\lim_{x \to \infty} \frac{g(x)}{f(x)} = 0 \quad \text{or, equivalently, if} \quad \lim_{x \to \infty} \frac{f(x)}{g(x)} = \infty.$$

The functions f and g have **comparable growth rates** if

$$\lim_{x \to \infty} \frac{f(x)}{g(x)} = M,$$

where $0 < M < \infty$ (M is nonzero and finite).

The idea of growth rates is illustrated nicely with graphs. Figure 6 shows a family of linear functions of the form $y = mx$, where $m > 0$, and powers of x of the form $y = x^p$, where $p > 1$. We see that powers of x grow faster (their curves rise at a greater rate) than the linear functions as $x \to \infty$.

Figure 7 shows that exponential functions of the form $y = b^x$, where $b > 1$, grow faster than powers of x of the form $y = x^p$, where $p > 0$, as $x \to \infty$ (Example 8).

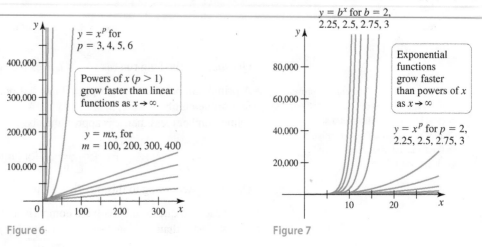

Figure 6

Figure 7

QUICK CHECK 6 Compare the growth rates of $f(x) = x^2$ and $g(x) = x^3$ as $x \to \infty$. Compare the growth rates of $f(x) = x^2$ and $g(x) = 10x^2$ as $x \to \infty$. ◄

We now begin a systematic comparison of growth rates. Note that a growth rate limit involves an indeterminate form ∞ / ∞, so l'Hôpital's Rule is always in the picture.

EXAMPLE 7   Powers of x vs. powers of ln x Compare the growth rates as $x \to \infty$ of the following pairs of functions.

a. $f(x) = \ln x$ and $g(x) = x^p$, where $p > 0$

b. $f(x) = \ln^q x$ and $g(x) = x^p$, where $p > 0$ and $q > 0$

SOLUTION

a. The limit of the ratio of the two functions is

$$\lim_{x \to \infty} \frac{\ln x}{x^p} = \lim_{x \to \infty} \frac{1/x}{px^{p-1}} \quad \text{L'Hôpital's Rule}$$

$$= \lim_{x \to \infty} \frac{1}{px^p} \quad \text{Simplify.}$$

$$= 0. \quad \text{Evaluate the limit.}$$

We see that any positive power of x grows faster than $\ln x$.

b. We compare $\ln^q x$ and x^p by observing that

$$\lim_{x \to \infty} \frac{\ln^q x}{x^p} = \lim_{x \to \infty} \left(\frac{\ln x}{x^{p/q}} \right)^q = \left(\underbrace{\lim_{x \to \infty} \frac{\ln x}{x^{p/q}}}_{0} \right)^q.$$

By part (a), $\displaystyle\lim_{x \to \infty} \frac{\ln x}{x^{p/q}} = 0$ (because $p/q > 0$). Therefore, $\displaystyle\lim_{x \to \infty} \frac{\ln^q x}{x^p} = 0$ (because $q > 0$). We conclude that any positive power of x grows faster than any positive power of $\ln x$.

Related Exercises 69–80 ◄

EXAMPLE 8 Powers of x vs. exponentials Compare the rates of growth of $f(x) = x^p$ and $g(x) = e^x$ as $x \to \infty$, where p is a positive real number.

SOLUTION The goal is to evaluate $\lim\limits_{x \to \infty} \dfrac{x^p}{e^x}$, for $p > 0$. This comparison is most easily done using Example 7 and a change of variables. We let $x = \ln t$ and note that as $x \to \infty$, we also have $t \to \infty$. With this substitution, $x^p = \ln^p t$ and $e^x = e^{\ln t} = t$. Therefore,

$$\lim_{x \to \infty} \frac{x^p}{e^x} = \lim_{t \to \infty} \frac{\ln^p t}{t} = 0. \quad \text{Example 7}$$

We see that increasing exponential functions grow faster than positive powers of x (Figure 7).

Related Exercises 69–80 ◄

These examples, together with the comparison of exponential functions b^x and the superexponential x^x (Exercise 120), establish a ranking of growth rates.

THEOREM 3 Ranking Growth Rates as $x \to \infty$

Let $f \ll g$ mean that g grows faster than f as $x \to \infty$. With positive real numbers p, q, r, and s and $b > 1$,

$$\ln^q x \ll x^p \ll x^p \ln^r x \ll x^{p+s} \ll b^x \ll x^x.$$

You should try to build these relative growth rates into your intuition and they can be used to evaluate limits at infinity quickly.

Pitfalls in Using l'Hôpital's Rule

We close with a list of common pitfalls when using l'Hôpital's Rule.

1. L'Hôpital's Rule says $\lim\limits_{x \to a} \dfrac{f(x)}{g(x)} = \lim\limits_{x \to a} \dfrac{f'(x)}{g'(x)}$, not

$$\lim_{x \to a} \frac{f(x)}{g(x)} = \lim_{x \to a} \left(\frac{f(x)}{g(x)} \right)' \quad \text{or} \quad \lim_{x \to a} \frac{f(x)}{g(x)} = \lim_{x \to a} \left(\frac{1}{g(x)} \right)' f'(x).$$

In other words, you should evaluate $f'(x)$ and $g'(x)$, form their quotient, and then take the limit. Don't confuse l'Hôpital's Rule with the Quotient Rule.

2. Be sure that the given limit involves the indeterminate form $0/0$ or ∞/∞ before applying l'Hôpital's Rule. For example, consider the following erroneous use of l'Hôpital's Rule:

$$\lim_{x \to 0} \frac{1 - \sin x}{\cos x} = \lim_{x \to 0} \frac{-\cos x}{\sin x},$$

which does not exist. The original limit is not an indeterminate form in the first place. This limit should be evaluated by direct substitution:

$$\lim_{x \to 0} \frac{1 - \sin x}{\cos x} = \frac{1 - \sin 0}{1} = 1.$$

3. When using l'Hôpital's Rule repeatedly, be sure to simplify expressions as much as possible at each step and evaluate the limit as soon as the new limit is no longer an indeterminate form.

4. Repeated use of l'Hôpital's Rule occasionally leads to unending cycles, in which case other methods must be used. For example, limits of the form $\lim\limits_{x \to \infty} \dfrac{\sqrt{ax + 1}}{\sqrt{bx + 1}}$, where a and b are real numbers, lead to such behavior (Exercise 111).

5. Be sure that the limit produced by l'Hôpital's Rule exists. Consider $\lim\limits_{x\to\infty}\dfrac{3x+\cos x}{x}$, which has the form ∞/∞. Applying l'Hôpital's Rule, we have

$$\lim_{x\to\infty}\frac{3x+\cos x}{x}=\lim_{x\to\infty}\frac{3-\sin x}{1}.$$

It is tempting to conclude that because the limit on the right side does not exist, the original limit also does not exist. In fact, the original limit has a value of 3 (divide numerator and denominator by x). To reach a conclusion from l'Hôpital's Rule, the limit produced by l'Hôpital's Rule must exist (or be $\pm\infty$).

EXERCISES

Review Questions

1. Explain with examples what is meant by the indeterminate form $0/0$.

2. Why are special methods, such as l'Hôpital's Rule, needed to evaluate indeterminate forms (as opposed to substitution)?

3. Explain the steps used to apply l'Hôpital's Rule to a limit of the form $0/0$.

4. To which indeterminate forms does l'Hôpital's Rule apply *directly*?

5. Explain how to convert a limit of the form $0\cdot\infty$ to a limit of the form $0/0$ or ∞/∞.

6. Give an example of a limit of the form ∞/∞ as $x\to0$.

7. Explain why the form 1^∞ is indeterminate and cannot be evaluated by substitution. Explain how the competing functions behave.

8. Give the two-step method for attacking an indeterminate limit of the form $\lim\limits_{x\to a}f(x)^{g(x)}$.

9. In terms of limits, what does it mean for f to grow faster than g as $x\to\infty$?

10. In terms of limits, what does it mean for the rates of growth of f and g to be comparable as $x\to\infty$?

11. Rank the functions x^3, $\ln x$, x^x, and 2^x in order of increasing growth rates as $x\to\infty$.

12. Rank the functions x^{100}, $\ln x^{10}$, x^x, and 10^x in order of increasing growth rates as $x\to\infty$.

Basic Skills

13–22. 0/0 form *Evaluate the following limits using l'Hôpital's Rule.*

13. $\lim\limits_{x\to2}\dfrac{x^2-2x}{8-6x+x^2}$

14. $\lim\limits_{x\to-1}\dfrac{x^4+x^3+2x+2}{x+1}$

15. $\lim\limits_{x\to1}\dfrac{\ln x}{4x-x^2-3}$

16. $\lim\limits_{x\to0}\dfrac{e^x-1}{x^2+3x}$

17. $\lim\limits_{x\to e}\dfrac{\ln x-1}{x-e}$

18. $\lim\limits_{x\to1}\dfrac{4\tan^{-1}x-\pi}{x-1}$

19. $\lim\limits_{x\to0}\dfrac{3\sin4x}{5x}$

20. $\lim\limits_{x\to2\pi}\dfrac{x\sin x+x^2-4\pi^2}{x-2\pi}$

21. $\lim\limits_{u\to\pi/4}\dfrac{\tan u-\cot u}{u-\pi/4}$

22. $\lim\limits_{z\to0}\dfrac{\tan4z}{\tan7z}$

23–36. 0/0 form *Evaluate the following limits.*

23. $\lim\limits_{x\to0}\dfrac{1-\cos3x}{8x^2}$

24. $\lim\limits_{x\to0}\dfrac{\sin^23x}{x^2}$

25. $\lim\limits_{x\to\pi}\dfrac{\cos x+1}{(x-\pi)^2}$

26. $\lim\limits_{x\to0}\dfrac{e^x-x-1}{5x^2}$

27. $\lim\limits_{x\to0}\dfrac{e^x-\sin x-1}{x^4+8x^3+12x^2}$

28. $\lim\limits_{x\to0}\dfrac{\sin x-x}{7x^3}$

29. $\lim\limits_{x\to\infty}\dfrac{e^{1/x}-1}{1/x}$

30. $\lim\limits_{x\to\infty}\dfrac{\tan^{-1}x-\pi/2}{1/x}$

31. $\lim\limits_{x\to-1}\dfrac{x^3-x^2-5x-3}{x^4+2x^3-x^2-4x-2}$

32. $\lim\limits_{x\to1}\dfrac{x^n-1}{x-1}$, n is a positive integer

33. $\lim\limits_{v\to3}\dfrac{v-1-\sqrt{v^2-5}}{v-3}$

34. $\lim\limits_{y\to2}\dfrac{y^2+y-6}{\sqrt{8-y^2}-y}$

35. $\lim\limits_{x\to2}\dfrac{x^2-4x+4}{\sin^2(\pi x)}$

36. $\lim\limits_{x\to2}\dfrac{\sqrt[3]{3x+2}-2}{x-2}$

37–44. ∞/∞ form *Evaluate the following limits.*

37. $\lim\limits_{x\to\infty}\dfrac{3x^4-x^2}{6x^4+12}$

38. $\lim\limits_{x\to\infty}\dfrac{4x^3-2x^2+6}{\pi x^3+4}$

39. $\lim\limits_{x\to\pi/2^-}\dfrac{\tan x}{3/(2x-\pi)}$

40. $\lim\limits_{x\to\infty}\dfrac{e^{3x}}{3e^{3x}+5}$

41. $\lim\limits_{x\to\infty}\dfrac{\ln(3x+5)}{\ln(7x+3)+1}$

42. $\lim\limits_{x\to\infty}\dfrac{\ln(3x+5e^x)}{\ln(7x+3e^{2x})}$

43. $\lim\limits_{x\to\infty}\dfrac{x^2-\ln(2/x)}{3x^2+2x}$

44. $\lim\limits_{x\to\pi/2}\dfrac{2\tan x}{\sec^2 x}$

45–50. 0·∞ form *Evaluate the following limits.*

45. $\lim\limits_{x\to0}x\csc x$

46. $\lim\limits_{x\to1^-}(1-x)\tan\left(\dfrac{\pi x}{2}\right)$

47. $\lim\limits_{x\to0}\csc6x\sin7x$

48. $\lim\limits_{x\to\infty}(\csc(1/x)(e^{1/x}-1))$

49. $\lim\limits_{x\to\pi/2^-}\left(\dfrac{\pi}{2}-x\right)\sec x$

50. $\lim\limits_{x\to0^+}(\sin x)\sqrt{\dfrac{1-x}{x}}$

51–54. $\infty - \infty$ **form** *Evaluate the following limits.*

51. $\lim\limits_{x \to 0^+} \left(\cot x - \dfrac{1}{x} \right)$ **52.** $\lim\limits_{x \to \infty} (x - \sqrt{x^2 + 1})$

53. $\lim\limits_{\theta \to \pi/2^-} (\tan \theta - \sec \theta)$ **54.** $\lim\limits_{x \to \infty} (x - \sqrt{x^2 + 4x})$

55–68. $1^\infty, 0^0, \infty^0$ **forms** *Evaluate the following limits or explain why they do not exist. Check your results by graphing.*

55. $\lim\limits_{x \to 0^+} x^{2x}$ **56.** $\lim\limits_{x \to 0} (1 + 4x)^{3/x}$

57. $\lim\limits_{\theta \to \pi/2^-} (\tan \theta)^{\cos \theta}$ **58.** $\lim\limits_{\theta \to 0^+} (\sin \theta)^{\tan \theta}$

59. $\lim\limits_{x \to 0^+} (1 + x)^{\cot x}$ **60.** $\lim\limits_{x \to \infty} \left(1 + \dfrac{1}{x} \right)^{\ln x}$

61. $\lim\limits_{x \to \infty} \left(1 + \dfrac{a}{x} \right)^x$, for a constant a

62. $\lim\limits_{x \to 0} (e^{5x} + x)^{1/x}$

63. $\lim\limits_{x \to 0} (e^{ax} + x)^{1/x}$, for a constant a

64. $\lim\limits_{x \to 0} (2^{ax} + x)^{1/x}$, for a constant a

65. $\lim\limits_{x \to 0^+} (\tan x)^x$ **66.** $\lim\limits_{z \to \infty} \left(1 + \dfrac{10}{z^2} \right)^{z^2}$

67. $\lim\limits_{x \to 0} (x + \cos x)^{1/x}$ **68.** $\lim\limits_{x \to 0^+} \left(\dfrac{1}{3} \cdot 3^x + \dfrac{2}{3} \cdot 2^x \right)^{1/x}$

69–80. Comparing growth rates *Use limit methods to determine which of the two given functions grows faster or state that they have comparable growth rates.*

69. x^{10}; $e^{0.01x}$ **70.** $x^2 \ln x$; $\ln^2 x$ **71.** $\ln x^{20}$; $\ln x$

72. $\ln x$; $\ln (\ln x)$ **73.** 100^x; x^x **74.** $x^2 \ln x$; x^3

75. x^{20}; 1.00001^x **76.** $x^{10} \ln^{10} x$; x^{11} **77.** x^x; $(x/2)^x$

78. $\ln \sqrt{x}$; $\ln^2 x$ **79.** e^{x^2}; e^{10x} **80.** e^{x^2}; $x^{x/10}$

Further Explorations

81. Explain why or why not Determine whether the following statements are true and give an explanation or counterexample.

  a. By l'Hôpital's Rule, $\lim\limits_{x \to 2} \dfrac{x - 2}{x^2 - 1} = \lim\limits_{x \to 2} \dfrac{1}{2x} = \dfrac{1}{4}$.

  b. $\lim\limits_{x \to 0} (x \sin x) = \lim\limits_{x \to 0} f(x) g(x) =$
    $\lim\limits_{x \to 0} f'(x) \lim\limits_{x \to 0} g'(x) = (\lim\limits_{x \to 0} 1)(\lim\limits_{x \to 0} \cos x) = 1$.

  c. $\lim\limits_{x \to 0^+} x^{1/x}$ is an indeterminate form.

  d. The number 1 raised to any fixed power is 1. Therefore, because $(1 + x) \to 1$ as $x \to 0$, $(1 + x)^{1/x} \to 1$ as $x \to 0$.

  e. The functions $\ln x^{100}$ and $\ln x$ have comparable growth rates as $x \to \infty$.

  f. The function e^x grows faster than 2^x as $x \to \infty$.

82–83. Two methods *Evaluate the following limits in two different ways: Use the methods of Chapter 2 and use l'Hôpital's Rule.*

82. $\lim\limits_{x \to \infty} \dfrac{100x^3 - 3}{x^4 - 2}$ **83.** $\lim\limits_{x \to \infty} \dfrac{2x^3 - x^2 + 1}{5x^3 + 2x}$

84. L'Hôpital's example Evaluate one of the limits l'Hôpital used in his own textbook in about 1700:

$$\lim\limits_{x \to a} \dfrac{\sqrt{2a^3 x - x^4} - a\sqrt[3]{a^2 x}}{a - \sqrt[4]{ax^3}}, \text{ where } a \text{ is a real number.}$$

85–102. Miscellaneous limits by any means *Use analytical methods to evaluate the following limits.*

85. $\lim\limits_{x \to 6} \dfrac{\sqrt[5]{5x + 2} - 2}{1/x - 1/6}$ **86.** $\lim\limits_{x \to \infty} x^2 \ln \left(\cos \dfrac{1}{x} \right)$

87. $\lim\limits_{x \to \infty} (\sqrt{x - 2} - \sqrt{x - 4})$ **88.** $\lim\limits_{x \to \pi/2} (\pi - 2x) \tan x$

89. $\lim\limits_{x \to \infty} x^3 \left(\dfrac{1}{x} - \sin \dfrac{1}{x} \right)$ **90.** $\lim\limits_{x \to \infty} (x^2 e^{1/x} - x^2 - x)$

91. $\lim\limits_{x \to 1^+} \left(\dfrac{1}{x - 1} - \dfrac{1}{\sqrt{x - 1}} \right)$ **92.** $\lim\limits_{x \to 0^+} x^{1/\ln x}$

93. $\lim\limits_{x \to \infty} \dfrac{\log_2 x}{\log_3 x}$ **94.** $\lim\limits_{x \to \infty} (\log_2 x - \log_3 x)$

95. $\lim\limits_{n \to \infty} \dfrac{1 + 2 + \cdots + n}{n^2}$

    $\left(\text{Hint: Use } 1 + 2 + \cdots + n = \dfrac{n(n + 1)}{2}. \right)$

96. $\lim\limits_{x \to 0} \left(\dfrac{\sin x}{x} \right)^{1/x^2}$ **97.** $\lim\limits_{x \to 1} \dfrac{x \ln x - x + 1}{x \ln^2 x}$

98. $\lim\limits_{x \to 1} \dfrac{x \ln x + \ln x - 2x + 2}{x^2 \ln^3 x}$ **99.** $\lim\limits_{x \to 0^+} x^{1/(1 + \ln x)}$

100. $\lim\limits_{n \to \infty} \left(\cot \dfrac{1}{n} - n \right)$ **101.** $\lim\limits_{n \to \infty} \left(n \cot \dfrac{1}{n} - n^2 \right)$

102. $\lim\limits_{n \to \infty} n^2 \ln \left(n \sin \dfrac{1}{n} \right)$

103. It may take time The ranking of growth rates given in the text applies for $x \to \infty$. However, these rates may not be evident for small values of x. For example, an exponential grows faster than any power of x. However, for $1 < x < 19{,}800$, x^2 is greater than $e^{x/1000}$. For the following pairs of functions, estimate the point at which the faster-growing function overtakes the slower-growing function (for the last time).

  a. $\ln^3 x$ and $x^{0.3}$ **b.** $2^{x/100}$ and x^3
  c. $x^{x/100}$ and e^x **d.** $\ln^{10} x$ and $e^{x/10}$

104–107. Limits with parameters *Evaluate the following limits in terms of the parameters a and b, which are positive real numbers. In each case, graph the function for specific values of the parameters to check your results.*

104. $\lim\limits_{x \to 0} (1 + ax)^{b/x}$

105. $\lim\limits_{x \to 0^+} (a^x - b^x)^x$, $a > b > 0$

106. $\lim\limits_{x \to 0^+} (a^x - b^x)^{1/x}$, $a > b > 0$

107. $\lim\limits_{x \to 0} \dfrac{a^x - b^x}{x}$

Applications

108. An optics limit The theory of interference of coherent oscillators requires the limit $\lim\limits_{\delta \to 2m\pi} \dfrac{\sin^2(N\delta/2)}{\sin^2(\delta/2)}$, where N is a positive integer and m is any integer. Show that the value of this limit is N^2.

109. Compound interest Suppose you make a deposit of $\$P$ into a savings account that earns interest at a rate of $100\,r\%$ per year.

  a. Show that if interest is compounded once per year, then the balance after t years is $B(t) = P(1 + r)^t$.

  b. If interest is compounded m times per year, then the balance after t years is $B(t) = P(1 + r/m)^{mt}$. For example, $m = 12$ corresponds to monthly compounding, and the interest rate for each month is $r/12$. In the limit $m \to \infty$, the compounding is said to be *continuous*. Show that with continuous compounding, the balance after t years is $B(t) = Pe^{rt}$.

110. Algorithm complexity The complexity of a computer algorithm is the number of operations or steps the algorithm needs to complete its task assuming there are n pieces of input (for example, the number of steps needed to put n numbers in ascending order). Four algorithms for doing the same task have complexities of A: $n^{3/2}$, B: $n \log_2 n$, C: $n(\log_2 n)^2$, and D: $\sqrt{n} \log_2 n$. Rank the algorithms in order of increasing efficiency for large values of n. Graph the complexities as they vary with n and comment on your observations.

Additional Exercises

111. L'Hôpital loops Consider the limit $\lim\limits_{x \to \infty} \dfrac{\sqrt{ax + b}}{\sqrt{cx + d}}$, where a, b, c, and d are positive real numbers. Show that l'Hôpital's Rule fails for this limit. Find the limit using another method.

112. General $\infty - \infty$ result Let a and b be positive real numbers. Evaluate $\lim\limits_{x \to \infty} (ax - \sqrt{a^2x^2 - bx})$ in terms of a and b.

113. Exponential functions and powers Show that any exponential function b^x, for $b > 1$, grows faster than x^p, for $p > 0$.

114. Exponentials with different bases Show that $f(x) = a^x$ grows faster than $g(x) = b^x$ as $x \to \infty$ if $1 < b < a$.

115. Logs with different bases Show that $f(x) = \log_a x$ and $g(x) = \log_b x$, where $a > 1$ and $b > 1$, grow at a comparable rate as $x \to \infty$.

116. Factorial growth rate The factorial function is defined for positive integers as $n! = n(n-1)(n-2) \cdots 3 \cdot 2 \cdot 1$. For example, $5! = 5 \cdot 4 \cdot 3 \cdot 2 \cdot 1 = 120$. A valuable result that gives good approximations to $n!$ for large values of n is *Stirling's formula*, $n! \approx \sqrt{2\pi n}\, n^n e^{-n}$. Use this formula and a calculator to determine where the factorial function appears in the ranking of growth rates given in Theorem 4.15. (See the Guided Project *Stirling's Formula*.)

117. A geometric limit Let $f(\theta)$ be the area of the triangle ABP (see figure) and let $g(\theta)$ be the area of the region between the chord PB and the arc PB. Evaluate $\lim\limits_{\theta \to 0} g(\theta)/f(\theta)$.

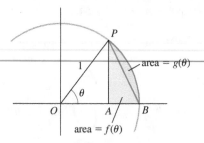

118. A fascinating function Consider the function
$$f(x) = (ab^x + (1 - a)c^x)^{1/x},$$
where a, b, and c are positive real numbers with $0 < a < 1$.

  a. Graph f for several sets of (a, b, c). Verify that in all cases f is an increasing function with a single inflection point, for all x.

  b. Use analytical methods to determine $\lim\limits_{x \to 0} f(x)$ in terms of a, b, and c.

  c. Show that $\lim\limits_{x \to \infty} f(x) = \max\{b, c\}$ and $\lim\limits_{x \to -\infty} f(x) = \min\{b, c\}$, for any $0 < a < 1$.

  d. Estimate the location of the inflection point of f.

119. Exponential limit Prove that $\lim\limits_{x \to \infty} \left(1 + \dfrac{a}{x}\right)^x = e^a$, for $a \neq 0$.

120. Exponentials vs. super exponentials Show that x^x grows faster than b^x as $x \to \infty$, for $b > 1$.

121. Exponential growth rates

  a. For what values of $b > 0$ does b^x grow faster than e^x as $x \to \infty$?

  b. Compare the growth rates of e^x and e^{ax} as $x \to \infty$, for $a > 0$.

QUICK CHECK ANSWERS

1. g and h **2.** g and h **3.** $0 \cdot \infty; (x - \pi/2)/\cot x$
4. The form 0^∞ (for example, $\lim\limits_{x \to 0^+} x^{1/x}$) is not indeterminate, because as the base goes to zero, raising it to larger and larger powers drives the entire function to zero.   **6.** x^3 grows faster than x^2 as $x \to \infty$, whereas x^2 and $10x^2$ have comparable growth rates as $x \to \infty$. ◀

8 Extension

Partial Fractions

This section shows how to express a rational function (a quotient of polynomials) as a sum of simpler fractions, called *partial fractions*, which are easily integrated. For instance, the rational function $(5x - 3)/(x^2 - 2x - 3)$ can be rewritten as

$$\frac{5x - 3}{x^2 - 2x - 3} = \frac{2}{x + 1} + \frac{3}{x - 3}.$$

You can verify this equation algebraically by placing the fractions on the right side over a common denominator $(x + 1)(x - 3)$. The skill acquired in writing rational functions as such a sum is useful in other settings as well (for instance, when using certain transform methods to solve differential equations). To integrate the rational function $(5x - 3)/(x^2 - 2x - 3)$ on the left side of our previous expression, we simply sum the integrals of the fractions on the right side:

$$\int \frac{5x - 3}{(x + 1)(x - 3)} \, dx = \int \frac{2}{x + 1} \, dx + \int \frac{3}{x - 3} \, dx$$

$$= 2 \ln|x + 1| + 3 \ln|x - 3| + C.$$

The method for rewriting rational functions as a sum of simpler fractions is called **the method of partial fractions**. In the case of the preceding example, it consists of finding constants A and B such that

$$\frac{5x - 3}{x^2 - 2x - 3} = \frac{A}{x + 1} + \frac{B}{x - 3}. \tag{1}$$

(Pretend for a moment that we do not know that $A = 2$ and $B = 3$ will work.) We call the fractions $A/(x + 1)$ and $B/(x - 3)$ **partial fractions** because their denominators are only part of the original denominator $x^2 - 2x - 3$. We call A and B **undetermined coefficients** until suitable values for them have been found.

To find A and B, we first clear Equation (1) of fractions and regroup in powers of x, obtaining

$$5x - 3 = A(x - 3) + B(x + 1) = (A + B)x - 3A + B.$$

This will be an identity in x if and only if the coefficients of like powers of x on the two sides are equal:

$$A + B = 5, \qquad -3A + B = -3.$$

Solving these equations simultaneously gives $A = 2$ and $B = 3$.

General Description of the Method

Success in writing a rational function $f(x)/g(x)$ as a sum of partial fractions depends on two things:

- *The degree of $f(x)$ must be less than the degree of $g(x)$.* That is, the fraction must be proper. If it isn't, divide $f(x)$ by $g(x)$ and work with the remainder term. Example 3 of this section illustrates such a case.

- *We must know the factors of $g(x)$.* In theory, any polynomial with real coefficients can be written as a product of real linear factors and real quadratic factors. In practice, the factors may be hard to find.

Here is how we find the partial fractions of a proper fraction $f(x)/g(x)$ when the factors of g are known. A quadratic polynomial (or factor) is **irreducible** if it cannot be written as the product of two linear factors with real coefficients. That is, the polynomial has no real roots.

Method of Partial Fractions when $f(x)/g(x)$ is Proper

1. Let $x - r$ be a linear factor of $g(x)$. Suppose that $(x - r)^m$ is the highest power of $x - r$ that divides $g(x)$. Then, to this factor, assign the sum of the m partial fractions:

$$\frac{A_1}{(x - r)} + \frac{A_2}{(x - r)^2} + \cdots + \frac{A_m}{(x - r)^m}.$$

Do this for each distinct linear factor of $g(x)$.

2. Let $x^2 + px + q$ be an irreducible quadratic factor of $g(x)$ so that $x^2 + px + q$ has no real roots. Suppose that $(x^2 + px + q)^n$ is the highest power of this factor that divides $g(x)$. Then, to this factor, assign the sum of the n partial fractions:

$$\frac{B_1 x + C_1}{(x^2 + px + q)} + \frac{B_2 x + C_2}{(x^2 + px + q)^2} + \cdots + \frac{B_n x + C_n}{(x^2 + px + q)^n}.$$

Do this for each distinct quadratic factor of $g(x)$.

3. Set the original fraction $f(x)/g(x)$ equal to the sum of all these partial fractions. Clear the resulting equation of fractions and arrange the terms in decreasing powers of x.

4. Equate the coefficients of corresponding powers of x and solve the resulting equations for the undetermined coefficients.

EXAMPLE 1   Use partial fractions to evaluate

$$\int \frac{x^2 + 4x + 1}{(x - 1)(x + 1)(x + 3)} \, dx.$$

Solution   The partial fraction decomposition has the form

$$\frac{x^2 + 4x + 1}{(x - 1)(x + 1)(x + 3)} = \frac{A}{x - 1} + \frac{B}{x + 1} + \frac{C}{x + 3}.$$

To find the values of the undetermined coefficients A, B, and C, we clear fractions and get

$$x^2 + 4x + 1 = A(x + 1)(x + 3) + B(x - 1)(x + 3) + C(x - 1)(x + 1)$$
$$= A(x^2 + 4x + 3) + B(x^2 + 2x - 3) + C(x^2 - 1)$$
$$= (A + B + C)x^2 + (4A + 2B)x + (3A - 3B - C).$$

The polynomials on both sides of the above equation are identical, so we equate coefficients of like powers of x, obtaining

$$\text{Coefficient of } x^2: \quad A + B + C = 1$$
$$\text{Coefficient of } x^1: \quad 4A + 2B \quad\quad = 4$$
$$\text{Coefficient of } x^0: \quad 3A - 3B - C = 1$$

There are several ways of solving such a system of linear equations for the unknowns A, B, and C, including elimination of variables or the use of a calculator or computer. Whatever method is used, the solution is $A = 3/4$, $B = 1/2$, and $C = -1/4$. Hence we have

$$\int \frac{x^2 + 4x + 1}{(x-1)(x+1)(x+3)}\,dx = \int \left[\frac{3}{4}\frac{1}{x-1} + \frac{1}{2}\frac{1}{x+1} - \frac{1}{4}\frac{1}{x+3}\right]dx$$

$$= \frac{3}{4}\ln|x-1| + \frac{1}{2}\ln|x+1| - \frac{1}{4}\ln|x+3| + K,$$

where K is the arbitrary constant of integration (to avoid confusion with the undetermined coefficient we labeled as C). ∎

EXAMPLE 2   Use partial fractions to evaluate

$$\int \frac{6x+7}{(x+2)^2}\,dx.$$

Solution   First we express the integrand as a sum of partial fractions with undetermined coefficients.

$$\frac{6x+7}{(x+2)^2} = \frac{A}{x+2} + \frac{B}{(x+2)^2}$$

$$6x + 7 = A(x+2) + B \quad\quad \text{Multiply both sides by } (x+2)^2.$$

$$= Ax + (2A + B)$$

Equating coefficients of corresponding powers of x gives

$$A = 6 \quad\text{and}\quad 2A + B = 12 + B = 7, \quad\text{or}\quad A = 6 \quad\text{and}\quad B = -5.$$

Therefore,

$$\int \frac{6x+7}{(x+2)^2}\,dx = \int \left(\frac{6}{x+2} - \frac{5}{(x+2)^2}\right)dx$$

$$= 6\int \frac{dx}{x+2} - 5\int (x+2)^{-2}\,dx$$

$$= 6\ln|x+2| + 5(x+2)^{-1} + C. \quad\quad ■$$

The next example shows how to handle the case when $f(x)/g(x)$ is an improper fraction. It is a case where the degree of f is larger than the degree of g.

EXAMPLE 3   Use partial fractions to evaluate

$$\int \frac{2x^3 - 4x^2 - x - 3}{x^2 - 2x - 3}\,dx.$$

Solution   First we divide the denominator into the numerator to get a polynomial plus a proper fraction.

$$
\begin{array}{r}
2x \phantom{{}-4x^2-x-3} \\
x^2 - 2x - 3 \overline{\smash{)}\,2x^3 - 4x^2 - x - 3} \\
\underline{2x^3 - 4x^2 - 6x - 3} \\
5x - 3
\end{array}
$$

Then we write the improper fraction as a polynomial plus a proper fraction.

$$\frac{2x^3 - 4x^2 - x - 3}{x^2 - 2x - 3} = 2x + \frac{5x - 3}{x^2 - 2x - 3}$$

We found the partial fraction decomposition of the fraction on the right in the opening example, so

$$\int \frac{2x^3 - 4x^2 - x - 3}{x^2 - 2x - 3} \, dx = \int 2x \, dx + \int \frac{5x - 3}{x^2 - 2x - 3} \, dx$$

$$= \int 2x \, dx + \int \frac{2}{x + 1} \, dx + \int \frac{3}{x - 3} \, dx$$

$$= x^2 + 2 \ln |x + 1| + 3 \ln |x - 3| + C. \quad \blacksquare$$

EXAMPLE 4   Use partial fractions to evaluate

$$\int \frac{-2x + 4}{(x^2 + 1)(x - 1)^2} \, dx.$$

Solution   The denominator has an irreducible quadratic factor as well as a repeated linear factor, so we write

$$\frac{-2x + 4}{(x^2 + 1)(x - 1)^2} = \frac{Ax + B}{x^2 + 1} + \frac{C}{x - 1} + \frac{D}{(x - 1)^2}. \tag{2}$$

Clearing the equation of fractions gives

$$-2x + 4 = (Ax + B)(x - 1)^2 + C(x - 1)(x^2 + 1) + D(x^2 + 1)$$
$$= (A + C)x^3 + (-2A + B - C + D)x^2$$
$$+ (A - 2B + C)x + (B - C + D).$$

Equating coefficients of like terms gives

Coefficients of x^3:	$0 = A + C$
Coefficients of x^2:	$0 = -2A + B - C + D$
Coefficients of x^1:	$-2 = A - 2B + C$
Coefficients of x^0:	$4 = B - C + D$

We solve these equations simultaneously to find the values of A, B, C, and D:

$-4 = -2A, \quad A = 2$	Subtract fourth equation from second.
$C = -A = -2$	From the first equation
$B = (A + C + 2)/2 = 1$	From the third equation and $C = -A$
$D = 4 - B + C = 1.$	From the fourth equation.

We substitute these values into Equation (2), obtaining

$$\frac{-2x + 4}{(x^2 + 1)(x - 1)^2} = \frac{2x + 1}{x^2 + 1} - \frac{2}{x - 1} + \frac{1}{(x - 1)^2}.$$

Finally, using the expansion above we can integrate:

$$\int \frac{-2x + 4}{(x^2 + 1)(x - 1)^2} \, dx = \int \left(\frac{2x + 1}{x^2 + 1} - \frac{2}{x - 1} + \frac{1}{(x - 1)^2} \right) dx$$

$$= \int \left(\frac{2x}{x^2 + 1} + \frac{1}{x^2 + 1} - \frac{2}{x - 1} + \frac{1}{(x - 1)^2} \right) dx$$

$$= \ln (x^2 + 1) + \tan^{-1} x - 2 \ln |x - 1| - \frac{1}{x - 1} + C. \quad \blacksquare$$

EXAMPLE 5   Use partial fractions to evaluate

$$\int \frac{dx}{x(x^2+1)^2}.$$

Solution   The form of the partial fraction decomposition is

$$\frac{1}{x(x^2+1)^2} = \frac{A}{x} + \frac{Bx+C}{x^2+1} + \frac{Dx+E}{(x^2+1)^2}.$$

Multiplying by $x(x^2+1)^2$, we have

$$1 = A(x^2+1)^2 + (Bx+C)x(x^2+1) + (Dx+E)x$$
$$= A(x^4+2x^2+1) + B(x^4+x^2) + C(x^3+x) + Dx^2 + Ex$$
$$= (A+B)x^4 + Cx^3 + (2A+B+D)x^2 + (C+E)x + A.$$

If we equate coefficients, we get the system

$$A+B=0, \quad C=0, \quad 2A+B+D=0, \quad C+E=0, \quad A=1.$$

Solving this system gives $A=1$, $B=-1$, $C=0$, $D=-1$, and $E=0$. Thus,

$$\int \frac{dx}{x(x^2+1)^2} = \int \left[\frac{1}{x} + \frac{-x}{x^2+1} + \frac{-x}{(x^2+1)^2} \right] dx$$

$$= \int \frac{dx}{x} - \int \frac{x\,dx}{x^2+1} - \int \frac{x\,dx}{(x^2+1)^2}$$

$$= \int \frac{dx}{x} - \frac{1}{2}\int \frac{du}{u} - \frac{1}{2}\int \frac{du}{u^2} \qquad \begin{array}{l} u = x^2+1, \\ du = 2x\,dx \end{array}$$

$$= \ln|x| - \frac{1}{2}\ln|u| + \frac{1}{2u} + K$$

$$= \ln|x| - \frac{1}{2}\ln(x^2+1) + \frac{1}{2(x^2+1)} + K$$

$$= \ln \frac{|x|}{\sqrt{x^2+1}} + \frac{1}{2(x^2+1)} + K.$$ ∎

HISTORICAL BIOGRAPHY

Oliver Heaviside
(1850–1925)

The Heaviside "Cover-up" Method for Linear Factors

When the degree of the polynomial $f(x)$ is less than the degree of $g(x)$ and

$$g(x) = (x-r_1)(x-r_2)\cdots(x-r_n)$$

is a product of n distinct linear factors, each raised to the first power, there is a quick way to expand $f(x)/g(x)$ by partial fractions.

EXAMPLE 6   Find A, B, and C in the partial fraction expansion

$$\frac{x^2+1}{(x-1)(x-2)(x-3)} = \frac{A}{x-1} + \frac{B}{x-2} + \frac{C}{x-3}. \tag{3}$$

Solution   If we multiply both sides of Equation (3) by $(x-1)$ to get

$$\frac{x^2+1}{(x-2)(x-3)} = A + \frac{B(x-1)}{x-2} + \frac{C(x-1)}{x-3}$$

and set $x=1$, the resulting equation gives the value of A:

$$\frac{(1)^2+1}{(1-2)(1-3)} = A + 0 + 0,$$

$$A = 1.$$

Thus, the value of A is the number we would have obtained if we had covered the factor $(x - 1)$ in the denominator of the original fraction

$$\frac{x^2 + 1}{(x - 1)(x - 2)(x - 3)} \tag{4}$$

and evaluated the rest at $x = 1$:

$$A = \frac{(1)^2 + 1}{\boxed{(x - 1)}\,(1 - 2)(1 - 3)} = \frac{2}{(-1)(-2)} = 1.$$

$$\underset{\text{Cover}}{\uparrow}$$

Similarly, we find the value of B in Equation (3) by covering the factor $(x - 2)$ in Expression (4) and evaluating the rest at $x = 2$:

$$B = \frac{(2)^2 + 1}{(2 - 1)\,\boxed{(x - 2)}\,(2 - 3)} = \frac{5}{(1)(-1)} = -5.$$

$$\underset{\text{Cover}}{\uparrow}$$

Finally, C is found by covering the $(x - 3)$ in Expression (4) and evaluating the rest at $x = 3$:

$$C = \frac{(3)^2 + 1}{(3 - 1)(3 - 2)\,\boxed{(x - 3)}} = \frac{10}{(2)(1)} = 5. \qquad \blacksquare$$

$$\underset{\text{Cover}}{\uparrow}$$

Heaviside Method

1. *Write the quotient with $g(x)$ factored:*

$$\frac{f(x)}{g(x)} = \frac{f(x)}{(x - r_1)(x - r_2) \cdots (x - r_n)}.$$

2. *Cover the factors $(x - r_i)$ of $g(x)$ one at a time*, each time replacing all the uncovered x's by the number r_i. This gives a number A_i for each root r_i:

$$A_1 = \frac{f(r_1)}{(r_1 - r_2) \cdots (r_1 - r_n)}$$

$$A_2 = \frac{f(r_2)}{(r_2 - r_1)(r_2 - r_3) \cdots (r_2 - r_n)}$$

$$\vdots$$

$$A_n = \frac{f(r_n)}{(r_n - r_1)(r_n - r_2) \cdots (r_n - r_{n-1})}.$$

3. *Write the partial fraction expansion of $f(x)/g(x)$ as*

$$\frac{f(x)}{g(x)} = \frac{A_1}{(x - r_1)} + \frac{A_2}{(x - r_2)} + \cdots + \frac{A_n}{(x - r_n)}.$$

EXAMPLE 7   Use the Heaviside Method to evaluate

$$\int \frac{x + 4}{x^3 + 3x^2 - 10x}\, dx.$$

Solution The degree of $f(x) = x + 4$ is less than the degree of the cubic polynomial $g(x) = x^3 + 3x^2 - 10x$, and, with $g(x)$ factored,

$$\frac{x + 4}{x^3 + 3x^2 - 10x} = \frac{x + 4}{x(x - 2)(x + 5)}.$$

The roots of $g(x)$ are $r_1 = 0$, $r_2 = 2$, and $r_3 = -5$. We find

$$A_1 = \frac{0 + 4}{\boxed{x}\,(0 - 2)(0 + 5)} = \frac{4}{(-2)(5)} = -\frac{2}{5}$$

$$\uparrow$$
Cover

$$A_2 = \frac{2 + 4}{2\,\boxed{(x - 2)}\,(2 + 5)} = \frac{6}{(2)(7)} = \frac{3}{7}$$

$$\uparrow$$
Cover

$$A_3 = \frac{-5 + 4}{(-5)(-5 - 2)\,\boxed{(x + 5)}} = \frac{-1}{(-5)(-7)} = -\frac{1}{35}.$$

$$\uparrow$$
Cover

Therefore,

$$\frac{x + 4}{x(x - 2)(x + 5)} = -\frac{2}{5x} + \frac{3}{7(x - 2)} - \frac{1}{35(x + 5)},$$

and

$$\int \frac{x + 4}{x(x - 2)(x + 5)}\,dx = -\frac{2}{5}\ln|x| + \frac{3}{7}\ln|x - 2| - \frac{1}{35}\ln|x + 5| + C. \quad \blacksquare$$

Other Ways to Determine the Coefficients

Another way to determine the constants that appear in partial fractions is to differentiate, as in the next example. Still another is to assign selected numerical values to x.

EXAMPLE 8   Find A, B, and C in the equation

$$\frac{x - 1}{(x + 1)^3} = \frac{A}{x + 1} + \frac{B}{(x + 1)^2} + \frac{C}{(x + 1)^3}$$

by clearing fractions, differentiating the result, and substituting $x = -1$.

Solution We first clear fractions:

$$x - 1 = A(x + 1)^2 + B(x + 1) + C.$$

Substituting $x = -1$ shows $C = -2$. We then differentiate both sides with respect to x, obtaining

$$1 = 2A(x + 1) + B.$$

Substituting $x = -1$ shows $B = 1$. We differentiate again to get $0 = 2A$, which shows $A = 0$. Hence,

$$\frac{x - 1}{(x + 1)^3} = \frac{1}{(x + 1)^2} - \frac{2}{(x + 1)^3}. \quad \blacksquare$$

In some problems, assigning small values to x, such as $x = 0, \pm 1, \pm 2$, to get equations in A, B, and C provides a fast alternative to other methods.

EXAMPLE 9 Find A, B, and C in the expression

$$\frac{x^2 + 1}{(x - 1)(x - 2)(x - 3)} = \frac{A}{x - 1} + \frac{B}{x - 2} + \frac{C}{x - 3}$$

by assigning numerical values to x.

Solution Clear fractions to get

$$x^2 + 1 = A(x - 2)(x - 3) + B(x - 1)(x - 3) + C(x - 1)(x - 2).$$

Then let $x = 1, 2, 3$ successively to find A, B, and C:

$$x = 1: \quad (1)^2 + 1 = A(-1)(-2) + B(0) + C(0)$$
$$2 = 2A$$
$$A = 1$$

$$x = 2: \quad (2)^2 + 1 = A(0) + B(1)(-1) + C(0)$$
$$5 = -B$$
$$B = -5$$

$$x = 3: \quad (3)^2 + 1 = A(0) + B(0) + C(2)(1)$$
$$10 = 2C$$
$$C = 5.$$

Conclusion:

$$\frac{x^2 + 1}{(x - 1)(x - 2)(x - 3)} = \frac{1}{x - 1} - \frac{5}{x - 2} + \frac{5}{x - 3}.$$

Exercises

Expanding Quotients into Partial Fractions

Expand the quotients in Exercises 1–8 by partial fractions.

1. $\dfrac{5x - 13}{(x - 3)(x - 2)}$

2. $\dfrac{5x - 7}{x^2 - 3x + 2}$

3. $\dfrac{x + 4}{(x + 1)^2}$

4. $\dfrac{2x + 2}{x^2 - 2x + 1}$

5. $\dfrac{z + 1}{z^2(z - 1)}$

6. $\dfrac{z}{z^3 - z^2 - 6z}$

7. $\dfrac{t^2 + 8}{t^2 - 5t + 6}$

8. $\dfrac{t^4 + 9}{t^4 + 9t^2}$

Nonrepeated Linear Factors

In Exercises 9–16, express the integrand as a sum of partial fractions and evaluate the integrals.

9. $\displaystyle\int \frac{dx}{1 - x^2}$

10. $\displaystyle\int \frac{dx}{x^2 + 2x}$

11. $\displaystyle\int \frac{x + 4}{x^2 + 5x - 6} dx$

12. $\displaystyle\int \frac{2x + 1}{x^2 - 7x + 12} dx$

13. $\displaystyle\int_4^8 \frac{y\, dy}{y^2 - 2y - 3}$

14. $\displaystyle\int_{1/2}^1 \frac{y + 4}{y^2 + y} dy$

15. $\displaystyle\int \frac{dt}{t^3 + t^2 - 2t}$

16. $\displaystyle\int \frac{x + 3}{2x^3 - 8x} dx$

Repeated Linear Factors

In Exercises 17–20, express the integrand as a sum of partial fractions and evaluate the integrals.

17. $\displaystyle\int_0^1 \frac{x^3\, dx}{x^2 + 2x + 1}$

18. $\displaystyle\int_{-1}^0 \frac{x^3\, dx}{x^2 - 2x + 1}$

19. $\displaystyle\int \frac{dx}{(x^2 - 1)^2}$

20. $\displaystyle\int \frac{x^2\, dx}{(x - 1)(x^2 + 2x + 1)}$

Irreducible Quadratic Factors

In Exercises 21–32, express the integrand as a sum of partial fractions and evaluate the integrals.

21. $\displaystyle\int_0^1 \frac{dx}{(x + 1)(x^2 + 1)}$

22. $\displaystyle\int_1^{\sqrt{3}} \frac{3t^2 + t + 4}{t^3 + t} dt$

23. $\displaystyle\int \frac{y^2 + 2y + 1}{(y^2 + 1)^2} dy$

24. $\displaystyle\int \frac{8x^2 + 8x + 2}{(4x^2 + 1)^2} dx$

25. $\displaystyle\int \frac{2s + 2}{(s^2 + 1)(s - 1)^3} ds$

26. $\displaystyle\int \frac{s^4 + 81}{s(s^2 + 9)^2} ds$

27. $\displaystyle\int \frac{x^2 - x + 2}{x^3 - 1} dx$

28. $\displaystyle\int \frac{1}{x^4 + x} dx$

29. $\displaystyle\int \frac{x^2}{x^4 - 1} dx$

30. $\displaystyle\int \frac{x^2 + x}{x^4 - 3x^2 - 4} dx$

31. $\displaystyle\int \frac{2\theta^3 + 5\theta^2 + 8\theta + 4}{(\theta^2 + 2\theta + 2)^2} d\theta$

32. $\displaystyle\int \frac{\theta^4 - 4\theta^3 + 2\theta^2 - 3\theta + 1}{(\theta^2 + 1)^3} d\theta$

Improper Fractions

In Exercises 33–38, perform long division on the integrand, write the proper fraction as a sum of partial fractions, and then evaluate the integral.

33. $\int \frac{2x^3 - 2x^2 + 1}{x^2 - x}\,dx$

34. $\int \frac{x^4}{x^2 - 1}\,dx$

35. $\int \frac{9x^3 - 3x + 1}{x^3 - x^2}\,dx$

36. $\int \frac{16x^3}{4x^2 - 4x + 1}\,dx$

37. $\int \frac{y^4 + y^2 - 1}{y^3 + y}\,dy$

38. $\int \frac{2y^4}{y^3 - y^2 + y - 1}\,dy$

Evaluating Integrals

Evaluate the integrals in Exercises 39–50.

39. $\int \frac{e^t\,dt}{e^{2t} + 3e^t + 2}$

40. $\int \frac{e^{4t} + 2e^{2t} - e^t}{e^{2t} + 1}\,dt$

41. $\int \frac{\cos y\,dy}{\sin^2 y + \sin y - 6}$

42. $\int \frac{\sin \theta\,d\theta}{\cos^2 \theta + \cos \theta - 2}$

43. $\int \frac{(x - 2)^2 \tan^{-1}(2x) - 12x^3 - 3x}{(4x^2 + 1)(x - 2)^2}\,dx$

44. $\int \frac{(x + 1)^2 \tan^{-1}(3x) + 9x^3 + x}{(9x^2 + 1)(x + 1)^2}\,dx$

45. $\int \frac{1}{x^{3/2} - \sqrt{x}}\,dx$

46. $\int \frac{1}{(x^{1/3} - 1)\sqrt{x}}\,dx$

(*Hint:* Let $x = u^6$.)

47. $\int \frac{\sqrt{x + 1}}{x}\,dx$

48. $\int \frac{1}{x\sqrt{x + 9}}\,dx$

(*Hint:* Let $x + 1 = u^2$.)

49. $\int \frac{1}{x(x^4 + 1)}\,dx$

50. $\int \frac{1}{x^6(x^5 + 4)}\,dx$

$\left(\text{\textit{Hint:} Multiply by } \dfrac{x^3}{x^3}.\right)$

Initial Value Problems

Solve the initial value problems in Exercises 51–54 for x as a function of t.

51. $(t^2 - 3t + 2)\dfrac{dx}{dt} = 1 \quad (t > 2), \quad x(3) = 0$

52. $(3t^4 + 4t^2 + 1)\dfrac{dx}{dt} = 2\sqrt{3}, \quad x(1) = -\pi\sqrt{3}/4$

53. $(t^2 + 2t)\dfrac{dx}{dt} = 2x + 2 \quad (t, x > 0), \quad x(1) = 1$

54. $(t + 1)\dfrac{dx}{dt} = x^2 + 1 \quad (t > -1), \quad x(0) = 0$

Applications and Examples

In Exercises 55 and 56, find the volume of the solid generated by revolving the shaded region about the indicated axis.

55. The x-axis

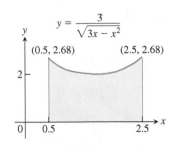

56. The y-axis

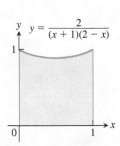

T 57. Find, to two decimal places, the x-coordinate of the centroid of the region in the first quadrant bounded by the x-axis, the curve $y = \tan^{-1} x$, and the line $x = \sqrt{3}$.

T 58. Find the x-coordinate of the centroid of this region to two decimal places.

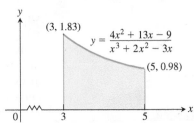

T 59. Social diffusion Sociologists sometimes use the phrase "social diffusion" to describe the way information spreads through a population. The information might be a rumor, a cultural fad, or news about a technical innovation. In a sufficiently large population, the number of people x who have the information is treated as a differentiable function of time t, and the rate of diffusion, dx/dt, is assumed to be proportional to the number of people who have the information times the number of people who do not. This leads to the equation

$$\frac{dx}{dt} = kx(N - x),$$

where N is the number of people in the population.

Suppose t is in days, $k = 1/250$, and two people start a rumor at time $t = 0$ in a population of $N = 1000$ people.

a. Find x as a function of t.

b. When will half the population have heard the rumor? (This is when the rumor will be spreading the fastest.)

T 60. Second-order chemical reactions Many chemical reactions are the result of the interaction of two molecules that undergo a change to produce a new product. The rate of the reaction typically depends on the concentrations of the two kinds of molecules. If a is the amount of substance A and b is the amount of substance B at time $t = 0$, and if x is the amount of product at time t, then the rate of formation of x may be given by the differential equation

$$\frac{dx}{dt} = k(a - x)(b - x),$$

or

$$\frac{1}{(a - x)(b - x)}\frac{dx}{dt} = k,$$

where k is a constant for the reaction. Integrate both sides of this equation to obtain a relation between x and t **(a)** if $a = b$, and **(b)** if $a \neq b$. Assume in each case that $x = 0$ when $t = 0$.

8 Extension

Improper Integrals

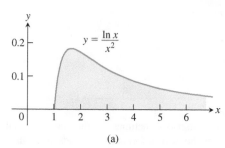

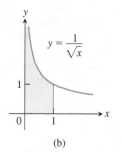

(a)

(b)

FIGURE 1   Are the areas under these infinite curves finite? We will see that the answer is yes for both curves.

Up to now, we have required definite integrals to have two properties. First, the domain of integration $[a, b]$ must be finite. Second, the range of the integrand must be finite on this domain. In practice, we may encounter problems that fail to meet one or both of these conditions. The integral for the area under the curve $y = (\ln x)/x^2$ from $x = 1$ to $x = \infty$ is an example for which the domain is infinite (Figure 1a). The integral for the area under the curve of $y = 1/\sqrt{x}$ between $x = 0$ and $x = 1$ is an example for which the range of the integrand is infinite (Figure 1b). In either case, the integrals are said to be *improper* and are calculated as limits. We will that improper integrals play an important role in probability. They are also useful when investigating the convergence of certain infinite series.

Infinite Limits of Integration

Consider the infinite region (unbounded on the right) that lies under the curve $y = e^{-x/2}$ in the first quadrant (Figure 2a). You might think this region has infinite area, but we will see that the value is finite. We assign a value to the area in the following way. First find the area $A(b)$ of the portion of the region that is bounded on the right by $x = b$ (Figure 2b).

$$A(b) = \int_0^b e^{-x/2}\, dx = -2e^{-x/2}\Big]_0^b = -2e^{-b/2} + 2$$

Then find the limit of $A(b)$ as $b \to \infty$

$$\lim_{b\to\infty} A(b) = \lim_{b\to\infty}\left(-2e^{-b/2} + 2\right) = 2.$$

The value we assign to the area under the curve from 0 to ∞ is

$$\int_0^\infty e^{-x/2}\, dx = \lim_{b\to\infty}\int_0^b e^{-x/2}\, dx = 2.$$

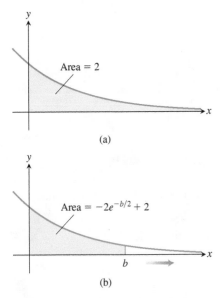

FIGURE 2 (a) The area in the first quadrant under the curve $y = e^{-x/2}$. (b) The area is an improper integral of the first type.

DEFINITION Integrals with infinite limits of integration are **improper integrals of Type I**.

1. If $f(x)$ is continuous on $[a, \infty)$, then

$$\int_a^\infty f(x)\, dx = \lim_{b \to \infty} \int_a^b f(x)\, dx.$$

2. If $f(x)$ is continuous on $(-\infty, b\,]$, then

$$\int_{-\infty}^b f(x)\, dx = \lim_{a \to -\infty} \int_a^b f(x)\, dx.$$

3. If $f(x)$ is continuous on $(-\infty, \infty)$, then

$$\int_{-\infty}^\infty f(x)\, dx = \int_{-\infty}^c f(x)\, dx + \int_c^\infty f(x)\, dx,$$

where c is any real number.

In each case, if the limit is finite we say that the improper integral **converges** and that the limit is the **value** of the improper integral. If the limit fails to exist, the improper integral **diverges**.

It can be shown that the choice of c in Part 3 of the definition is unimportant. We can evaluate or determine the convergence or divergence of $\int_{-\infty}^\infty f(x)\, dx$ with any convenient choice.

Any of the integrals in the above definition can be interpreted as an area if $f \geq 0$ on the interval of integration. For instance, we interpreted the improper integral in Figure 2 as an area. In that case, the area has the finite value 2. If $f \geq 0$ and the improper integral diverges, we say the area under the curve is **infinite**.

EXAMPLE 1 Is the area under the curve $y = (\ln x)/x^2$ from $x = 1$ to $x = \infty$ finite? If so, what is its value?

Solution We find the area under the curve from $x = 1$ to $x = b$ and examine the limit as $b \to \infty$. If the limit is finite, we take it to be the area under the curve (Figure 3). The area from 1 to b is

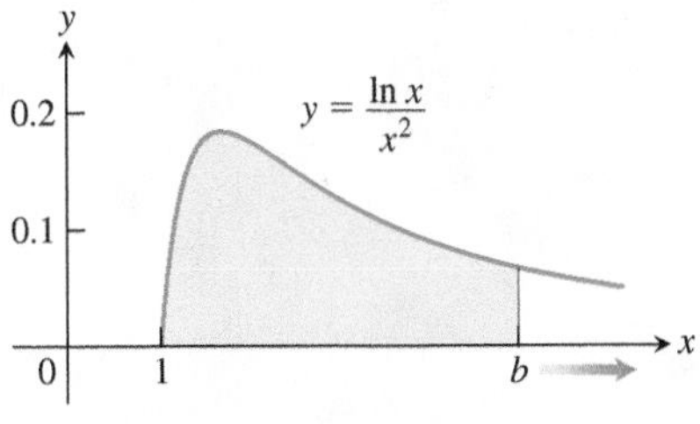

$$\int_1^b \frac{\ln x}{x^2}\, dx = \left[(\ln x)\left(-\frac{1}{x} \right) \right]_1^b - \int_1^b \left(-\frac{1}{x} \right)\left(\frac{1}{x} \right) dx$$

$$= -\frac{\ln b}{b} - \left[\frac{1}{x} \right]_1^b$$

$$= -\frac{\ln b}{b} - \frac{1}{b} + 1.$$

Integration by parts with $u = \ln x$, $dv = dx/x^2$, $du = dx/x$, $v = -1/x$

FIGURE 3 The area under this curve is an improper integral (Example 1).

The limit of the area as $b \to \infty$ is

$$\int_1^{\infty} \frac{\ln x}{x^2}\, dx = \lim_{b \to \infty} \int_1^b \frac{\ln x}{x^2}\, dx$$

$$= \lim_{b \to \infty} \left[-\frac{\ln b}{b} - \frac{1}{b} + 1 \right]$$

$$= -\left[\lim_{b \to \infty} \frac{\ln b}{b} \right] - 0 + 1$$

$$= -\left[\lim_{b \to \infty} \frac{1/b}{1} \right] + 1 = 0 + 1 = 1. \qquad \text{l'Hôpital's Rule}$$

Thus, the improper integral converges and the area has finite value 1. ∎

EXAMPLE 2 Evaluate

$$\int_{-\infty}^{\infty} \frac{dx}{1 + x^2}.$$

HISTORICAL BIOGRAPHY
Lejeune Dirichlet
(1805–1859)

Solution According to the definition (Part 3), we can choose $c = 0$ and write

$$\int_{-\infty}^{\infty} \frac{dx}{1 + x^2} = \int_{-\infty}^{0} \frac{dx}{1 + x^2} + \int_0^{\infty} \frac{dx}{1 + x^2}.$$

Next we evaluate each improper integral on the right side of the equation above.

$$\int_{-\infty}^{0} \frac{dx}{1 + x^2} = \lim_{a \to -\infty} \int_a^0 \frac{dx}{1 + x^2}$$

$$= \lim_{a \to -\infty} \tan^{-1} x \Big]_a^0$$

$$= \lim_{a \to -\infty} (\tan^{-1} 0 - \tan^{-1} a) = 0 - \left(-\frac{\pi}{2} \right) = \frac{\pi}{2}$$

$$\int_0^{\infty} \frac{dx}{1 + x^2} = \lim_{b \to \infty} \int_0^b \frac{dx}{1 + x^2}$$

$$= \lim_{b \to \infty} \tan^{-1} x \Big]_0^b$$

$$= \lim_{b \to \infty} (\tan^{-1} b - \tan^{-1} 0) = \frac{\pi}{2} - 0 = \frac{\pi}{2}$$

Thus,

$$\int_{-\infty}^{\infty} \frac{dx}{1 + x^2} = \frac{\pi}{2} + \frac{\pi}{2} = \pi.$$

$y = \dfrac{1}{1 + x^2}$ Area $= \pi$

NOT TO SCALE

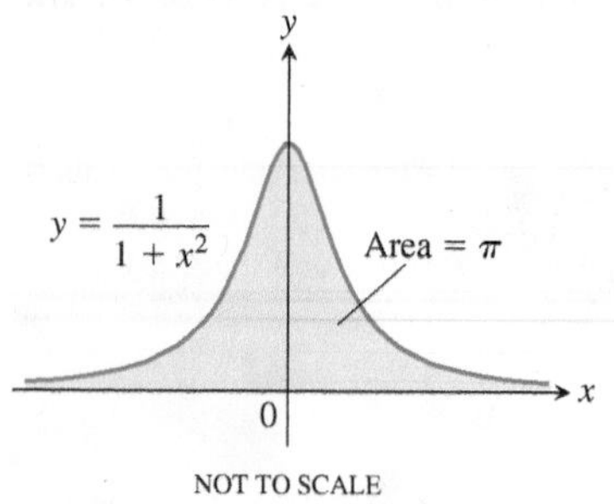

FIGURE 4 The area under this curve is finite (Example 2).

Since $1/(1 + x^2) > 0$, the improper integral can be interpreted as the (finite) area beneath the curve and above the x-axis (Figure 4). ∎

The Integral $\displaystyle\int_1^H \frac{dx}{x^p}$

The function $y = 1/x$ is the boundary between the convergent and divergent improper integrals with integrands of the form $y = 1/x^p$. As the next example shows, the improper integral converges if $p > 1$ and diverges if $p \leq 1$.

EXAMPLE 3   For what values of p does the integral $\int_1^\infty dx/x^p$ converge? When the integral does converge, what is its value?

Solution   If $p \neq 1$,

$$\int_1^b \frac{dx}{x^p} = \frac{x^{-p+1}}{-p+1}\Big]_1^b = \frac{1}{1-p}(b^{-p+1} - 1) = \frac{1}{1-p}\left(\frac{1}{b^{p-1}} - 1\right).$$

Thus,

$$\int_1^\infty \frac{dx}{x^p} = \lim_{b\to\infty}\int_1^b \frac{dx}{x^p}$$

$$= \lim_{b\to\infty}\left[\frac{1}{1-p}\left(\frac{1}{b^{p-1}} - 1\right)\right] = \begin{cases} \dfrac{1}{p-1}, & p > 1 \\ \infty, & p < 1 \end{cases}$$

because

$$\lim_{b\to\infty} \frac{1}{b^{p-1}} = \begin{cases} 0, & p > 1 \\ \infty, & p < 1. \end{cases}$$

Therefore, the integral converges to the value $1/(p-1)$ if $p > 1$ and it diverges if $p < 1$.

If $p = 1$, the integral also diverges:

$$\int_1^\infty \frac{dx}{x^p} = \int_1^\infty \frac{dx}{x}$$

$$= \lim_{b\to\infty}\int_1^b \frac{dx}{x}$$

$$= \lim_{b\to\infty} \ln x \Big]_1^b$$

$$= \lim_{b\to\infty} (\ln b - \ln 1) = \infty. \qquad \blacksquare$$

Integrands with Vertical Asymptotes

Another type of improper integral arises when the integrand has a vertical asymptote—an infinite discontinuity—at a limit of integration or at some point between the limits of integration. If the integrand f is positive over the interval of integration, we can again interpret the improper integral as the area under the graph of f and above the x-axis between the limits of integration.

Consider the region in the first quadrant that lies under the curve $y = 1/\sqrt{x}$ from $x = 0$ to $x = 1$ (Figure 8.1b). First we find the area of the portion from a to 1 (Figure 5):

$$\int_a^1 \frac{dx}{\sqrt{x}} = 2\sqrt{x}\Big]_a^1 = 2 - 2\sqrt{a}.$$

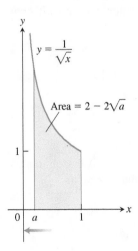

FIGURE 5   The area under this curve is an example of an improper integral of the second kind.

Then we find the limit of this area as $a \to 0^+$:

$$\lim_{a \to 0^+} \int_a^1 \frac{dx}{\sqrt{x}} = \lim_{a \to 0^+} \left(2 - 2\sqrt{a}\right) = 2.$$

Therefore the area under the curve from 0 to 1 is finite and is defined to be

$$\int_0^1 \frac{dx}{\sqrt{x}} = \lim_{a \to 0^+} \int_a^1 \frac{dx}{\sqrt{x}} = 2.$$

DEFINITION   Integrals of functions that become infinite at a point within the interval of integration are **improper integrals of Type II**.

1. If $f(x)$ is continuous on $(a, b]$ and discontinuous at a, then

$$\int_a^b f(x)\, dx = \lim_{c \to a^+} \int_c^b f(x)\, dx.$$

2. If $f(x)$ is continuous on $[a, b)$ and discontinuous at b, then

$$\int_a^b f(x)\, dx = \lim_{c \to b^-} \int_a^c f(x)\, dx.$$

3. If $f(x)$ is discontinuous at c, where $a < c < b$, and continuous on $[a, c) \cup (c, b]$, then

$$\int_a^b f(x)\, dx = \int_a^c f(x)\, dx + \int_c^b f(x)\, dx.$$

In each case, if the limit is finite we say the improper integral **converges** and that the limit is the **value** of the improper integral. If the limit does not exist, the integral **diverges**.

In Part 3 of the definition, the integral on the left side of the equation converges if *both* integrals on the right side converge; otherwise it diverges.

EXAMPLE 4   Investigate the convergence of

$$\int_0^1 \frac{1}{1-x}\, dx.$$

Solution   The integrand $f(x) = 1/(1-x)$ is continuous on $[0, 1)$ but is discontinuous at $x = 1$ and becomes infinite as $x \to 1^-$ (Figure 6). We evaluate the integral as

$$\lim_{b \to 1^-} \int_0^b \frac{1}{1-x}\, dx = \lim_{b \to 1^-} \left[-\ln|1-x| \right]_0^b$$

$$= \lim_{b \to 1^-} \left[-\ln(1-b) + 0 \right] = \infty.$$

The limit is infinite, so the integral diverges.

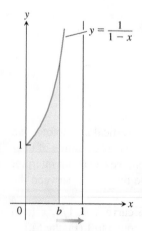

FIGURE 6   The area beneath the curve and above the x-axis for $[0, 1)$ is not a real number (Example 4).

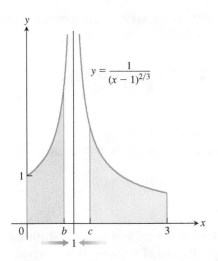

$$y = \frac{1}{(x-1)^{2/3}}$$

FIGURE 7   Example 5 shows that the area under the curve exists (so it is a real number).

EXAMPLE 5   Evaluate

$$\int_0^3 \frac{dx}{(x-1)^{2/3}}.$$

Solution   The integrand has a vertical asymptote at $x = 1$ and is continuous on $[0, 1)$ and $(1, 3]$ (Figure 7). Thus, by Part 3 of the definition above,

$$\int_0^3 \frac{dx}{(x-1)^{2/3}} = \int_0^1 \frac{dx}{(x-1)^{2/3}} + \int_1^3 \frac{dx}{(x-1)^{2/3}}.$$

Next, we evaluate each improper integral on the right-hand side of this equation.

$$\int_0^1 \frac{dx}{(x-1)^{2/3}} = \lim_{b \to 1^-} \int_0^b \frac{dx}{(x-1)^{2/3}}$$

$$= \lim_{b \to 1^-} 3(x-1)^{1/3} \Big]_0^b$$

$$= \lim_{b \to 1^-} \left[3(b-1)^{1/3} + 3 \right] = 3$$

$$\int_1^3 \frac{dx}{(x-1)^{2/3}} = \lim_{c \to 1^+} \int_c^3 \frac{dx}{(x-1)^{2/3}}$$

$$= \lim_{c \to 1^+} 3(x-1)^{1/3} \Big]_c^3$$

$$= \lim_{c \to 1^+} \left[3(3-1)^{1/3} - 3(c-1)^{1/3} \right] = 3\sqrt[3]{2}$$

We conclude that

$$\int_0^3 \frac{dx}{(x-1)^{2/3}} = 3 + 3\sqrt[3]{2}.$$ ■

Improper Integrals with a CAS

Computer algebra systems can evaluate many convergent improper integrals. To evaluate the integral

$$\int_2^\infty \frac{x+3}{(x-1)(x^2+1)}\, dx$$

(which converges) using Maple, enter

```
> f:= (x + 3)/((x − 1) * (x^2 + 1));
```

Then use the integration command

```
> int(f, x = 2..infinity);
```

Maple returns the answer

$$-\frac{1}{2}\pi + \ln(5) + \arctan(2).$$

To obtain a numerical result, use the evaluation command **evalf** and specify the number of digits as follows:

```
> evalf(%, 6);
```

The symbol % instructs the computer to evaluate the last expression on the screen, in this case $(-1/2)\pi + \ln(5) + \arctan(2)$. Maple returns 1.14579.

Using Mathematica, entering

In [1]:= Integrate $[(x + 3)/((x - 1)(x^2 + 1)), \{x, 2, \text{Infinity}\}]$

returns

$$Out [1] = \frac{-\pi}{2} + \text{ArcTan}[2] + \text{Log}[5].$$

To obtain a numerical result with six digits, use the command "N[%, 6]"; it also yields 1.14579.

Tests for Convergence and Divergence

When we cannot evaluate an improper integral directly, we try to determine whether it converges or diverges. If the integral diverges, that's the end of the story. If it converges, we can use numerical methods to approximate its value. The principal tests for convergence or divergence are the Direct Comparison Test and the Limit Comparison Test.

EXAMPLE 6   Does the integral $\int_1^\infty e^{-x^2}\, dx$ converge?

Solution   By definition,

$$\int_1^\infty e^{-x^2}\, dx = \lim_{b\to\infty} \int_1^b e^{-x^2}\, dx.$$

We cannot evaluate this integral directly because it is nonelementary. But we *can* show that its limit as $b \to \infty$ is finite. We know that $\int_1^b e^{-x^2}\, dx$ is an increasing function of b. Therefore either it becomes infinite as $b \to \infty$ or it has a finite limit as $b \to \infty$. It does not become infinite: For every value of $x \geq 1$, we have $e^{-x^2} \leq e^{-x}$ (Figure 8) so that

$$\int_1^b e^{-x^2}\, dx \leq \int_1^b e^{-x}\, dx = -e^{-b} + e^{-1} < e^{-1} \approx 0.36788.$$

Hence,

$$\int_1^\infty e^{-x^2}\, dx = \lim_{b\to\infty} \int_1^b e^{-x^2}\, dx$$

converges to some definite finite value. We do not know exactly what the value is except that it is something positive and less than 0.37. Here we are relying on the completeness property of the real numbers. ∎

The comparison of e^{-x^2} and e^{-x} in Example 6 is a special case of the following test.

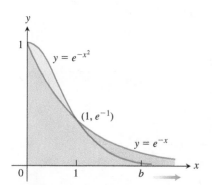

FIGURE 8   The graph of e^{-x^2} lies below the graph of e^{-x} for $x > 1$ (Example 6).

THEOREM 1—Direct Comparison Test   Let f and g be continuous on $[a, \infty)$ with $0 \leq f(x) \leq g(x)$ for all $x \geq a$. Then

1. $\displaystyle\int_a^\infty f(x)\, dx$ converges if $\displaystyle\int_a^\infty g(x)\, dx$ converges.

2. $\displaystyle\int_a^\infty g(x)\, dx$ diverges if $\displaystyle\int_a^\infty f(x)\, dx$ diverges.

Proof   The reasoning behind the argument establishing Theorem 1 is similar to that in Example 6. If $0 \le f(x) \le g(x)$ for $x \ge a$, then from Rule 7 in Theorem 2 we have

$$\int_a^b f(x) \, dx \le \int_a^b g(x) \, dx, \quad b > a.$$

From this it can be argued, as in Example 6, that

$$\int_a^\infty f(x) \, dx \quad \text{converges if} \quad \int_a^\infty g(x) \, dx \quad \text{converges.}$$

Turning this around says that

$$\int_a^\infty g(x) \, dx \quad \text{diverges if} \quad \int_a^\infty f(x) \, dx \quad \text{diverges.} \quad \blacksquare$$

Although the theorem is stated for Type I improper integrals, a similar result is true for integrals of Type II as well.

EXAMPLE 7   These examples illustrate how we use Theorem 1.

(a) $\displaystyle\int_1^\infty \frac{\sin^2 x}{x^2} \, dx$ converges because

$$0 \le \frac{\sin^2 x}{x^2} \le \frac{1}{x^2} \quad \text{on} \quad [1, \infty) \quad \text{and} \quad \int_1^\infty \frac{1}{x^2} \, dx \quad \text{converges.} \quad \text{Example 3}$$

(b) $\displaystyle\int_1^\infty \frac{1}{\sqrt{x^2 - 0.1}} \, dx$ diverges because

$$\frac{1}{\sqrt{x^2 - 0.1}} \ge \frac{1}{x} \quad \text{on} \quad [1, \infty) \quad \text{and} \quad \int_1^\infty \frac{1}{x} \, dx \quad \text{diverges.} \quad \text{Example 3}$$

(c) $\displaystyle\int_0^{\pi/2} \frac{\cos x}{\sqrt{x}} \, dx$ converges because

$$0 \le \frac{\cos x}{\sqrt{x}} \le \frac{1}{\sqrt{x}} \quad \text{on} \quad \left[0, \frac{\pi}{2}\right],$$

and

$$\int_0^{\pi/2} \frac{dx}{\sqrt{x}} = \lim_{a \to 0^+} \int_a^{\pi/2} \frac{dx}{\sqrt{x}}$$

$$= \lim_{a \to 0^+} \sqrt{4x} \,\Big]_a^{\pi/2} \qquad 2\sqrt{x} = \sqrt{4x}$$

$$= \lim_{a \to 0^+} \left(\sqrt{2\pi} - \sqrt{4a}\right) = \sqrt{2\pi} \quad \text{converges.} \quad \blacksquare$$

THEOREM 2—Limit Comparison Test   If the positive functions f and g are continuous on $[a, \infty)$, and if

$$\lim_{x \to \infty} \frac{f(x)}{g(x)} = L, \quad 0 < L < \infty,$$

then

$$\int_a^\infty f(x) \, dx \quad \text{and} \quad \int_a^\infty g(x) \, dx$$

both converge or both diverge.

We omit the proof of Theorem 2.

Although the improper integrals of two functions from a to ∞ may both converge, this does not mean that their integrals necessarily have the same value, as the next example shows.

EXAMPLE 8 Show that

$$\int_1^\infty \frac{dx}{1 + x^2}$$

converges by comparison with $\int_1^\infty (1/x^2)\,dx$. Find and compare the two integral values.

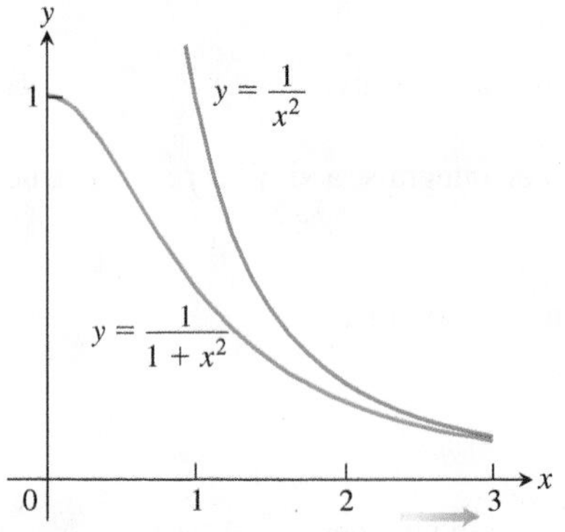

Solution The functions $f(x) = 1/x^2$ and $g(x) = 1/(1 + x^2)$ are positive and continuous on $[1, \infty)$. Also,

$$\lim_{x \to \infty} \frac{f(x)}{g(x)} = \lim_{x \to \infty} \frac{1/x^2}{1/(1 + x^2)} = \lim_{x \to \infty} \frac{1 + x^2}{x^2}$$

$$= \lim_{x \to \infty} \left(\frac{1}{x^2} + 1 \right) = 0 + 1 = 1,$$

FIGURE 9 The functions in Example 8.

a positive finite limit (Figure 9). Therefore, $\int_1^\infty \dfrac{dx}{1 + x^2}$ converges because $\int_1^\infty \dfrac{dx}{x^2}$ converges.

The integrals converge to different values, however:

$$\int_1^\infty \frac{dx}{x^2} = \frac{1}{2 - 1} = 1 \qquad \text{Example 3}$$

and

$$\int_1^\infty \frac{dx}{1 + x^2} = \lim_{b \to \infty} \int_1^b \frac{dx}{1 + x^2}$$

$$= \lim_{b \to \infty} \left[\tan^{-1} b - \tan^{-1} 1 \right] = \frac{\pi}{2} - \frac{\pi}{4} = \frac{\pi}{4}. \qquad \blacksquare$$

EXAMPLE 9 Investigate the convergence of $\displaystyle\int_1^\infty \frac{1 - e^{-x}}{x}\,dx$.

Solution The integrand suggests a comparison of $f(x) = (1 - e^{-x})/x$ with $g(x) = 1/x$. However, we cannot use the Direct Comparison Test because $f(x) \leq g(x)$ and the integral of $g(x)$ *diverges*. On the other hand, using the Limit Comparison Test we find that

$$\lim_{x \to \infty} \frac{f(x)}{g(x)} = \lim_{x \to \infty} \left(\frac{1 - e^{-x}}{x} \right)\left(\frac{x}{1} \right) = \lim_{x \to \infty} (1 - e^{-x}) = 1,$$

which is a positive finite limit. Therefore, $\displaystyle\int_1^\infty \frac{1 - e^{-x}}{x}\,dx$ diverges because $\displaystyle\int_1^\infty \frac{dx}{x}$ diverges. Approximations to the improper integral are given in Table 1. Note that the values do not appear to approach any fixed limiting value as $b \to \infty$. $\blacksquare$

TABLE 1

b	$\displaystyle\int_1^b \frac{1 - e^{-x}}{x}\,dx$
2	0.5226637569
5	1.3912002736
10	2.0832053156
100	4.3857862516
1000	6.6883713446
10000	8.9909564376
100000	11.2935415306

Exercises

Evaluating Improper Integrals

The integrals in Exercises 1–34 converge. Evaluate the integrals without using tables.

1. $\displaystyle\int_0^\infty \frac{dx}{x^2 + 1}$

2. $\displaystyle\int_1^\infty \frac{dx}{x^{1.001}}$

3. $\displaystyle\int_0^1 \frac{dx}{\sqrt{x}}$

4. $\displaystyle\int_0^4 \frac{dx}{\sqrt{4 - x}}$

5. $\displaystyle\int_{-1}^1 \frac{dx}{x^{2/3}}$

6. $\displaystyle\int_{-8}^1 \frac{dx}{x^{1/3}}$

7. $\displaystyle\int_0^1 \frac{dx}{\sqrt{1 - x^2}}$

8. $\displaystyle\int_0^1 \frac{dr}{r^{0.999}}$

9. $\displaystyle\int_{-\infty}^{-2} \frac{2\,dx}{x^2 - 1}$

10. $\displaystyle\int_{-\infty}^2 \frac{2\,dx}{x^2 + 4}$

11. $\displaystyle\int_2^\infty \frac{2}{v^2 - v}\,dv$

12. $\displaystyle\int_2^\infty \frac{2\,dt}{t^2 - 1}$

13. $\displaystyle\int_{-\infty}^\infty \frac{2x\,dx}{(x^2 + 1)^2}$

14. $\displaystyle\int_{-\infty}^\infty \frac{x\,dx}{(x^2 + 4)^{3/2}}$

15. $\displaystyle\int_0^1 \frac{\theta + 1}{\sqrt{\theta^2 + 2\theta}}\,d\theta$

16. $\displaystyle\int_0^2 \frac{s + 1}{\sqrt{4 - s^2}}\,ds$

17. $\displaystyle\int_0^\infty \frac{dx}{(1 + x)\sqrt{x}}$

18. $\displaystyle\int_1^\infty \frac{1}{x\sqrt{x^2 - 1}}\,dx$

19. $\displaystyle\int_0^\infty \frac{dv}{(1 + v^2)(1 + \tan^{-1} v)}$

20. $\displaystyle\int_0^\infty \frac{16\tan^{-1} x}{1 + x^2}\,dx$

21. $\displaystyle\int_{-\infty}^0 \theta e^\theta\,d\theta$

22. $\displaystyle\int_0^\infty 2e^{-\theta}\sin\theta\,d\theta$

23. $\displaystyle\int_{-\infty}^0 e^{-|x|}\,dx$

24. $\displaystyle\int_{-\infty}^\infty 2xe^{-x^2}\,dx$

25. $\displaystyle\int_0^1 x \ln x\,dx$

26. $\displaystyle\int_0^1 (-\ln x)\,dx$

27. $\displaystyle\int_0^2 \frac{ds}{\sqrt{4 - s^2}}$

28. $\displaystyle\int_0^1 \frac{4r\,dr}{\sqrt{1 - r^4}}$

29. $\displaystyle\int_1^2 \frac{ds}{s\sqrt{s^2 - 1}}$

30. $\displaystyle\int_2^4 \frac{dt}{t\sqrt{t^2 - 4}}$

31. $\displaystyle\int_{-1}^4 \frac{dx}{\sqrt{|x|}}$

32. $\displaystyle\int_0^2 \frac{dx}{\sqrt{|x - 1|}}$

33. $\displaystyle\int_{-1}^\infty \frac{d\theta}{\theta^2 + 5\theta + 6}$

34. $\displaystyle\int_0^\infty \frac{dx}{(x + 1)(x^2 + 1)}$

Testing for Convergence

In Exercises 35–64, use integration, the Direct Comparison Test, or the Limit Comparison Test to test the integrals for convergence. If more than one method applies, use whatever method you prefer.

35. $\displaystyle\int_0^{\pi/2} \tan\theta\,d\theta$

36. $\displaystyle\int_0^{\pi/2} \cot\theta\,d\theta$

37. $\displaystyle\int_0^1 \frac{\ln x}{x^2}\,dx$

38. $\displaystyle\int_1^2 \frac{dx}{x \ln x}$

39. $\displaystyle\int_0^{\ln 2} x^{-2}e^{-1/x}\,dx$

40. $\displaystyle\int_0^1 \frac{e^{-\sqrt{x}}}{\sqrt{x}}\,dx$

41. $\displaystyle\int_0^\pi \frac{dt}{\sqrt{t} + \sin t}$

42. $\displaystyle\int_0^1 \frac{dt}{t - \sin t}$ (Hint: $t \geq \sin t$ for $t \geq 0$)

43. $\displaystyle\int_0^2 \frac{dx}{1 - x^2}$

44. $\displaystyle\int_0^2 \frac{dx}{1 - x}$

45. $\displaystyle\int_{-1}^2 \ln|x|\,dx$

46. $\displaystyle\int_{-1}^1 -x \ln|x|\,dx$

47. $\displaystyle\int_1^\infty \frac{dx}{x^3 + 1}$

48. $\displaystyle\int_4^\infty \frac{dx}{\sqrt{x} - 1}$

49. $\displaystyle\int_2^\infty \frac{dv}{\sqrt{v - 1}}$

50. $\displaystyle\int_0^\infty \frac{d\theta}{1 + e^\theta}$

51. $\displaystyle\int_0^\infty \frac{dx}{\sqrt{x^6 + 1}}$

52. $\displaystyle\int_2^\infty \frac{dx}{\sqrt{x^2 - 1}}$

53. $\displaystyle\int_1^\infty \frac{\sqrt{x + 1}}{x^2}\,dx$

54. $\displaystyle\int_2^\infty \frac{x\,dx}{\sqrt{x^4 - 1}}$

55. $\displaystyle\int_\pi^\infty \frac{2 + \cos x}{x}\,dx$

56. $\displaystyle\int_\pi^\infty \frac{1 + \sin x}{x^2}\,dx$

57. $\displaystyle\int_4^\infty \frac{2\,dt}{t^{3/2} - 1}$

58. $\displaystyle\int_2^\infty \frac{1}{\ln x}\,dx$

59. $\displaystyle\int_1^\infty \frac{e^x}{x}\,dx$

60. $\displaystyle\int_{e^e}^\infty \ln(\ln x)\,dx$

61. $\displaystyle\int_1^\infty \frac{1}{\sqrt{e^x - x}}\,dx$

62. $\displaystyle\int_1^\infty \frac{1}{e^x - 2^x}\,dx$

63. $\displaystyle\int_{-\infty}^\infty \frac{dx}{\sqrt{x^4 + 1}}$

64. $\displaystyle\int_{-\infty}^\infty \frac{dx}{e^x + e^{-x}}$

Theory and Examples

65. Find the values of p for which each integral converges.

a. $\displaystyle\int_1^2 \frac{dx}{x(\ln x)^p}$

b. $\displaystyle\int_2^\infty \frac{dx}{x(\ln x)^p}$

66. $\displaystyle\int_{-\infty}^\infty f(x)$ **may not equal** $\displaystyle\lim_{b \to \infty}\int_{-b}^b f(x)\,dx$ Show that

$$\int_0^\infty \frac{2x\,dx}{x^2 + 1}$$

diverges and hence that

$$\int_{-\infty}^\infty \frac{2x\,dx}{x^2 + 1}$$

diverges. Then show that

$$\lim_{b \to \infty}\int_{-b}^b \frac{2x\,dx}{x^2 + 1} = 0.$$

Exercises 67–70 are about the infinite region in the first quadrant between the curve $y = e^{-x}$ and the x-axis.

67. Find the area of the region.

68. Find the centroid of the region.

69. Find the volume of the solid generated by revolving the region about the y-axis.

70. Find the volume of the solid generated by revolving the region about the x-axis.

71. Find the area of the region that lies between the curves $y = \sec x$ and $y = \tan x$ from $x = 0$ to $x = \pi/2$.

72. The region in Exercise 71 is revolved about the x-axis to generate a solid.

   a. Find the volume of the solid.

   b. Show that the inner and outer surfaces of the solid have infinite area.

73. Evaluate the integrals.

   a. $\displaystyle\int_0^1 \frac{dt}{\sqrt{t}(1+t)}$ **b.** $\displaystyle\int_0^\infty \frac{dt}{\sqrt{t}(1+t)}$

74. Evaluate $\displaystyle\int_3^\infty \frac{dx}{x\sqrt{x^2-9}}$.

75. Estimating the value of a convergent improper integral whose domain is infinite

   a. Show that

$$\int_3^\infty e^{-3x}\,dx = \frac{1}{3}e^{-9} < 0.000042,$$

   and hence that $\int_3^\infty e^{-x^2}\,dx < 0.000042$. Explain why this means that $\int_0^\infty e^{-x^2}\,dx$ can be replaced by $\int_0^3 e^{-x^2}\,dx$ without introducing an error of magnitude greater than 0.000042.

   [T] b. Evaluate $\int_0^3 e^{-x^2}\,dx$ numerically.

76. The infinite paint can or Gabriel's horn As Example 3 shows, the integral $\int_1^\infty (dx/x)$ diverges. This means that the integral

$$\int_1^\infty 2\pi \frac{1}{x}\sqrt{1+\frac{1}{x^4}}\,dx,$$

which measures the *surface area* of the solid of revolution traced out by revolving the curve $y = 1/x$, $1 \le x$, about the x-axis, diverges also. By comparing the two integrals, we see that, for every finite value $b > 1$,

$$\int_1^b 2\pi \frac{1}{x}\sqrt{1+\frac{1}{x^4}}\,dx > 2\pi\int_1^b \frac{1}{x}\,dx.$$

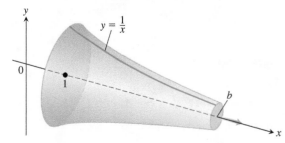

However, the integral

$$\int_1^\infty \pi\left(\frac{1}{x}\right)^2 dx$$

for the *volume* of the solid converges.

   a. Calculate it.

   b. This solid of revolution is sometimes described as a can that does not hold enough paint to cover its own interior. Think

about that for a moment. It is common sense that a finite amount of paint cannot cover an infinite surface. But if we fill the horn with paint (a finite amount), then we *will* have covered an infinite surface. Explain the apparent contradiction.

77. Sine-integral function The integral

$$\text{Si}(x) = \int_0^x \frac{\sin t}{t}\,dt,$$

called the *sine-integral function*, has important applications in optics.

   [T] a. Plot the integrand $(\sin t)/t$ for $t > 0$. Is the sine-integral function everywhere increasing or decreasing? Do you think $\text{Si}(x) = 0$ for $x > 0$? Check your answers by graphing the function $\text{Si}(x)$ for $0 \le x \le 25$.

   b. Explore the convergence of

$$\int_0^\infty \frac{\sin t}{t}\,dt.$$

   If it converges, what is its value?

78. Error function The function

$$\text{erf}(x) = \int_0^x \frac{2e^{-t^2}}{\sqrt{\pi}}\,dt,$$

called the *error function*, has important applications in probability and statistics.

   [T] a. Plot the error function for $0 \le x \le 25$.

   b. Explore the convergence of

$$\int_0^\infty \frac{2e^{-t^2}}{\sqrt{\pi}}\,dt.$$

   If it converges, what appears to be its value? You will see how to confirm your estimate.

79. Normal probability distribution The function

$$f(x) = \frac{1}{\sigma\sqrt{2\pi}}e^{-\frac{1}{2}\left(\frac{x-\mu}{\sigma}\right)^2}$$

is called the *normal probability density function* with mean μ and standard deviation σ. The number μ tells where the distribution is centered, and σ measures the "scatter" around the mean.

From the theory of probability, it is known that

$$\int_{-\infty}^\infty f(x)\,dx = 1.$$

In what follows, let $\mu = 0$ and $\sigma = 1$.

   [T] a. Draw the graph of f. Find the intervals on which f is increasing, the intervals on which f is decreasing, and any local extreme values and where they occur.

   b. Evaluate

$$\int_{-n}^n f(x)\,dx$$

   for $n = 1, 2,$ and 3.

c. Give a convincing argument that

$$\int_{-\infty}^{\infty} f(x)\,dx = 1.$$

(*Hint:* Show that $0 < f(x) < e^{-x/2}$ for $x > 1$, and for $b > 1$,

$$\int_{b}^{\infty} e^{-x/2}\,dx \to 0 \quad \text{as} \quad b \to \infty.)$$

80. Show that if $f(x)$ is integrable on every interval of real numbers and a and b are real numbers with $a < b$, then

   a. $\int_{-\infty}^{a} f(x)\,dx$ and $\int_{a}^{\infty} f(x)\,dx$ both converge if and only if $\int_{-\infty}^{b} f(x)\,dx$ and $\int_{b}^{\infty} f(x)\,dx$ both converge.

   b. $\int_{-\infty}^{a} f(x)\,dx + \int_{a}^{\infty} f(x)\,dx = \int_{-\infty}^{b} f(x)\,dx + \int_{b}^{\infty} f(x)\,dx$ when the integrals involved converge.

COMPUTER EXPLORATIONS

In Exercises 81–84, use a CAS to explore the integrals for various values of p (include noninteger values). For what values of p does the integral converge? What is the value of the integral when it does converge? Plot the integrand for various values of p.

81. $\displaystyle\int_{0}^{e} x^{p} \ln x\,dx$

82. $\displaystyle\int_{e}^{\infty} x^{p} \ln x\,dx$

83. $\displaystyle\int_{0}^{\infty} x^{p} \ln x\,dx$

84. $\displaystyle\int_{-\infty}^{\infty} x^{p} \ln |x|\,dx$

Use a CAS to evaluate the integrals.

85. $\displaystyle\int_{0}^{2/\pi} \sin \frac{1}{x}\,dx$

86. $\displaystyle\int_{0}^{2/\pi} x \sin \frac{1}{x}\,dx$

10.2

Extension

Matrix Notation

Additional material to supplement Section 10.2 of *Calculus for the Life Sciences.*

We often want to work with a specific entry of an $m \times n$ matrix A. In order to do so, the entry in row i and column j, appropriately called the "ij^{th} entry of the matrix A," is written $(A)_{ij}$ or more simply a_{ij} For example, if A is the matrix

$$A = \begin{bmatrix} 3 & -2 & 4 \\ -1 & 10 & -12 \end{bmatrix},$$

then $a_{11} = 3$, $a_{12} = -2$, and so forth. More generally, any $m \times n$ matrix can be written explicitly in terms of its entries as

$$A = \begin{bmatrix} a_{11} & a_{12} & \cdots & a_{1n} \\ a_{21} & a_{22} & \cdots & a_{2n} \\ \vdots & \vdots & & \vdots \\ a_{m1} & a_{m2} & \cdots & a_{mn} \end{bmatrix}.$$

This notation has many handy uses. For the moment, notice that the rule for matrix addition can now be made more explicit: $A + B = C$ if $a_{ij} + b_{ij} = c_{ij}$ for all i and j.

EXERCISES

Given the matrix

$$A = \begin{bmatrix} 4 & 5 & 6 \\ -1 & -2 & -3 \\ 17 & 18 & 19 \end{bmatrix},$$

find each of the following.
1. a_{23} 2. a_{31}

ANSWERS

1. -3 2. 17

10.3

Extension

Matrix Linear Equations

Additional material to supplement Section 10.3, p. 550, of *Calculus for the Life Sciences.*

Matrix multiplication will turn out to have many applications. Before exploring some of these, it's worth noting that our introduction to matrices in Section 10.1 – specifically, rewriting a system of linear equations as an augmented matrix – is matrix multiplication in disguise. For example, consider the following system of linear equations from Example 4 in Section 10.1.

$$x + 2y - z = 0$$
$$3x - y + z = 6$$
$$-2x - 4y + 2z = 0$$

Instead of x, y, and z, let us label the variables as x_1, x_2, and x_3 (a useful notation when there are lots of variables), resulting in the following system.

$$x_1 + 2x_2 - x_3 = 0$$
$$3x_1 - x_2 + x_3 = 6$$
$$-2x_1 - 4x_2 + 2x_3 = 0$$

If we let

$$A = \begin{bmatrix} 1 & 2 & -1 \\ 3 & -1 & 1 \\ -2 & -4 & 2 \end{bmatrix}, \quad X = \begin{bmatrix} x_1 \\ x_2 \\ x_3 \end{bmatrix}, \quad \text{and} \quad B = \begin{bmatrix} 0 \\ 6 \\ 0 \end{bmatrix},$$

then the linear system is equivalent to the matrix equation $AX = B$. For example, the first row of the product AX is $1 \cdot x_1 + 2 \cdot x_2 - 1 \cdot x_3$, and the first row of matrix B is 0. Setting these two equal to each other gives the first equation in the linear system. The matrix equation $AX = B$ gives

$$\begin{bmatrix} 1 & 2 & -1 \\ 3 & -1 & 1 \\ -2 & -4 & 2 \end{bmatrix} \begin{bmatrix} x_1 \\ x_2 \\ x_3 \end{bmatrix} = \begin{bmatrix} 0 \\ 6 \\ 0 \end{bmatrix},$$

which is equivalent to the original linear system. See Exercises 37 and 38 for more practice on this idea.

10.5
Extension

Diagonalization

Additional material to supplement Section 10.5, p.574, of *Calculus for Life Sciences*.

There is a remarkable fact about eigenvalues and eigenvectors that makes them particularly useful for determining long-term trends.

Diagonalization of a Matrix

Suppose M is an $n \times n$ matrix with n distinct eigenvalues $\lambda_1, \lambda_2, \ldots, \lambda_n$ and corresponding eigenvectors $V_1, V_2, \ldots, V_n$. Let $P = [V_1, V_2, \ldots, V_n]$ be an $n \times n$ matrix with columns consisting of the eigenvectors of M. Then P is invertible, and M can be written as

$$M = PDP^{-1},$$

where D is an $n \times n$ diagonal matrix with diagonal elements equal to the corresponding eigenvalues of M; that is,

$$D = \begin{bmatrix} \lambda_1 & 0 & \cdots & 0 \\ 0 & \lambda_2 & \cdots & 0 \\ 0 & 0 & \cdots & \lambda_n \end{bmatrix}.$$

For example, consider the matrix $M = \begin{bmatrix} 0.6 & 0.8 \\ 0.9 & 0 \end{bmatrix}$ in Example 6. The eigenvalues are $\lambda_1 = 1.2$ and $\lambda_2 = -0.6$, and the corresponding eigenvectors are $V_1 = \begin{bmatrix} 4 \\ 3 \end{bmatrix}$ and $V_2 = \begin{bmatrix} 2 \\ -3 \end{bmatrix}$, so

$$P = [V_1, V_2] = \begin{bmatrix} 4 & 2 \\ 3 & -3 \end{bmatrix}.$$

Using the techniques of Section 10.4, we can verify that

$$P^{-1} = \begin{bmatrix} 1/6 & 1/9 \\ 1/6 & -2/9 \end{bmatrix}$$

and that D is the diagonal matrix with diagonal entries equal to 1.2 and -0.6, namely,

$$D = \begin{bmatrix} 1.2 & 0 \\ 0 & -0.6 \end{bmatrix}.$$

(We must be careful here. Because V_1 is the first column of P, we must be sure that the corresponding eigenvalue λ_1 is in the first row, first column of D.) Now verify by direct multiplication that $M = PDP^{-1}$, that is,

$$\begin{bmatrix} 0.6 & 0.8 \\ 0.9 & 0 \end{bmatrix} = \begin{bmatrix} 4 & 2 \\ 3 & -3 \end{bmatrix} \begin{bmatrix} 1.2 & 0 \\ 0 & -0.6 \end{bmatrix} \begin{bmatrix} 1/6 & 1/9 \\ 1/6 & -2/9 \end{bmatrix}.$$

To see why diagonalization is important, consider the Leslie matrix M^2 for a two year period.

$$
\begin{aligned}
M^2 &= (PDP^{-1})(PDP^{-1}) & \text{Diagonalization} \\
&= PD(P^{-1}P)DP^{-1} & \text{Associative property of matrix multiplication} \\
&= PDIDP^{-1} & \text{Property of inverse matrices} \\
&= PD^2P^{-1} & \text{Property of the identity matrix}
\end{aligned}
$$

Similarly, for any positive integer n,

$$
\begin{aligned}
M^n &= (PDP^{-1})(PDP^{-1})\cdots(PDP^{-1}) & n \text{ times} \\
&= PD(P^{-1}P)D(P^{-1}P)\cdots(P^{-1}P)DP^{-1} \\
&= PDD\cdots DP^{-1} & n \text{ times} \\
&= PD^nP^{-1}.
\end{aligned}
$$

Furthermore, $\lim_{n\to\infty}(-0.6)^n = 0$, so in this example,

$$
D^n = \begin{bmatrix} 1.2^n & 0 \\ 0 & (-0.6)^n \end{bmatrix} \approx \begin{bmatrix} 1.2^n & 0 \\ 0 & 0 \end{bmatrix}
$$

for large n. Thus, in the long run, it is the positive eigenvalue that determines the growth rate, and

$$
\begin{aligned}
M^n &= PD^nP^{-1} \\
&\approx \begin{bmatrix} 4 & 2 \\ 3 & -3 \end{bmatrix}\begin{bmatrix} 1.2^n & 0 \\ 0 & 0 \end{bmatrix}\begin{bmatrix} 1/6 & 1/9 \\ 1/6 & -2/9 \end{bmatrix} \\
&= \begin{bmatrix} 4 & 2 \\ 3 & -3 \end{bmatrix}\begin{bmatrix} (1/6)1.2^n & (1/9)1.2^n \\ 0 & 0 \end{bmatrix} & \text{Multiply the matrices.} \\
&= \begin{bmatrix} (2/3)1.2^n & (4/9)1.2^n \\ (1/2)1.2^n & (1/3)1.2^n \end{bmatrix} \\
&= \begin{bmatrix} 2/3 & 4/9 \\ 1/2 & 1/3 \end{bmatrix}1.2^n.
\end{aligned}
$$

Notice that both columns of this last matrix are multiples of the eigenvector $\begin{bmatrix} 4 \\ 3 \end{bmatrix}$ and are thus eigenvectors themselves. Finally, for large n,

$$
\begin{aligned}
M^n\begin{bmatrix} x_1(0) \\ x_2(0) \end{bmatrix} &\approx 1.2^n\begin{bmatrix} 2/3 & 4/9 \\ 1/2 & 1/3 \end{bmatrix}\begin{bmatrix} x_1(0) \\ x_2(0) \end{bmatrix} \\
&= 1.2^n\begin{bmatrix} (2/3)x_1(0)+(4/9)x_2(0) \\ (1/2)x_1(0)+(1/3)x_2(0) \end{bmatrix} \\
&= 1.2^n\left\{ x_1(0)\begin{bmatrix} 2/3 \\ 1/2 \end{bmatrix} + x_2(0)\begin{bmatrix} 4/9 \\ 1/3 \end{bmatrix} \right\} \\
&= 1.2^n\left\{ \frac{x_1(0)}{6}\begin{bmatrix} 4 \\ 3 \end{bmatrix} + \frac{x_2(0)}{9}\begin{bmatrix} 4 \\ 3 \end{bmatrix} \right\} \\
&= 1.2^n\left(\frac{x_1(0)}{6} + \frac{x_2(0)}{9} \right)\begin{bmatrix} 4 \\ 3 \end{bmatrix}.
\end{aligned}
$$

Thus, as our initial calculations suggest, in the long term the population grows by a factor of approximately $\lambda_1 = 1.2$, and the eventual proportion of adults and juveniles within the population is determined by $V_1 = \begin{bmatrix} 4 \\ 3 \end{bmatrix}$.

EXERCISES

For the following exercises in Section 10.5, suppose that the population is large enough that the eventual long term growth or decay is apparent. Find **(a)** the long term rate of growth or decay, and **(b)** the eventual distribution of the categories as a proportion of the entire population.

1. Exercise 18   **2.** Exercise 19

3. Exercise 20   **4.** Exercise 21

5. Exercise 22   **6.** Exercise 23

ANSWERS

1. (a) 1.6 **(b)** 1/2 1/2   **2. (a)** 1.4 **(b)** 1/2 1/2   **3. (a)** 1 **(b)** 3/8 5/8   **4. (a)** 0.9 **(b)** 1/2 1/2
5. (a) 0.8 **(b)** 2/3 1/3   **6. (a)** 0.9 **(b)** 3/5 2/5

11

Introduction to Differential Equations

Chapter Preview If you wanted to demonstrate the utility of mathematics to a skeptic, perhaps the most convincing way would be to talk about *differential equations*. This vast subject lies at the heart of mathematical modeling and is used in engineering, physics, chemistry, biology, geophysics, economics and finance, and health sciences. Its many applications in these areas include analyzing the stability of buildings and bridges, simulating planet and satellite orbits, describing chemical reactions, modeling populations and epidemics, predicting weather, locating oil reserves, forecasting financial markets, producing medical images, and simulating drug kinetics. Differential equations rely heavily on calculus, and are usually studied in advanced courses that follow calculus. Nevertheless, you have now seen enough calculus to take a brief tour of this rich and powerful subject.

11.1 Basic Ideas

If you studied antiderivatives or velocity and net change, then you saw a preview of differential equations. Given the derivative of a function (for example, a velocity), the study of these topics showed how to find the function itself by integration. This process amounts to solving a differential equation.

A differential equation involves an unknown function y and its derivatives. The unknown in a differential equation is not a number (as in an algebraic equation), but rather a *function*. Examples of differential equations are

> Common choices for the independent variable in a differential equation are x and t, with t being used for time-dependent problems.

$$\text{(A)} \frac{dy}{dx} + 4y = \cos x, \quad \text{(B)} \frac{d^2y}{dx^2} + 16y = 0, \quad \text{and} \quad \text{(C)} \, y'(t) = 0.1y(100 - y).$$

In each case, the goal is to find functions y that satisfy the equation. Just to be clear about what we mean by a solution, consider equation (B). If we substitute $y = \cos 4x$ and $y'' = -16 \cos 4x$ into this equation, we find that

$$\underbrace{-16 \cos 4x}_{y''} + \underbrace{16 \cos 4x}_{16y} = 0,$$

which implies that $y = \cos 4x$ is a solution of the equation. You should verify that $y = C \cos 4x$ is also a solution, for any real number C (as is $y = C \sin 4x$).

Let's begin with a brief discussion of the terminology associated with differential equations. The **order** of a differential equation is the order of the highest-order derivative that appears in the equation. Of the three differential equations just given, (A) and (C) are first order, and (B) is second order. A differential equation is **linear** if the unknown

> A *linear* differential equation cannot have terms such as y^2, yy', or $\sin y$, where y is the unknown function.

function y and its derivatives appear only to the first power and are not composed with other functions. Furthermore, a linear equation cannot have products or quotients of y and its derivatives. Of the equations just given, (A) and (B) are linear, but (C) is **nonlinear** (because the right side contains y^2).

In this chapter, we work primarily with first-order differential equations. The most general **first-order linear differential equation** has the form

$$\frac{dy}{dx} + p(x)y = q(x),$$

where p and q are given functions of x. Notice that y and y' appear to the first power and not in products or compositions that involve y or y', which makes the equation linear.

> To keep matters simple, we will use *general solution* to refer to the most general family of solutions of any differential equation. However, some nonlinear equations may have isolated solutions that are not included in this family of solutions. For example, you should check that for real numbers C, the functions $y = 1/(C - t)$ satisfy the equation $y'(t) = y^2$. Therefore, we call $y = 1/(C - t)$ the general solution of the equation, even though it doesn't include the solution $y = 0$.

Solving a first-order differential equation requires integration—you must "undo" the derivative y' in order to find y. Integration introduces an arbitrary constant, so the most general solution of a first-order differential equation typically involves one arbitrary constant. Similarly, the most general solution of a second-order differential equation involves two arbitrary constants, and for an nth-order differential equation, the most general solution involves n arbitrary constants. The most general family of functions that solves a differential equation, including the appropriate number of arbitrary constants, is called (not surprisingly) the **general solution**.

A differential equation is often accompanied by **initial conditions** that specify the values of y, and possibly its derivatives, at a particular point. In general, an nth-order equation requires n initial conditions, which can be used to determine the n arbitrary constants in the general solution. A differential equation, together with the appropriate number of initial conditions, is called an **initial value problem**. A typical first-order initial value problem has the form

$$y'(t) = f(t, y) \quad \text{Differential equation where } f \text{ is given}$$
$$y(0) = A. \quad \text{Initial condition where } A \text{ is given}$$

EXAMPLE 1 Verifying solutions Exponential growth processes (for example, cell populations and bank accounts) involve functions of the form $y(t) = Ce^{kt}$, where C and $k > 0$ are real numbers.

a. Show by substitution that the function $y(t) = Ce^{2.5t}$ is a solution of the differential equation $y'(t) = 2.5y(t)$, where C is an arbitrary constant.

b. Show by substitution that the function $y(t) = 3.2e^{2.5t}$ satisfies the initial value problem

$$y'(t) = 2.5y(t) \quad \text{Differential equation}$$
$$y(0) = 3.2. \quad \text{Initial condition}$$

SOLUTION

a. We differentiate $y(t) = Ce^{2.5t}$ to get $y'(t) = 2.5Ce^{2.5t}$. Substituting into the differential equation, we find that

$$y'(t) = \underbrace{2.5Ce^{2.5t}}_{y'(t)} = 2.5\underbrace{Ce^{2.5t}}_{y(t)} = 2.5y(t).$$

In other words, the function $y(t) = Ce^{2.5t}$ satisfies the equation $y'(t) = 2.5y(t)$, for any value of C. Therefore, $y(t) = Ce^{2.5t}$ is a family of solutions of the differential equation.

> The term *initial condition* originates with equations in which the independent variable is *time*. In such problems, the initial state of the system (for example, position and velocity) is specified at some initial time (often $t = 0$).

b. By part (a) with $C = 3.2$, the function $y(t) = 3.2e^{2.5t}$ satisfies the differential equation $y'(t) = 2.5y(t)$. We can also check that this function satisfies the initial condition $y(0) = 3.2$:

$$y(0) = 3.2e^{2.5 \cdot 0} = 3.2 \cdot e^0 = 3.2.$$

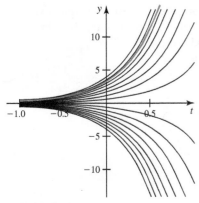

FIGURE 11.1

Therefore, $y(t) = 3.2e^{2.5t}$ is a solution of the initial value problem. Figure 11.1 shows the general solution as a family of curves with several different values of the constant C. It also shows the function $y(t) = 3.2e^{2.5t}$ highlighted in red, which is the solution of the initial value problem.

Related Exercises 7–14 ◄

EXAMPLE 2   General solutions Find the general solution of the following differential equations.

a. $y'(t) = 5 \cos t + 6 \sin 3t$

b. $y''(t) = 10t^3 - 144t^7 + 12t$

SOLUTION

a. The solution of the equation consists of the antiderivatives of $5 \cos t + 6 \sin 3t$. Taking the indefinite integral of both sides of the equation, we have

$$\int y'(t)\, dt = \int (5 \cos t + 6 \sin 3t)\, dt \quad \text{Integrate both sides with respect to } t.$$

$$y(t) = 5 \sin t - 2 \cos 3t + C, \quad \text{Evaluate integrals.}$$

where C is an arbitrary constant. The function $y(t) = 5 \sin t - 2 \cos 3t + C$ is the general solution of the differential equation.

b. In this second-order equation, we are given $y''(t)$ in terms of the independent variable t. Taking the indefinite integral of both sides of the equation yields

$$\int y''(t)\, dt = \int (10t^3 - 144t^7 + 12t)\, dt \quad \text{Integrate both sides with respect to } t.$$

$$y'(t) = \frac{5}{2}t^4 - 18t^8 + 6t^2 + C_1. \quad \text{Evaluate integrals.}$$

Integrating once gives $y'(t)$ and introduces an arbitrary constant that we call C_1. We now integrate again:

$$\int y'(t)\, dt = \int \left(\frac{5}{2}t^4 - 18t^8 + 6t^2 + C_1 \right) dt \quad \text{Integrate both sides with respect to } t.$$

$$y(t) = \frac{1}{2}t^5 - 2t^9 + 2t^3 + C_1 t + C_2. \quad \text{Evaluate integrals.}$$

This function, which involves two arbitrary constants, is the general solution of the differential equation.

Related Exercises 15–22 ◄

QUICK CHECK 1 What are the orders of the equations in Example 2? Are they linear or nonlinear? ◄

EXAMPLE 3   An initial value problem Solve the initial value problem

$$y'(t) = 10e^{-t/2}, \quad y(0) = 4, \text{ for } t \geq 0.$$

SOLUTION The general solution is found by taking the indefinite integral of both sides of the differential equation with respect to t:

$$\int y'(t)\, dt = \int 10e^{-t/2}\, dt \quad \text{Integrate both sides with respect to } t.$$

$$y(t) = -20e^{-t/2} + C. \quad \text{Evaluate integrals.}$$

We have found the general solution, which involves one arbitrary constant. To determine its value, we use the initial condition by substituting $t = 0$ and $y = 4$ into the general solution:

$$\underbrace{y(0)}_{4} = -20e^{-0/2} + C = -20 + C,$$

> If an initial value problem represents a system that evolves in time (for example, a population or a trajectory), then the initial condition $y(0) = A$ gives the initial state of the system. In such cases, the solution is usually graphed only for $t \geq 0$. More generally, if a specific interval of interest is not specified, the solution is customarily represented on the domain of the solution; that is, the initial condition may not appear at an endpoint of the solution curve.

QUICK CHECK 2 What is the solution of the initial value problem in Example 3 with the initial condition $y(0) = 16$? ◄

which implies that $4 = -20 + C$ or $C = 24$. Therefore, the solution of the initial value problem is $y(t) = -20e^{-t/2} + 24$ (Figure 11.2). You should check that this function satisfies both the differential equation and the initial condition.

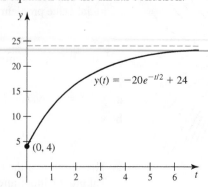

FIGURE 11.2

Related Exercises 23–28 ◄

Differential Equations in Action

We close this section with three examples of differential equations that are used to model particular physical systems. It is useful to revisit an example of one-dimensional motion in a gravitational field using the language of differential equations. The equations in Examples 5 and 6 reappear later in the chapter when we show how to solve them.

EXAMPLE 4   Motion in a gravitational field A stone is launched vertically upward with a velocity of v_0 meters/second from a point s_0 meters above the ground, where $v_0 > 0$ and $s_0 \geq 0$. Assume that the stone is launched at time $t = 0$ and that $s(t)$ is the position of the stone at time $t \geq 0$ (the positive s-axis points in the upward direction). By Newton's Second Law of Motion, assuming no air resistance, the position of the stone is governed by the differential equation $s''(t) = -g$, where $g = 9.8$ m/s^2 is the acceleration due to gravity (in the downward direction).

a. Find the position $s(t)$ of the stone for all times at which the stone is above the ground.

b. At what time does the stone reach its highest point and what is its height above the ground?

c. Does the stone go higher if it is launched at $v(0) = v_0 = 39.2$ m/s from the ground ($s_0 = 0$) or at $v_0 = 19.6$ m/s from a height of $s_0 = 50$ m?

SOLUTION

a. Integrating both sides of the differential equation $s''(t) = -9.8$ gives the velocity $v(t)$:

$$\int s''(t)\, dt = -\int 9.8\, dt \qquad \text{Integrate both sides.}$$

$$s'(t) = v(t) = -9.8t + C_1. \quad \text{Evaluate integrals.}$$

To evaluate the constant C_1, we use the initial condition $v(0) = v_0$, finding that $v(0) = -9.8 \cdot 0 + C_1 = C_1 = v_0$. Therefore, $C_1 = v_0$ and the velocity is $v(t) = s'(t) = -9.8t + v_0$.

Integrating both sides of this velocity equation gives the position function:

$$\int s'(t)\, dt = \int (-9.8t + v_0)\, dt \quad \text{Integrate both sides.}$$

$$s(t) = -4.9t^2 + v_0 t + C_2. \quad \text{Evaluate integrals.}$$

We now use the initial condition $s(0) = s_0$ to evaluate C_2, finding that

$$s(0) = -4.9 \cdot 0^2 + v_0 \cdot 0 + C_2 = C_2 = s_0.$$

Therefore, $C_2 = s_0$ and the position function is $s(t) = -4.9t^2 + v_0 t + s_0$, where v_0 and s_0 are given. This function is valid while the stone is in flight. Notice that we have solved an initial value problem for the position of the stone.

To find the time at which the stone reaches its highest point, we could also locate the local maximum of the position function, which also requires solving $s'(t) = v(t) = 0$.

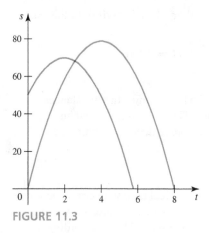

FIGURE 11.3

The curves in Figure 11.3 are not the trajectories of the stones. The motion is one-dimensional because the stones travel along a vertical line.

b. The stone reaches its highest point when $v(t) = 0$. Solving $v(t) = -9.8t + v_0 = 0$, we find that the stone reaches its highest point when $t = v_0/9.8$, measured in seconds. So the position at the highest point is

$$s_{max} = s\left(\frac{v_0}{9.8}\right) = -4.9\left(\frac{v_0}{9.8}\right)^2 + v_0\left(\frac{v_0}{9.8}\right) + s_0 = \frac{v_0^2}{19.6} + s_0.$$

c. Now it is a matter of substituting the given values of s_0 and v_0. In the first case, with $v_0 = 39.2$ and $s_0 = 0$, we have $s_{max} = 78.4$ m. In the second case, with $v_0 = 19.6$ and $s_0 = 50$, we have $s_{max} = 69.6$ m. The position functions in the two cases are shown in Figure 11.3. We see that the stone goes higher with $v_0 = 39.2$ and $s_0 = 0$.

Related Exercises 29–30 ◀

QUICK CHECK 3 In Example 4, find the highest point of the stone if it is launched upward at 9.8 m/s from an initial height of 100 m. ◀

EXAMPLE 5   A harvesting model A simple model of a harvested resource (for example, timber or fish) assumes a competition between the harvesting and the natural growth of the resource. This process may be described by the differential equation

$$\underbrace{p'(t)}_{\substack{\text{rate of}\\\text{change}}} = \underbrace{rp(t)}_{\substack{\text{natural}\\\text{growth rate}}} - \underbrace{H}_{\text{harvesting}}, \quad \text{for} \quad t \geq 0,$$

where $p(t)$ is the amount (or population) of the resource at time $t \geq 0$, $r > 0$ is the natural growth rate of the resource, and $H > 0$ is the harvesting rate. An initial condition $p(0) = p_0$ is also specified to create an initial value problem. Notice that the rate of change $p'(t)$ has a positive contribution from the natural growth rate and a negative contribution from the harvesting term.

a. For given constants p_0, r, and H, verify that the function

$$p(t) = \left(p_0 - \frac{H}{r}\right)e^{rt} + \frac{H}{r}$$

is a solution of the initial value problem.

b. Let $p_0 = 1000$ and $r = 0.1$. Graph the solutions for $H = 50, 90, 130,$ and 170. Describe and interpret the four curves.

c. What value of H gives a constant value of p, for all $t \geq 0$?

SOLUTION

a. Differentiating the given solution, we find that

$$p'(t) = \left(p_0 - \frac{H}{r}\right)re^{rt} = (rp_0 - H)e^{rt}.$$

Simplifying the right side of the differential equation, we find that

$$rp(t) - H = r\left[\left(p_0 - \frac{H}{r}\right)e^{rt} + \frac{H}{r}\right] - H = (rp_0 - H)e^{rt}.$$

Therefore, the left and right sides of the equation $p'(t) = rp(t) - H$ are equal, so the equation is satisfied by the given function. You can verify that $p(0) = p_0$, which means p satisfies the initial value problem.

b. Letting $p_0 = 1000$ and $r = 0.1$, the function

$$p(t) = (1000 - 10H)e^{0.1t} + 10H$$

is graphed in Figure 11.4, for $H = 50, 90, 130,$ and 170. We see that for small values of H ($H = 50$ and $H = 90$), the amount of the resource increases with time. On the other hand, for large values of H ($H = 130$ and $H = 170$), the amount of the resource

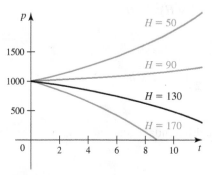

FIGURE 11.4

decreases with time, eventually reaching zero. The model predicts that if the harvesting rate is too large, the resource will eventually disappear.

c. The solution

$$p(t) = (1000 - 10H)e^{0.1t} + 10H$$

is constant (independent of t) when $1000 - 10H = 0$ or when $H = 100$. In this case, the solution is

$$p(t) = \underbrace{(1000 - 10H)}_{0} e^{0.1t} + 10H = 1000.$$

Therefore, if the harvesting rate is $H = 100$, then the harvesting exactly balances the natural growth of the resource, and p is constant. This solution is called an *equilibrium solution*. For $H > 100$, the amount of resource decreases in time, and for $H < 100$, it increases in time.

Related Exercises 31–32 ◄

▷ Evangelista Torricelli was an Italian mathematician and physicist who lived from 1608 to 1647. He is credited with inventing the barometer.

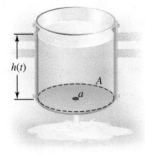

FIGURE 11.5

EXAMPLE 6   **Flow from a tank**   Imagine a large cylindrical tank with cross-sectional area A. The bottom of the tank has a circular drain with cross-sectional area a. Assume the tank is initially filled with water to a height $h(0) = H$ (Figure 11.5). According to Torricelli's law, the height of the water as it flows out of the tank is described by the differential equation

$$h'(t) = -k\sqrt{h}, \quad \text{where } t \geq 0, k = \frac{a}{A}\sqrt{2g},$$

and $g = 9.8 \text{ m/s}^2$ is the acceleration due to gravity.

a. According to the differential equation, is h an increasing or decreasing function of t, for $t \geq 0$?

b. Verify by substitution that the solution of the initial value problem is

$$h(t) = \left(\sqrt{H} - \frac{kt}{2} \right)^2.$$

c. Graph the solution for $H = 1.44 \text{ m}$, $A = 1 \text{ m}^2$, and $a = 0.05 \text{ m}^2$.

d. After how many seconds is the tank in part (c) empty?

SOLUTION

a. Because $k > 0$, the differential equation implies that $h'(t) < 0$, for $t \geq 0$. Therefore, the height of the water decreases in time, consistent with the fact that the tank is being drained.

b. We first check the initial condition. Substituting $t = 0$ into the proposed solution, we see that

$$h(0) = \left(\sqrt{H} - \frac{k \cdot 0}{2} \right)^2 = (\sqrt{H})^2 = H.$$

Differentiating the proposed solution, we have

$$h'(t) = 2\left(\underbrace{\sqrt{H} - \frac{kt}{2}}_{\sqrt{h(t)}} \right)\left(-\frac{k}{2} \right) = -k\sqrt{h}.$$

Therefore, h satisfies the initial condition and the differential equation.

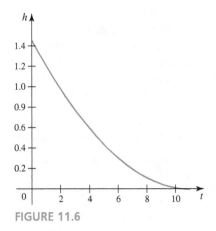

FIGURE 11.6

QUICK CHECK 4 In Example 6, if the height function were given by $h(t) = (4.2 - 0.14t)^2$, at what time would the tank be empty? ◄

c. With the given values of the parameters,

$$k = \frac{a}{A}\sqrt{2g} = \frac{0.05 \text{ m}^2}{1 \text{ m}^2}\sqrt{2 \cdot 9.8 \text{ m/s}^2} \approx 0.22 \text{ m}^{1/2}/s,$$

and the solution becomes

$$h(t) = \left(\sqrt{H} - \frac{kt}{2}\right)^2 \approx (\sqrt{1.44} - 0.11t)^2 = (1.2 - 0.11t)^2.$$

The graph of the solution (Figure 11.6) shows the height of the water decreasing from $h(0) = 1.44$ to zero at approximately $t \approx 11$ s.

d. Solving the equation

$$h(t) = (1.2 - 0.11t)^2 = 0,$$

we find that the tank is empty at $t \approx 10.9$ s.

Related Exercises 33–34 ◄

Final Note   Throughout this section, we found solutions to initial value problems without worrying about whether there might be other solutions. Once we find a solution to an initial value problem, how can we be sure there aren't other solutions? More generally, given a particular initial value problem, how do we know whether a solution exists and whether it is unique?

These theoretical questions have answers, and they are provided by powerful *existence and uniqueness theorems*. These theorems and their proofs are quite technical and are handled in advanced courses. Here is an informal statement of an existence and uniqueness theorem for a particular class of initial value problems encountered in this chapter:

The solution of the general first-order initial value problem

$$y'(t) = f(t, y), y(a) = A$$

exists and is unique in some region that contains the point (a, A) provided f is a "well-behaved" function in that region.

The technical challenges arise in defining *well-behaved* in the most general way possible. The initial value problems we consider in this chapter satisfy the conditions of this theorem, and can be assumed to have unique solutions.

SECTION 11.1 EXERCISES

Review Questions

1. What is the order of $y''(t) + 9y(t) = 10$?

2. Is $y''(t) + 9y(t) = 10$ linear or nonlinear?

3. How many arbitrary constants appear in the general solution of $y''(t) + 9y(t) = 10$?

4. If the general solution of a differential equation is $y(t) = Ce^{-3t} + 10$, what is the solution that satisfies the initial condition $y(0) = 5$?

5. Does the function $y(t) = 2t$ satisfy the differential equation $y'''(t) + y'(t) = 2$?

6. Does the function $y(t) = 6e^{-3t}$ satisfy the initial value problem $y'(t) - 3y(t) = 0, y(0) = 6$?

Basic Skills

7–10. Verifying general solutions *Verify that the given function y is a solution of the differential equation that follows it. Assume that C is an arbitrary constant.*

7. $y(t) = Ce^{-5t}$; $y'(t) + 5y(t) = 0$

8. $y(t) = Ct^{-3}$; $ty'(t) + 3y(t) = 0$

9. $y(t) = C_1 \sin 4t + C_2 \cos 4t$; $y''(t) + 16y(t) = 0$

10. $y(x) = C_1e^{-x} + C_2e^x$; $y''(x) - y(x) = 0$

11–14. Verifying solutions of initial value problems *Verify that the given function y is a solution of the initial value problem that follows it.*

11. $y(t) = 16e^{2t} - 10$; $y'(t) - 2y(t) = 20, y(0) = 6$

12. $y(t) = 8t^6 - 3$; $ty'(t) - 6y(t) = 18, y(1) = 5$

13. $y(t) = -3 \cos 3t$; $y''(t) + 9y(t) = 0, y(0) = -3, y'(0) = 0$

14. $y(x) = \frac{1}{4}(e^{2x} - e^{-2x})$; $y''(x) - 4y(x) = 0, y(0) = 0, y'(0) = 1$

15–22. Finding general solutions *Find the general solution of each differential equation. Use $C, C_1, C_2, \ldots$ to denote arbitrary constants.*

15. $y'(t) = 3 + e^{-2t}$

16. $y'(t) = 12t^5 - 20t^4 + 2 - 6t^{-2}$

17. $y'(x) = 4 \tan 2x - 3 \cos x$

18. $p'(x) = \dfrac{16}{x^9} - 5 + 14x^6$

19. $y''(t) = 60t^4 - 4 + 12t^{-3}$

20. $y''(t) = 15e^{3t} + \sin 4t$

21. $u''(x) = 55x^9 + 36x^7 - 21x^5 + 10x^{-3}$

22. $v''(x) = xe^x$

23–28. Solving initial value problems *Solve the following initial value problems.*

23. $y'(t) = 1 + e^t, y(0) = 4$

24. $y'(t) = \sin t + \cos 2t, y(0) = 4$

25. $y'(x) = 3x^2 - 3x^{-4}, y(1) = 0$

26. $y'(x) = 4 \sec^2 2x, y(0) = 8$

27. $y''(t) = 12t - 20t^3, y(0) = 1, y'(0) = 0$

28. $u''(x) = 4e^{2x} - 8e^{-2x}, u(0) = 1, u'(0) = 3$

29–30. Motion in a gravitational field *An object is fired vertically upward with an initial velocity $v(0) = v_0$ from an initial position $s(0) = s_0$.*

a. *For the following values of v_0 and s_0, find the position and velocity functions for all times at which the object is above the ground.*

b. *Find the time at which the highest point of the trajectory is reached and the height of the object at that time.*

29. $v_0 = 29.4 \text{ m/s}, s_0 = 30 \text{ m}$

30. $v_0 = 49 \text{ m/s}, s_0 = 60 \text{ m}$

31–32. Harvesting problems *Consider the harvesting problem in Example 5.*

31. If $r = 0.05$ and $p_0 = 1500$, for what values of H is the amount of the resource increasing? For what value of H is the amount of the resource constant? If $H = 100$, when does the resource vanish?

32. If $r = 0.05$ and $H = 500$, for what values of p_0 is the amount of the resource decreasing? For what value of p_0 is the amount of the resource constant? If $p_0 = 9000$, when does the resource vanish?

33–34. Draining tanks *Consider the tank problem in Example 6. For the following parameter values, find the water height function. Then determine the approximate time at which the tank is first empty and graph the solution.*

33. $H = 1.96 \text{ m}, A = 1.5 \text{ m}^2, a = 0.3 \text{ m}^2$

34. $H = 2.25 \text{ m}, A = 2 \text{ m}^2, a = 0.5 \text{ m}^2$

Further Explorations

35. Explain why or why not Determine whether the following statements are true and give an explanation or counterexample.

a. The general solution of the differential equation $y'(t) = 1$ is $y(t) = t$.

b. The differential equation $y''(t) - y(t)y'(t) = 0$ is second order and linear.

c. To find the solution of an initial value problem, you usually begin by finding a general solution of the differential equation.

36–39. General solutions *Find the general solution of the following differential equations.*

36. $y'(t) = t \ln t + 1$

37. $u'(x) = \dfrac{2(x - 1)}{x^2 + 4}$

38. $v'(t) = \dfrac{4}{t^2 - 4}$

39. $y''(x) = \dfrac{x}{(1 - x^2)^{3/2}}$

40–43. Solving initial value problems *Find the solution of the following initial value problems.*

40. $y'(t) = te^t, y(0) = -1$

41. $u'(x) = \dfrac{1}{x^2 + 16} - 4, u(0) = 2$

42. $p'(x) = \dfrac{2}{x^2 + x}, p(1) = 0$

43. $y''(t) = te^t, y(0) = 0, y'(0) = 1$

44–49. Verifying general solutions *Verify that the given function is a solution of the differential equation that follows it.*

44. $u(t) = Ce^{1/(4t^4)}$; $u'(t) + \dfrac{1}{t^5} u(t) = 0$

45. $u(t) = C_1 e^t + C_2 te^t$; $u''(t) - 2u'(t) + u(t) = 0$

46. $g(x) = C_1 e^{-2x} + C_2 xe^{-2x} + 2$; $g''(x) + 4g'(x) + 4g(x) = 8$

47. $u(t) = C_1 t^2 + C_2 t^3$; $t^2 u''(t) - 4tu'(t) + 6u(t) = 0$

48. $u(t) = C_1 t^5 + C_2 t^{-4} - t^3$; $t^2 u''(t) - 20u(t) = 14t^3$

49. $z(t) = C_1 e^{-t} + C_2 e^{2t} + C_3 e^{-3t} - e^t$; $z'''(t) + 2z''(t) - 5z'(t) - 6z(t) = 8e^t$

50. A second-order equation Consider the differential equation $y''(t) - k^2 y(t) = 0$, where $k > 0$ is a real number.

a. Verify by substitution that when $k = 1$, a solution of the equation is $y(t) = C_1 e^t + C_2 e^{-t}$. You may assume that this function is the general solution.

b. Verify by substitution that when $k = 2$, the general solution of the equation is $y(t) = C_1 e^{2t} + C_2 e^{-2t}$.

c. Give the general solution of the equation for arbitrary $k > 0$ and verify your conjecture.

d. For a positive real number k, verify that the general solution of the equation may also be expressed in the form $y(t) = C_1 \cosh kt + C_2 \sinh kt$, where cosh and sinh are the hyperbolic cosine and hyperbolic sine, respectively.

51. Another second-order equation Consider the differential equation $y''(t) + k^2 y(t) = 0$, where k is a positive real number.

   a. Verify by substitution that when $k = 1$, a solution of the equation is $y(t) = C_1 \sin t + C_2 \cos t$. You may assume that this function is the general solution.

   b. Verify by substitution that when $k = 2$, the general solution of the equation is $y(t) = C_1 \sin 2t + C_2 \cos 2t$.

   c. Give the general solution of the equation for arbitrary $k > 0$ and verify your conjecture.

Applications

In this section, several models are presented and the solution of the associated differential equation is given. Later in the chapter, we present methods for solving these differential equations.

52. Drug infusion The delivery of a drug (such as an antibiotic) through an intravenous line may be modeled by the differential equation $m'(t) + km(t) = I$, where $m(t)$ is the mass of the drug in the blood at time $t \geq 0$, k is a constant that describes the rate at which the drug is absorbed, and I is the infusion rate.

   a. Show by substitution that if the initial mass of drug in the blood is zero $(m(0) = 0)$, then the solution of the initial value problem is $m(t) = \dfrac{I}{k}(1 - e^{-kt})$.

   b. Graph the solution for $I = 10$ mg/hr and $k = 0.05$ hr^{-1}.

   c. Evaluate $\lim_{t \to \infty} m(t)$, the steady-state drug level, and verify the result using the graph in part (b).

53. Logistic population growth Widely used models for population growth involve the *logistic equation* $P'(t) = rP\left(1 - \dfrac{P}{K}\right)$, where $P(t)$ is the population, for $t \geq 0$, and $r > 0$ and $K > 0$ are given constants.

   a. Verify by substitution that the general solution of the equation is $P(t) = \dfrac{K}{1 + Ce^{-rt}}$, where C is an arbitrary constant.

   b. Find that value of C that corresponds to the initial condition $P(0) = 50$.

   c. Graph the solution for $P(0) = 50$, $r = 0.1$, and $K = 300$.

   d. Find $\lim_{t \to \infty} P(t)$ and check that the result is consistent with the graph in part (c).

54. Free fall One possible model that describes the free fall of an object in a gravitational field subject to air resistance uses the equation $v'(t) = g - bv$, where $v(t)$ is the velocity of the object for $t \geq 0$,

$g = 9.8$ m/s^2 is the acceleration due to gravity, and $b > 0$ is a constant that involves the mass of the object and the air resistance.

   a. Verify by substitution that a solution of the equation, subject to the initial condition $v(0) = 0$, is $v(t) = \dfrac{g}{b}(1 - e^{-bt})$.

   b. Graph the solution with $b = 0.1$ s^{-1}.

   c. Using the graph in part (c), estimate the terminal velocity $\lim_{t \to \infty} v(t)$.

55. Chemical rate equations The reaction of certain chemical compounds can be modeled using a differential equation of the form $y'(t) = -ky^n(t)$, where $y(t)$ is the concentration of the compound for $t \geq 0$, $k > 0$ is a constant that determines the speed of the reaction, and n is a positive integer called the *order* of the reaction. Assume that the initial concentration of the compound is $y(0) = y_0 > 0$.

   a. Consider a first-order reaction $(n = 1)$ and show that the solution of the initial value problem is $y(t) = y_0 e^{-kt}$.

   b. Consider a second-order reaction $(n = 2)$ and show that the solution of the initial value problem is $y(t) = \dfrac{y_0}{y_0 kt + 1}$.

   c. Let $y_0 = 1$ and $k = 0.1$. Graph the first-order and second-order solutions found in parts (a) and (b). Compare the two reactions.

56. Tumor growth The growth of cancer tumors may be modeled by the Gompertz growth equation. Let $M(t)$ be the mass of a tumor, for $t \geq 0$. The relevant initial value problem is

$$\frac{dM}{dt} = -rM(t) \ln\left(\frac{M(t)}{K}\right), \quad M(0) = M_0,$$

where r and K are positive constants and $0 < M_0 < K$.

   a. Show by substitution that the solution of the initial value problem is

$$M(t) = K\left(\frac{M_0}{K}\right)^{\exp(-rt)}.$$

   b. Graph the solution for $M_0 = 100$ and $r = 0.05$.

   c. Using the graph in part (b), estimate $\lim_{t \to \infty} M(t)$, the limiting size of the tumor.

QUICK CHECK ANSWERS

1. The first equation is first order and linear. The second equation is second order and linear.   **2.** $y(t) = -20e^{-t/2} + 36$ **3.** $s_{\max} = 104.9$ m   **4.** The tank is empty at $t = 30$ s. ◄

11.2 Direction Fields and Euler's Method

The goal of this chapter is to present methods for finding solutions of various kinds of differential equations. However, before taking up that task, we spend a few pages investigating a remarkable fact: It is possible to visualize and draw approximate graphs of the solutions of a differential equation without ever solving the equation. You might wonder how one can graph a function without knowing a formula for it. It turns out that the differential equation itself contains enough information to draw accurate graphs of its solutions. The tool that makes this visualization possible and allows us to explore the geometry of a differential equation is called the *direction field* (or *slope field*).

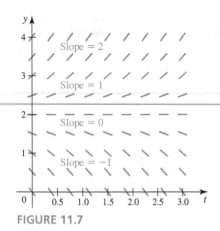

FIGURE 11.7

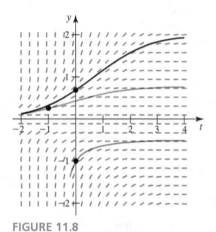

FIGURE 11.8

> If the function f in the differential equation is even slightly complicated, drawing the direction field by hand is tedious. It's best to use a calculator or software. Examples 1 and 2 show some basic steps in plotting fairly simple direction fields by hand.

Direction Fields

We work with first-order differential equations of the form

$$\frac{dy}{dt} = f(t, y),$$

where the notation $f(t, y)$ means an expression involving the independent variable t and/or the unknown solution y. If a solution of this equation is displayed in the ty-plane, then the differential equation simply says that at each point (t, y) of the solution curve, the slope of the curve is $y'(t) = f(t, y)$ (Figure 11.7). A **direction field** is a picture that shows the slope of the solution at selected points of the ty-plane.

For example, consider the equation $y'(t) = f(t, y) = y^2 e^{-t}$. We choose a regular grid of points in the ty-plane and at each point $P(t, y)$ we make a small line segment with slope $y^2 e^{-t}$. The line segment at a point P gives the slope of the solution curve that passes through P (Figure 11.8). We see that along the t-axis $(y = 0)$, the slopes of the line segments are $f(t, 0) = 0$, which means the line segments are horizontal. Along the y-axis $(t = 0)$, the slopes of the line segments are $f(0, y) = y^2$, which means the slopes of the line segments increase as we move up or down the y-axis.

Now suppose an initial condition $y(0) = \frac{2}{3}$ is given. We start at the point $(0, \frac{2}{3})$ in the ty-plane and sketch a curve that follows the flow of the direction field (black curve in Figure 11.8). At each point of the solution curve, the slope matches the direction field. Different initial conditions ($y(-1) = \frac{1}{3}$ and $y(0) = -1$ in Figure 11.8) give different solution curves. The collection of solution curves for several different initial conditions is a representation of the general solution of the equation.

EXAMPLE 1   Direction field for a linear differential equation Figure 11.9 shows the direction field for the equation $y'(t) = y - 2$, for $t \geq 0$ and $y \geq 0$. For what initial conditions at $t = 0$ are the solutions constant? Increasing? Decreasing?

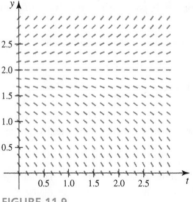

FIGURE 11.9

SOLUTION The direction field has horizontal line segments (slope zero) for $y = 2$. Therefore, $y'(t) = 0$ when $y = 2$, for all $t \geq 0$. These horizontal line segments correspond to a solution that is constant in time; that is, if the initial condition is $y(0) = 2$, then the solution is $y(t) = 2$, for all $t \geq 0$.

We also see that the direction field has line segments with positive slopes above the line $y = 2$ (with increasing slopes as you move away from $y = 2$). Therefore, $y'(t) > 0$ when $y > 2$, and solutions are increasing in this region.

Similarly, the direction field has line segments with negative slopes below the line $y = 2$ (with increasingly negative slopes as you move away from $y = 2$). Therefore, $y'(t) < 0$ when $y < 2$, and solutions are decreasing in this region.

Combining these observations, we see that if the initial condition satisfies $y(0) > 2$, the resulting solution is increasing, for $t \geq 0$. If the initial condition satisfies $y(0) < 2$, the resulting solution is decreasing, for $t \geq 0$. Figure 11.10 shows the solution curves with initial conditions $y(0) = 2.25$, $y(0) = 2$, and $y(0) = 1.75$.

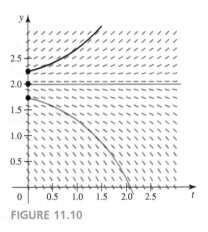

FIGURE 11.10

Related Exercises 5–16◄

QUICK CHECK 1 Assuming that solutions are unique (at most one solution curve passes through each point), explain why a solution curve cannot cross the line $y = 2$ in Example 1. ◄

> ▷ A differential equation in which the function f is independent of t is said to be **autonomous**.

For a differential equation of the form $y'(t) = f(y)$ (that is, the function f depends only on y), the following steps are useful in sketching the direction field. Notice that because the direction field depends only on y, it has the same slope on any given horizontal line. A detailed direction field is usually not required. You need to draw only a few line segments to indicate which direction the solution is changing.

PROCEDURE   Sketching a Direction Field by Hand for $y'(t) = f(y)$

1. Find the values of y for which $f(y) = 0$. For example, suppose that $f(a) = 0$. Then we have $y'(t) = 0$ whenever $y = a$, and the direction field at all points (t, a) consists of horizontal line segments. If the initial condition is $y(0) = a$, then the solution is $y(t) = a$, for all $t \geq 0$. Such a constant solution is called an **equilibrium solution**.

2. Find the values of y for which $f(y) > 0$. For example, suppose that $f(b) > 0$. Then $y'(t) > 0$ whenever $y = b$. It follows that the direction field at all points (t, b) has line segments with positive slopes, and the solution is increasing at those points.

3. Find the values of y for which $f(y) < 0$. For example, suppose that $f(c) < 0$. Then $y'(t) < 0$ whenever $y = c$. It follows that the direction field at all points (t, c) has line segments with negative slopes and the solution is decreasing at those points.

EXAMPLE 2   Direction field for a simple nonlinear equation Consider the differential equation $y'(t) = y(y - 2)$, for $t \geq 0$.

a. For what initial conditions $y(0) = a$ is the resulting solution constant? Increasing? Decreasing?

b. Sketch the direction field for the equation.

SOLUTION

a. We follow the steps given earlier.

1. Letting $f(y) = y(y - 2)$, we see that $f(y) = 0$ when $y = 0$ or $y = 2$. Therefore, the direction field has horizontal line segments when $y = 0$ and $y = 2$. As a result, the constant functions $y(t) = 0$ and $y(t) = 2$, for $t \geq 0$, are equilibrium solutions (Figure 11.11).

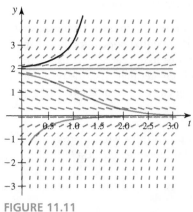

FIGURE 11.11

2. The solutions of the inequality $f(y) = y(y - 2) > 0$ are $y < 0$ or $y > 2$. Therefore, below the line $y = 0$ or above the line $y = 2$, the direction field has positive slopes and the solutions are increasing in these regions.

3. The solution of the inequality $f(y) = y(y - 2) < 0$ is $0 < y < 2$. Therefore, between the lines $y = 0$ and $y = 2$, the direction field has negative slopes and the solutions are decreasing in this region.

b. The direction field is shown in Figure 11.11 with several representative solutions.

Related Exercises 17–20◄

QUICK CHECK 2 In Example 2, is the solution to the equation increasing or decreasing if the initial condition is $y(0) = 2.01$? Is it increasing or decreasing if the initial condition is $y(1) = -1$? ◄

EXAMPLE 3   Direction field for the logistic equation   The logistic equation is commonly used to model populations with a stable equilibrium solution (called the *carrying capacity*). Consider the logistic equation

$$\frac{dP}{dt} = 0.1P\left(1 - \frac{P}{300}\right), \text{ for } t \geq 0.$$

a. Sketch the direction field of the equation.

b. Sketch solution curves corresponding to the initial conditions $P(0) = 50$, $P(0) = 150$, and $P(0) = 350$.

c. Find and interpret $\lim_{t \to \infty} P(t)$.

SOLUTION

a. We follow the steps in the summary box for sketching the direction field. Because P represents a population, we assume that $P \geq 0$.

> The constant solutions $P = 0$ and $P = 300$ are equilibrium solutions. The solution $P = 0$ is an *unstable* equilibrium because nearby solution curves move away from $P = 0$. By contrast, the solution $P = 300$ is a *stable equilibrium* because nearby solution curves are attracted to $P = 300$.

1. Notice that $P'(t) = 0$ when $P = 0$ or $P = 300$. Therefore, if the initial population is either $P = 0$ or $P = 300$, then $P'(t) = 0$, for all $t \geq 0$, and the solution is constant. For this reason we expect the direction field to show horizontal lines (with zero slope) at $P = 0$ and $P = 300$.

2. The equation implies that $P'(t) > 0$ provided $0 < P < 300$. Therefore, the direction field has positive slopes and the solutions are increasing, for $t \geq 0$ and $0 < P < 300$.

3. The equation also implies that $P'(t) < 0$ provided $P > 300$ (it was assumed that $P \geq 0$). Therefore, the direction field has negative slopes and the solutions are decreasing, for $t \geq 0$ and $P > 300$.

b. Figure 11.12 shows the direction field with three solution curves corresponding to the three different initial conditions.

c. The horizontal line $P = 300$ corresponds to the carrying capacity of the population. We see that if the initial population is less than 300, the resulting solution increases to the carrying capacity from below. If the initial population is greater than 300, the resulting solution decreases to the carrying capacity from above.

Related Exercises 21–24◄

QUICK CHECK 3 According to Figure 11.12, for what approximate value of P is the growth rate of the solution the greatest? ◄

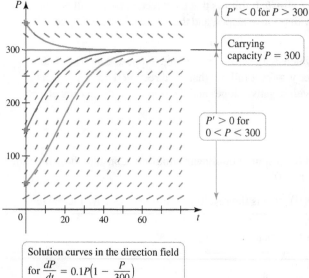

$P' < 0$ for $P > 300$

Carrying capacity $P = 300$

$P' > 0$ for $0 < P < 300$

Solution curves in the direction field for $\dfrac{dP}{dt} = 0.1P\left(1 - \dfrac{P}{300}\right)$

FIGURE 11.12

Euler's Method

Direction fields are useful for at least two reasons. As shown in previous examples, a direction field provides valuable qualitative information about the solutions of a differential equation *without solving the equation*. In addition, it turns out that direction fields are the basis for many computer-based methods for approximating solutions of a differential equation. The computer begins with the initial condition and advances the solution in small steps, always following the direction field at each time step. The simplest method that uses this idea is called *Euler's method*.

Suppose we wish to approximate the solution to the initial value problem $y'(t) = f(t, y), y(0) = A$ on an interval $[0, T]$. We begin by dividing the interval $[0, T]$ into N **time steps** of equal length $\Delta t = \dfrac{T}{N}$. In so doing, we create a set of grid points (Figure 11.13)

$$t_0 = 0, t_1 = \Delta t, t_2 = 2\Delta t, \ldots, t_k = k\Delta t, \ldots, t_N = N\Delta t = T.$$

The exact solution of the initial value problem at the grid points is $y(t_k)$, for $k = 0, 1, 2, \ldots, N$, which is generally unknown unless we are able to solve the original differential equation. The goal is to compute a set of *approximations* to the exact solution at the grid points, which we denote u_k, for $k = 0, 1, 2, \ldots, N$; that is, $u_k \approx y(t_k)$.

The initial condition says that $u_0 = y(0) = A$ (exactly). We now make one step forward in time of length Δt and compute an approximation u_1 to $y(t_1)$. The key observation is that, according to the direction field, the solution at the point (t_0, u_0) has slope $f(t_0, u_0)$. We obtain u_1 from u_0 by drawing a line segment starting at (t_0, u_0) with horizontal extent Δt and slope $f(t_0, u_0)$. The other endpoint of the line segment is (t_1, u_1) (Figure 11.14). Applying the slope formula to the two points (t_0, u_0) and (t_1, u_1), we have

$$f(t_0, u_0) = \frac{u_1 - u_0}{t_1 - t_0}.$$

Solving for u_1 and noting that $t_1 - t_0 = \Delta t$, we have

$$u_1 = u_0 + f(t_0, u_0)\Delta t.$$

This basic *Euler step* is now repeated over each time step until we reach $t = T$. That is, having computed u_1, we apply the same argument to obtain u_2. From u_2, we compute u_3. In general, u_{k+1} is computed from u_k, for $k = 0, 1, 2, \ldots, N - 1$. Hand calculations with Euler's method quickly become laborious. The method is usually carried out on a calculator or with a computer program. It is also included in many software packages.

> Euler proposed his method for finding approximate solutions to differential equations 200 years before digital computers were invented.

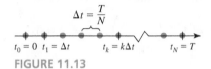

FIGURE 11.13

> See Exercise 45 for setting up Euler's method on a more general interval $[a, b]$.

> The argument used to derive the first step of Euler's method is really an application of linear approximation. We draw a line tangent to the curve at the point (t_0, u_0). The point on that line corresponding to $t = t_1$ is (t_1, u_1), where u_1 is the Euler approximation to $y(t_1)$.

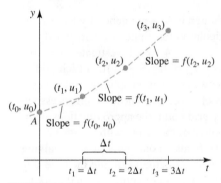

FIGURE 11.14

PROCEDURE   **Euler's Method for $y'(t) = f(t, y), y(0) = A$ on $[0, T]$**

1. Choose either a time step Δt or a positive integer N such that $\Delta t = \dfrac{T}{N}$ and $t_k = k\Delta t$, for $k = 0, 1, 2, \ldots, N - 1$.

2. Let $u_0 = y(0) = A$.

3. For $k = 0, 1, 2, \ldots, N - 1$, compute

$$u_{k+1} = u_k + f(t_k, u_k)\Delta t.$$

Each u_k is an approximation to the exact solution $y(t_k)$.

EXAMPLE 4   Using Euler's method Find an approximate solution to the initial value problem $y'(t) = t - \dfrac{y}{2}, y(0) = 1$, on the interval $[0, 2]$. Use the time steps $\Delta t = 0.2$ ($N = 10$) and $\Delta t = 0.1$ ($N = 20$). Which time step gives a better approximation to the exact solution, which is $y(t) = 5e^{-t/2} + 2t - 4$?

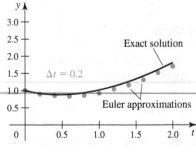

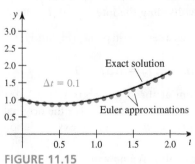

FIGURE 11.15

SOLUTION With a time step of $\Delta t = 0.2$, the grid points on the interval $[0, 2]$ are

$$t_0 = 0.0, t_1 = 0.2, t_2 = 0.4, \ldots, t_{10} = 2.0.$$

We identify $f(t, y) = t - \dfrac{y}{2}$, and let u_k be the Euler approximation to $y(t_k)$. Euler's method takes the form

$$u_0 = y(0) = 1, \quad u_{k+1} = u_k + f(t_k, u_k)\Delta t = u_k + \left(t_k - \frac{u_k}{2} \right)\Delta t,$$

where $k = 0, 1, 2, \ldots, 9$. For example, the value of the approximation u_1 is given by

$$u_1 = u_0 + f(t_0, u_0)\Delta t = u_0 + \left(t_0 - \frac{u_0}{2} \right)\Delta t = 1 + \left(0 - \frac{1}{2} \right) \cdot 0.2 = 0.900,$$

and the value of u_2 is given by

$$u_2 = u_1 + f(t_1, u_1)\Delta t = u_1 + \left(t_1 - \frac{u_1}{2} \right)\Delta t = 0.9 + \left(0.2 - \frac{0.9}{2} \right) \cdot 0.2 = 0.850.$$

A similar procedure is used with $\Delta t = 0.1$. In this case, $N = 20$ time steps are needed to cover the interval $[0, 2]$. The results of the two calculations are shown in Figure 11.15, where the exact solution appears as a solid curve and the Euler approximations are shown as points. From these graphs, it appears that the time step $\Delta t = 0.1$ gives better approximations to the solution.

A more detailed account of these calculations is given in Table 11.1, which shows the numerical values of the Euler approximations for $\Delta t = 0.2$ and $\Delta t = 0.1$. Notice that the approximations with $\Delta t = 0.1$ are tabulated at *every other* time step so that they may be compared to the $\Delta t = 0.2$ approximations.

How accurate are these approximations? Although it does not generally happen in practice, we can compute the solution of this particular initial value problem exactly. (You can check that the solution is $y(t) = 5e^{-t/2} + 2t - 4$.) We investigate the accuracy of the Euler approximations by computing the *error*, $e_k = |u_k - y(t_k)|$, at each grid point. The error simply measures the difference between the exact solution and the corresponding approximations. The last two columns of Table 11.1 show the errors associated with the approximations. We see that at every grid point, the approximations with $\Delta t = 0.1$ have errors with roughly half the magnitude of the errors with $\Delta t = 0.2$.

This pattern is typical of Euler's method. If we focus on one point in time, halving the time step roughly halves the errors. However, nothing is free: Halving the time step also requires twice as many time steps and twice the amount of computational work to cover the same time interval.

▷ Because computers produce small errors at each time step, taking a large number of time steps may eventually lead to an unacceptable accumulation of errors. When more accuracy is needed, it may be best to use other methods that require more work per time step, but also give more accurate results.

Table 11.1

t_k	$u_k(\Delta t = 0.2)$	$u_k(\Delta t = 0.1)$	$e_k(\Delta t = 0.2)$	$e_k(\Delta t = 0.1)$
0.0	1.000	1.000	0.000	0.000
0.2	0.900	0.913	0.0242	0.0117
0.4	0.850	0.873	0.0437	0.0211
0.6	0.845	0.875	0.0591	0.0286
0.8	0.881	0.917	0.0711	0.0345
1.0	0.952	0.994	0.0802	0.0390
1.2	1.057	1.102	0.0869	0.0423
1.4	1.191	1.238	0.0914	0.0446
1.6	1.352	1.401	0.0943	0.0460
1.8	1.537	1.586	0.0957	0.0468
2.0	1.743	1.792	0.0960	0.0470

Related Exercises 25–36 ◀

QUICK CHECK 4 Notice that the errors in Table 11.1 increase in time for both time steps. Give a possible explanation for this increase in the errors. ◄

Final Note   Euler's method is the simplest of a vast collection of *numerical methods* for approximating solutions of differential equations (often studied in courses on *numerical analysis*). As we have seen, Euler's method uses linear approximation; that is, the method follows the direction field using line segments. This idea works well provided the direction field varies smoothly and slowly. In less well behaved cases, Euler's method may encounter difficulties. More robust and accurate methods do a better job of following the direction field (for example, by using parabolas or higher-degree polynomials instead of linear approximation). While these refined methods are generally more accurate than Euler's method, they often require more computational work per time step. As with Euler's method, all methods have the property that their accuracy improves as the time step decreases. The upshot is that there are often trade-offs in choosing a method to approximate the solution of a differential equation. However, Euler's method is a good place to start and may be adequate.

SECTION 11.2 EXERCISES

Review Questions

1. Explain how to sketch the direction field of the equation $y'(t) = f(t, y)$, where f is given.

2. Consider the differential equation $y'(t) = t^2 - 3y^2$ and the solution curve that passes through the point $(3, 1)$. What is the slope of the curve at $(3, 1)$?

3. Consider the initial value problem $y'(t) = t^2 - 3y^2$, $y(3) = 1$. What is the approximation to $y(3.1)$ given by Euler's method with a time step of $\Delta t = 0.1$?

4. Give a geometrical explanation of how Euler's method works.

Basic Skills

5–6. Direction fields *A differential equation and its direction field are shown in the following figures. Sketch a graph of the solution curve that passes through the given initial conditions.*

5. $y'(t) = \dfrac{t^2}{y^2 + 1}$, $y(0) = -2$
   and $y(-2) = 0$.

6. $y'(t) = \dfrac{\sin t}{y}$, $y(-2) = -2$
   and $y(-2) = 2$

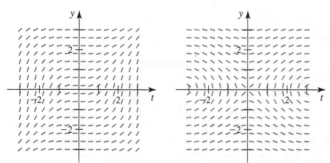

7. **Matching direction fields** Match equations a–d with direction fields A–D.

   a. $y'(t) = \dfrac{t}{2}$

   b. $y'(t) = \dfrac{y}{2}$

   c. $y'(t) = \dfrac{t^2 + y^2}{2}$

   d. $y'(t) = \dfrac{y}{t}$

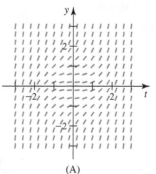

(A)

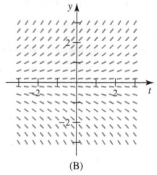

(B)

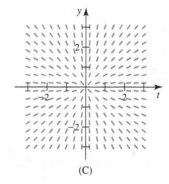

(C)

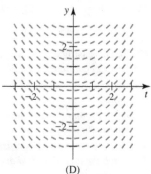

(D)

8. **Identifying direction fields** Which of the differential equations a–d corresponds to the following direction field? Explain your reasoning.

a. $y'(t) = 0.5(y + 1)(t - 1)$
b. $y'(t) = -0.5(y + 1)(t - 1)$
c. $y'(t) = 0.5(y - 1)(t + 1)$
d. $y'(t) = -0.5(y - 1)(t + 1)$

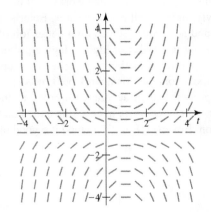

9–11. Direction fields with technology *Plot a direction field for the following differential equation with a graphing utility. Then find the solutions that are constant and determine which initial conditions $y(0) = A$ lead to solutions that are increasing in time.*

9. $y'(t) = 0.05(y + 1)^2(t - 1)^2, |t| \le 3$ and $|y| \le 3$

10. $y'(t) = (y - 1) \sin \pi t, \quad 0 \le t \le \pi, 0 \le y \le 2$

11. $y'(t) = t(y - 1), \quad 0 \le t \le 2, 0 \le y \le 2$

12–16. Sketching direction fields *Use the window $[-2, 2] \times [-2, 2]$ to sketch a direction field for the following equations. Then sketch the solution curve that corresponds to the given initial condition. A detailed direction field is not needed.*

12. $y'(t) = y - 3, y(0) = 1$

13. $y'(t) = 4 - y, y(0) = -1$

14. $y'(t) = y(2 - y), y(0) = 1$

15. $y'(x) = \sin x, y(-2) = 2$

16. $y'(x) = \sin y, y(-2) = \frac{1}{2}$

17–20. Increasing and decreasing solutions *Consider the following differential equations. A detailed direction field is not needed.*

a. Find the solutions that are constant, for all $t \ge 0$ (the equilibrium solutions).
b. In what regions are solutions increasing? Decreasing?
c. Which initial conditions $y(0) = A$ lead to solutions that are increasing in time? Decreasing?
d. Sketch the direction field and verify that it is consistent with parts (a)–(c).

17. $y'(t) = (y - 1)(1 + y)$

18. $y'(t) = (y - 2)(y + 1)$

19. $y'(t) = \cos y$, for $|y| \le \pi$

20. $y'(t) = y(y + 3)(4 - y)$

21–24. Logistic equations *Consider the following logistic equations, for $t \ge 0$. In each case, sketch the direction field, draw the solution curve for each initial condition, and find the equilibrium solutions. A detailed direction field is not needed. Assume $t \ge 0$ and $P \ge 0$.*

21. $P'(t) = 0.05P\left(1 - \dfrac{P}{500}\right); P(0) = 100, P(0) = 400,$
$P(0) = 700$

22. $P'(t) = 0.1P\left(1 - \dfrac{P}{1200}\right); P(0) = 600, P(0) = 800,$
$P(0) = 1600$

23. $P'(t) = 0.02P\left(4 - \dfrac{P}{800}\right); P(0) = 1600, P(0) = 2400,$
$P(0) = 4000$

24. $P'(t) = 0.05P - 0.001P^2; P(0) = 10, P(0) = 40,$
$P(0) = 80$

25–28. Two steps of Euler's method *For the following initial value problems, compute the first two approximations u_1 and u_2 given by Euler's method using the given time step.*

25. $y'(t) = 2y, y(0) = 2; \Delta t = 0.5$

26. $y'(t) = -y, y(0) = -1; \Delta t = 0.2$

27. $y'(t) = 2 - y, y(0) = 1; \Delta t = 0.1$

28. $y'(t) = t + y, y(0) = 4; \Delta t = 0.5$

29–32. Errors in Euler's method *Consider the following initial value problems.*

a. Find the approximations to $y(0.2)$ and $y(0.4)$ using Euler's method with time steps of $\Delta t = 0.2, 0.1, 0.05$, and 0.025.
b. Using the exact solution given, compute the errors in the Euler approximations at $t = 0.2$ and $t = 0.4$.
c. Which time step results in the more accurate approximation? Explain your observations.
d. In general, how does halving the time step affect the error at $t = 0.2$ and $t = 0.4$?

29. $y'(t) = -y, y(0) = 1; y(t) = e^{-t}$

30. $y'(t) = \dfrac{y}{2}, y(0) = 2; y(t) = 2e^{t/2}$

31. $y'(t) = 4 - y, y(0) = 3; y(t) = 4 - e^{-t}$

32. $y'(t) = 2t + 1, y(0) = 0; y(t) = t^2 + t$

33–36. Computing Euler approximations *Use a calculator or computer program to carry out the following steps.*

a. Approximate the value of $y(T)$ using Euler's method with the given time step on the interval $[0, T]$.
b. Using the exact solution (also given), find the error in the approximation to $y(T)$ (only at the right endpoint of the time interval).
c. Repeating parts (a) and (b) using half the time step used in those calculations, again find an approximation to $y(T)$.
d. Compare the errors in the approximations to $y(T)$.

33. $y'(t) = -2y, y(0) = 1; \Delta t = 0.2, T = 2; y(t) = e^{-2t}$

34. $y'(t) = 6 - 2y, y(0) = -1; \Delta t = 0.2, T = 3;$
$y(t) = 3 - 4e^{-2t}$

35. $y'(t) = t - y, y(0) = 4; \; \Delta t = 0.2, T = 4;$
$y(t) = 5e^{-t} + t - 1$

36. $y'(t) = \dfrac{t}{y}, y(0) = 4; \; \Delta t = 0.1, T = 2; \; y(t) = \sqrt{t^2 + 16}$

Further Explorations

37. Explain why or why not Determine whether the following statements are true and give an explanation or counterexample.

    a. A direction field allows you to visualize the solution of a differential equation, but it does not give exact values of the solution at particular points.

    b. Euler's method is used to compute exact values of the solution of an initial value problem.

38–43. Equilibrium solutions *A differential equation of the form $y'(t) = f(y)$ is said to be* **autonomous** *(the function f depends only on y). The constant function $y = y_0$ is an equilibrium solution of the equation provided $f(y_0) = 0$ (because then $y'(t) = 0$ and the solution remains constant for all t). Note that equilibrium solutions correspond to horizontal lines in the direction field. Note also that for autonomous equations, the direction field is independent of t. Carry out the following analysis on the given equations.*

    a. *Find the equilibrium solutions.*

    b. *Sketch the direction field, for $t \geq 0$.*

    c. *Sketch the solution curve that corresponds to the initial condition $y(0) = 1$.*

38. $y'(t) = 2y + 4$

39. $y'(t) = 6 - 2y$

40. $y'(t) = y(2 - y)$

41. $y'(t) = y(y - 3)$

42. $y'(t) = \sin y$

43. $y'(t) = y(y - 3)(y + 2)$

44. Direction field analysis Consider the first-order initial value problem $y'(t) = ay + b, y(0) = A$, for $t \geq 0$, where a, b, and A are real numbers.

    a. Explain why $y = -b/a$ is an equilibrium solution and corresponds to a horizontal line in the direction field.

    b. Draw a representative direction field in the case that $a > 0$. Show that if $A > -b/a$, then the solution increases for $t \geq 0$ and if $A < -b/a$, then the solution decreases for $t \geq 0$.

    c. Draw a representative direction field in the case that $a < 0$. Show that if $A > -b/a$, then the solution decreases for $t \geq 0$ and if $A < -b/a$, then the solution increases for $t \geq 0$.

45. Euler's method on more general grids Suppose the solution of the initial value problem $y'(t) = f(t, y), y(a) = A$ is to be approximated on the interval $[a, b]$.

    a. If $N + 1$ grid points are used (including the endpoints), what is the time step Δt?

    b. Write the first step of Euler's method to compute u_1.

    c. Write the general step of Euler's method that applies, for $k = 0, 1, \ldots, N - 1$.

Applications

46–48. Analyzing models *The following models were discussed in Section 11.1 and reappear in later sections of this chapter. In each case, carry out the indicated analysis using direction fields.*

46. Drug infusion The delivery of a drug (such as an antibiotic) through an intravenous line may be modeled by the differential equation $m'(t) + km(t) = I$, where $m(t)$ is the mass of the drug in the blood at time $t \geq 0$, k is a constant that describes the rate at which the drug is absorbed, and I is the infusion rate. Let $I = 10 \text{ mg/hr}$ and $k = 0.05 \text{ hr}^{-1}$.

    a. Draw the direction field, for $0 \leq t \leq 100, 0 \leq y \leq 600$.

    b. What is the equilibrium solution?

    c. For what initial values $m(0) = A$ are solutions increasing? Decreasing?

47. Free fall A model that describes the free fall of an object in a gravitational field subject to air resistance uses the equation $v'(t) = g - bv$, where $v(t)$ is the velocity of the object, for $t \geq 0$, $g = 9.8 \text{ m/s}^2$ is the acceleration due to gravity, and $b > 0$ is a constant that involves the mass of the object and the air resistance. Let $b = 0.1 \text{ s}^{-1}$.

    a. Draw the direction field for $0 \leq t \leq 60, 0 \leq y \leq 150$.

    b. For what initial values $v(0) = A$ are solutions increasing? Decreasing?

    c. What is the equilibrium solution?

48. Chemical rate equations Consider the chemical rate equations $y'(t) = -ky(t)$ and $y'(t) = -ky^2(t)$, where $y(t)$ is the concentration of the compound for $t \geq 0$ and $k > 0$ is a constant that determines the speed of the reaction. Assume that the initial concentration of the compound is $y(0) = y_0 > 0$.

    a. Let $k = 0.3$ and make a sketch of the direction fields for both equations. What is the equilibrium solution in both cases?

    b. According to the direction fields, which reaction approaches its equilibrium solution faster?

Additional Exercises

49. Convergence of Euler's method Suppose Euler's method is applied to the initial value problem $y'(t) = ay, y(0) = 1$, which has the exact solution $y(t) = e^{at}$. For this exercise, let h denote the time step (rather than Δt). The grid points are then given by $t_k = kh$. We let u_k be the Euler approximation to the exact solution $y(t_k)$, for $k = 0, 1, 2, \ldots$.

    a. Show that Euler's method applied to this problem can be written $u_0 = 1, u_{k+1} = (1 + ah)u_k$, for $k = 0, 1, 2, \ldots$.

    b. Show by substitution that $u_k = (1 + ah)^k$ is a solution of the equations in part (a), for $k = 0, 1, 2, \ldots$.

    c. Recall that $\lim\limits_{h \to 0} (1 + ah)^{1/h} = e^a$. Use this fact to show that as the time step goes to zero ($h \to 0$, with $t_k = kh$ fixed), the approximations given by Euler's method approach the exact solution of the initial value problem; that is,
$$\lim_{h \to 0} u_k = \lim_{h \to 0} (1 + ah)^k = y(t_k) = e^{at_k}.$$

50. Stability of Euler's method Consider the initial value problem $y'(t) = -ay, y(0) = 1$, where $a > 0$; it has the exact solution $y(t) = e^{-at}$, which is a decreasing function.

    a. Show that Euler's method applied to this problem with time step h can be written $u_0 = 1, u_{k+1} = (1 - ah)u_k$, for $k = 0, 1, 2, \ldots$.

b. Show by substitution that $u_k = (1 - ah)^k$ is a solution of the equations in part (a), for $k = 0, 1, 2, \ldots$.

c. Explain why as k increases the Euler approximations $u_k = (1 - ah)^k$ decrease in magnitude only if $|1 - ah| < 1$.

d. Show that the inequality in part (c) implies that the time step must satisfy the condition $0 < h < \dfrac{2}{a}$. If the time step does not satisfy this condition, then Euler's method is *unstable* and produces approximations that actually increase in time.

QUICK CHECK ANSWERS

1. To cross the line $y = 2$, the solution must have a slope different than zero when $y = 2$. However, according to the direction field, a solution on the line $y = 2$ must have zero slope.   **2.** The solutions originating at both initial conditions are increasing.   **3.** The direction field is steepest when $P = 150$.   **4.** Each step of Euler's method introduces an error. With each successive step of the calculation, the errors could accumulate (or propagate). ◄

Answers

CHAPTER 11

Section 11.1 Exercises, pp. 71–73

1. 2   **3.** 2   **5.** Yes   **15.** $y = 3t - \dfrac{e^{-2t}}{2} + C$

17. $y = 2 \ln \left| \sec 2x \right| - 3 \sin x + C$

19. $y = 2t^6 + 6t^{-1} - 2t^2 + C_1 t + C_2$

21. $u = \dfrac{x^{11}}{2} + \dfrac{x^9}{2} - \dfrac{x^7}{2} + \dfrac{5}{x} + C_1 x + C_2$

23. $y = e^t + t + 3$ **25.** $y = x^3 + x^{-3} - 2$ **27.** $y = -t^5 + 2t^3 + 1$

29. a. $s = -4.9t^2 + 29.4t + 30, v = -9.8t + 29.4$ **b.** Highest point of 74.1 m is reached at $t = 3$ s   **31.** The amount of resource is increasing for $H < 75$, and the amount of the resource is constant if $H = 75$. Approximately 28 time units.

33. $h = (1.4 - 0.2t\sqrt{2g})^2 \approx (1.4 - 0.44t)^2$; tank is empty after approximately 3.16 s.

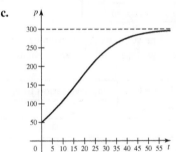

35. a. False   **b.** False   **c.** True

37. $u = \ln (x^2 + 4) - \tan^{-1}\dfrac{x}{2} + C$ **39.** $y = \sin^{-1} x + C_1 x + C_2$

41. $u = \dfrac{1}{4} \tan^{-1}\dfrac{x}{4} - 4x + 2$ **43.** $y = e^t(t - 2) + 2(t + 1)$

51. c. $y = C_1 \sin kt + C_2 \cos kt$ **53. b.** $C = \dfrac{K - 50}{50}$

c.   **d.** 300

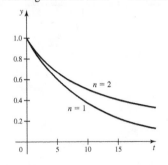

55. c. The decay rate is greater for the $n = 1$ model.

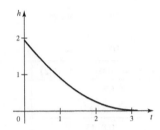

Section 11.2 Exercises, pp. 79–82

1. At selected points (t_0, y_0) in the region of interest draw a short line segment with slope $f(t_0, y_0)$.   **3.** $y(3.1) \approx 1.6$

5.

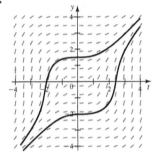

7. a. D   **b.** B   **c.** A   **d.** C   **9.** An initial condition of $y(0) = -1$ leads to a constant solution. For any other initial condition, the solutions are increasing over time.

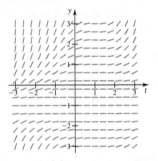

11. An initial condition of $y(0) = 1$ leads to a constant solution. Initial conditions $y(0) = A$ lead to solutions that are increasing over time if $A > 1$.

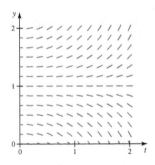

13.

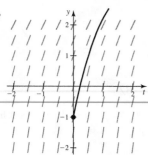

15.

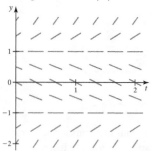

17. a. $y = 1, y = -1$ **b.** Solutions are increasing for $|y| > 1$; decreasing for $|y| < 1$. **c.** Initial conditions $y(0) = A$ lead to increasing solutions if $|A| > 1$ and decreasing solutions if $|A| < 1$.

d.

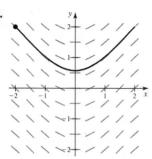

19. a. $y = \pi/2, y = -\pi/2$ **b.** Solutions are increasing for $|y| < \pi/2$, decreasing for $|y| > \pi/2$. **c.** Initial conditions $y(0) = A$ lead to increasing solutions if $|A| < \pi/2$ and decreasing solutions if $\pi/2 < |A| < \pi$. **d.**

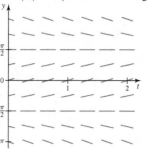

21. The equilibrium solutions are $P = 0$ and $P = 500$.

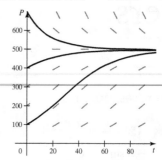

23. The equilibrium solutions are $P = 0$ and $P = 3200$.

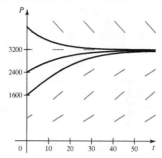

25. $y(0.5) \approx u_1 = 4; y(1) \approx u_2 = 8$

27. $y(0.1) \approx u_1 = 1.1; y(0.2) \approx u_2 = 1.19$

29. a.

Δt	approximation to $y(0.2)$	approximation to $y(0.4)$
0.20000	0.80000	0.64000
0.10000	0.81000	0.65610
0.05000	0.81451	0.66342
0.02500	0.81665	0.66692

b.

Δt	errors for $y(0.2)$	errors for $y(0.4)$
0.20000	0.01873	0.03032
0.10000	0.00873	0.01422
0.05000	0.00422	0.00690
0.02500	0.00208	0.00340

c. Time step $\Delta t = 0.025$; smaller time steps generally produce more accurate results. **d.** Halving the time steps results in approximately halving the error.

31. a.

Δt	approximation to $y(0.2)$	approximation to $y(0.4)$
0.20000	3.20000	3.36000
0.10000	3.19000	3.34390
0.05000	3.18549	3.33658
0.02500	3.18335	3.33308

b.

Δt	errors for $y(0.2)$	errors for $y(0.4)$
0.20000	0.01873	0.03032
0.10000	0.00873	0.01422
0.05000	0.00422	0.00690
0.02500	0.00208	0.00340

c. Time step $\Delta t = 0.025$; smaller time steps generally produce more accurate results.   **d.** Halving the time steps results in approximately halving the error.   **33. a.** $y(2) \approx 0.00604662$ **b.** 0.012269
c. $y(2) \approx 0.0115292$ **d.** Error in part (c) is approximately half of the error in part (b).   **35. a.** $y(4) \approx 3.05765$ **b.** 0.0339321
c. $y(4) \approx 3.0739$ **d.** Error in part (c) is approximately half of the error in part (b).   **37. a.** True   **b.** False   **39. a.** $y = 3$
b, c.

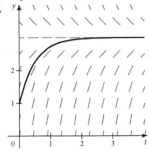

41. a. $y = 0$ and $y = 3$ **b, c.**

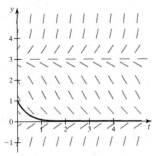

43. a. $y = -2, y = 0$, and $y = 3$
b, c.

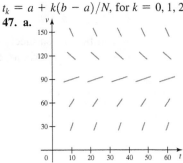

45. a. $\Delta t = \dfrac{b - a}{N}$ **b.** $u_1 = A + f(a, A)\dfrac{b - a}{N}$
c. $u_{k+1} = u_k + f(t_k, u_k)\dfrac{b - a}{N}$, where $u_0 = A$ and
$t_k = a + k(b - a)/N$, for $k = 0, 1, 2, \ldots, N - 1$.
47. a.

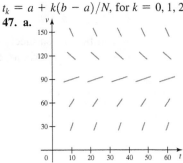

b. Increasing for $A < 98$ and decreasing for $A > 98$ **c.** $v(t) = 98$

Eigenvalues and Eigenvectors

Additional material to supplement Section 11.4, p. 613, of *Calculus for the Life Sciences*.

Notice that the general solution to the compartmental analysis problem

$$\frac{dX}{dt} = \begin{bmatrix} -2 & 2 \\ 1 & -3 \end{bmatrix} X$$
$$= MX$$

can be written nicely in terms of the eigenvalues and corresponding eigenvectors for the coefficient matrix M. Specifically,

$$\begin{bmatrix} x_1(t) \\ x_2(t) \end{bmatrix} = \begin{bmatrix} C_1 e^{-4t} + 2C_2 e^{-t} \\ -C_1 e^{-4t} + C_2 e^{-t} \end{bmatrix}$$
$$= \begin{bmatrix} 1 & 2 \\ -1 & 1 \end{bmatrix} \begin{bmatrix} C_1 e^{-4t} \\ C_2 e^{-t} \end{bmatrix}$$
$$= C_1 e^{-4t} \begin{bmatrix} 1 \\ -1 \end{bmatrix} + C_2 e^{-t} \begin{bmatrix} 2 \\ 1 \end{bmatrix}$$
$$= C_1 e^{\lambda_1 t} V_1 + C_2 e^{\lambda_2 t} V_2,$$

where λ_1 and λ_2 are the two eigenvalues of M, and V_1 and V_2 are the corresponding eigenvectors. This is true in general, as the following result states.

GENERAL SOLUTION TO A SYSTEM OF DIFFERENTIAL EQUATIONS

For a linear system of differential equations

$$\frac{dX}{dt} = MX$$

where M is an $n \times n$ coefficient matrix with n distinct eigenvalues $\lambda_1, \lambda_2, \ldots, \lambda_n$ and corresponding eigenvectors $V_1, V_2, \ldots, V_n$, the general solution can be written as

$$X = C_1 e^{\lambda_1 t} V_1 + C_2 e^{\lambda_2 t} V_2 + \cdots C_n e^{\lambda_n t} V_n,$$

where $C_1, C_2, \ldots, C_n$ are arbitrary constants.

To see why this is true, write X using summation notation and substitute into the system of differential equations, and use the property that for an eigenvalue λ_1 and corresponding eigenvector V_1 of a matrix M, $MV_1 = \lambda_1 V_1$. In the first step, we use the Constant Times a Function Rule and the Sum Rule for derivatives.

$$\frac{dX}{dt} = \frac{d}{dt} \sum_{i=1}^{n} C_i e^{\lambda_i t} V_i$$

$$= \sum_{i=1}^{n} C_i V_i \frac{d}{dt} e^{\lambda_i t}$$

$$= \sum_{i=1}^{n} C_i V_i \lambda_i e^{\lambda_i t} \qquad de^{\lambda t}/dt = \lambda e^{\lambda t}$$

$$= \sum_{i=1}^{n} C_i e^{\lambda_i t} \lambda_i V_i \qquad \text{Rearrange factors.}$$

$$= \sum_{i=1}^{n} C_i e^{\lambda_i t} M V_i \qquad M V_1 = \lambda_1 V_1$$

$$= M \sum_{i=1}^{n} C_i e^{\lambda_i t} V_i \qquad \text{Factor out } M.$$

$$= MX$$

Notice also that in the case with two eigenvalues λ_1 and λ_2, where $\lambda_1 < 0$ and $\lambda_2 > 0$, then $e^{\lambda_1 t}$ will get smaller and smaller as t increases, while $e^{\lambda_2 t}$ will get larger and larger, so that soon the solution will be approximately equal to $C_2 e^{\lambda_2 t}$. Even in the case with two negative eigenvalues or two positive eigenvalues, or in the case with a larger matrix with more than two eigenvalues, it is the largest eigenvalue that will dominate in the long run.

For example, consider once again the solution to the compartmental analysis problem with $C_1 = C_2 = 1$, so that

$$\begin{bmatrix} x_1(t) \\ x_2(t) \end{bmatrix} = \begin{bmatrix} e^{-4t} + 2e^{-t} \\ -e^{-4t} + e^{-t} \end{bmatrix}.$$

If we evaluate this solution for even a moderate sized value of t such as 5, then

$$\begin{bmatrix} x_1(5) \\ x_2(5) \end{bmatrix} = \begin{bmatrix} e^{-4 \cdot 5} + 2e^{-5} \\ -e^{-4 \cdot 5} + e^{-5} \end{bmatrix} \approx \begin{bmatrix} 0.013476 \\ 0.006738 \end{bmatrix}.$$

In comparison, if we only take the term with the largest eigenvalue of -1, then

$$\begin{bmatrix} x_1(5) \\ x_2(5) \end{bmatrix} \approx \begin{bmatrix} 2e^{-5} \\ e^{-5} \end{bmatrix} \approx \begin{bmatrix} 0.013476 \\ 0.006738 \end{bmatrix}.$$

Out to 6 decimal places, this is identical to our previous answer. We can generalize this result.

DOMINANT EIGENVALUE
For a linear system of differential equations

$$\frac{dX}{dt} = MX$$

where M is an $n \times n$ coefficient matrix with n distinct eigenvalues $\lambda_1, \lambda_2, \ldots, \lambda_n$ and corresponding eigenvectors $V_1, V_2, \ldots, V_n$, suppose that the largest eigenvalue is λ_k (that is, $\lambda_k > \lambda_i$ for $i \neq k$). Then, for large values of t the general solution can be approximated by

$$X \approx C_k e^{\lambda_k t} V_k,$$

where C_k is an arbitrary constant.

EXERCISES

Solve Exercises 1-8 in Section 11.4 (a) by converting the system to the form $dY/dt = P^{-1}MPY$, solving the system for Y, and then converting to a system for X, and (b) by using the formulas given in the box labeled "General Solution to a System of Differential Equations."

For the following exercises in Section 11.4, evaluate (a) the solution at the given value of t, and (b) the solution at the given value of t using only the term with the largest eigenvalue.

1. Exercise 9, $t = 5$
3. Exercise 11, $t = 1$

2. Exercise 10, $t = 2$
4. Exercise 12, $t = 1$

ANSWERS

1. (a) $x_1 = 88{,}551$, $x_2 = 44{,}498$ (b) $x_1 = 88{,}105$, $x_2 = 44{,}052$ 2. (a) $x_1 = 7{,}215{,}626$, $x_2 = 7{,}215{,}626$ (b) $x_1 = 7{,}215{,}626$, $x_2 = 7{,}215{,}626$ 3. (a) $x_1 = 56{,}692$, $x_2 = 170{,}180$ (b) $x_1 = 56{,}722$, $x_2 = 170{,}165$ 4. (a) $x_1 = 44{,}713.56$, $x_2 = 14{,}907.23$ (b) $x_1 = 44{,}714.37$, $x_2 = 14{,}904.79$

15

Markov Chains

In a Markov process, the next state of the system you are analyzing depends only on the current state and a set of transition probabilities. For example, the length of a waiting line in a bank a minute from now depends on the current length and the probabilities of a customer arriving or completing a transaction. This *queuing chain* model is studied in the exercises in Section 1.

Stochastic processes are mathematical models that evolve over time in a probabilistic manner. In this chapter we study a special kind of stochastic process called a *Markov chain,* where the outcome of an experiment depends only on the outcome of the previous experiment. In other words, the next **state** of the system depends only on the present state, not on preceding states. Such experiments are common enough in applications to make their study worthwhile. Markov chains are named after the Russian mathematician A.A. Markov (1856–1922), who initiated the theory of stochastic processes.

15.1 Basic Properties of Markov Chains

APPLY IT

Teaching Tip: This section requires matrix multiplication. Be sure to review the procedure with students.

If we know the probability that the child of an upper-class parent becomes middle-class or lower-class, and we know similar information for the child of a middle-class or lower-class parent, what is the probability that the grandchild or great-grandchild of an upper-class parent is middle- or lower-class?
Using Markov chains, we will learn the answer to this question in Example 2.

Transition Matrix

In sociology, it is convenient to classify people by income as *lower-class*, *middle-class*, and *upper-class*. Sociologists have found that the strongest determinant of the income class of an individual is the income class of the individual's parents. For example, if an individual in the lower-income class is said to be in *state 1*, an individual in the middle-income class is in *state 2*, and an individual in the upper-income class is in *state 3*, then the following probabilities of change in income class from one generation to the next might apply.*

Class Transition		Current Generation		
	State	1	2	3
Next Generation 1	1	0.65	0.15	0.12
2	2	0.28	0.67	0.36
3	3	0.07	0.18	0.52

This table shows that if an individual is in state 1 (lower-income class) then there is a probability of 0.65 that any offspring will be in the lower-income class, a probability of 0.28 that offspring will be in the middle-income class, and a probability of 0.07 that offspring will be in the upper-income class.

We can summarize this information geometrically with a **transition diagram**, as in Figure 1 on the next page. Here each oval represents one of the three possible states and each arrow between ovals represents the probability of moving from one state to another.

*For an example with actual data, see Exercise 34 in Section 2 of this chapter. For another example, see the landmark study by Glass, D. V., and J. R. Hall, "Social Mobility in Great Britain: A Study of Intergenerational Changes in Status," in *Social Mobility in Great Britain*, D. V. Glass, ed., Routledge & Kegan Paul, 1954. These data are analyzed using Markov chains in *Finite Markov Chains* by John G. Kemeny and J. Laurie Snell, Springer-Verlag, 1976.

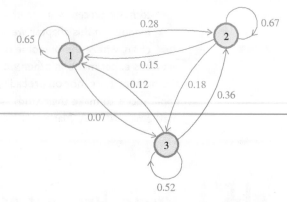

FIGURE 1

Furthermore, in order to work more easily with these probabilities, the transition diagram can be expressed as the matrix P.

$$
\begin{array}{c}
 \\
1 \\
2 \\
3
\end{array}
\begin{array}{ccc}
1 & 2 & 3 \\
\left[\begin{array}{ccc}
0.65 & 0.15 & 0.12 \\
0.28 & 0.67 & 0.36 \\
0.07 & 0.18 & 0.52
\end{array}\right] = P.
\end{array}
$$

The transition probabilities from our original table can be written as matrix entries. The symbol p_{ij} will be used for the probability of transition to state i from state j in one generation. For example, p_{32} represents the probability that a person in state 2 will have offspring in state 3; from the matrix above,

$$p_{32} = 0.18.$$

Also from the matrix, $p_{13} = 0.12$, $p_{22} = 0.67$, and so on. A **transition matrix** has several features:

1. It is square, since all possible states must be used both as rows and as columns.

2. All entries are between 0 and 1, inclusive, because all entries represent probabilities.

3. The sum of the entries in any column must be 1, since the numbers in the column give the probability of changing from the state at the top to one of the states indicated on the left.

Markov Chains

To generalize the previous example, assume that a series of experiments (like measuring a generation's socio-economic status) is performed at fixed time intervals (like once every generation), that the set of possible outcomes of the experiment is always the same, and that the probability of transitioning from one outcome to another never changes. This process is known as a Markov Chain, and is characterized by three key features.

Markov Chain

A sequence of trials of an experiment is a **Markov chain** if

1. the outcome of each experiment is one of a set of discrete states;

2. the outcome of an experiment depends only on the present state and not on any past states;

3. the transition probabilities remain constant from one transition to the next, and can be written in matrix form

$$P = \begin{bmatrix} p_{11} & p_{12} & \cdots & p_{1n} \\ \vdots & \vdots & & \vdots \\ p_{n1} & p_{n2} & \cdots & p_{nn} \end{bmatrix},$$

where p_{ij} is the probability of moving from state j to state i.

For example, in transition matrix P with constant probabilities, a person is assumed to be in one of three discrete states (lower, middle, or upper income), with each offspring in one of these same three discrete states.

EXAMPLE 1 Dry Cleaners

A small town has only two dry cleaners, Johnson and NorthClean. Johnson's manager hopes to increase the firm's market share by conducting an extensive advertising campaign. After the campaign, a market research firm finds that there is a probability of 0.8 that a customer of Johnson's will bring his next batch of dirty clothes to Johnson and a 0.35 chance that a North-Clean customer will switch to Johnson for his next batch. Write a transition matrix showing this information.

SOLUTION We must assume that the probability that a customer comes to a given dry cleaner depends only on where the last batch of clothes was taken. If there is a probability of 0.8 that a Johnson customer will return to Johnson, then there must be a $1 - 0.8 = 0.2$ chance that the customer will switch to NorthClean. In the same way, there is a $1 - 0.35 = 0.65$ chance that a NorthClean customer will return to NorthClean. These probabilities give the following transition matrix.

YOUR TURN 1 In Example 1, suppose there is a probability of 0.68 that a customer of Johnson's will bring his next batch of dirty clothes to Johnson and a 0.21 chance that a NorthClean customer will switch to Johnson for his next batch. Write a transition matrix showing this information.

$$\begin{array}{c} & \textit{First Batch} \\ & \begin{array}{cc} \text{Johnson} & \text{NorthClean} \end{array} \\ \textit{Second Batch} \begin{array}{c} \text{Johnson} \\ \text{NorthClean} \end{array} & \begin{bmatrix} 0.8 & 0.35 \\ 0.2 & 0.65 \end{bmatrix} \end{array}$$

We shall come back to this transition matrix later in this section (Example 3).

Figure 2 shows a transition diagram with the probabilities of using each dry cleaner for the second batch of dirty clothes.   **TRY YOUR TURN 1**

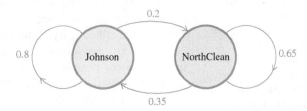

0.2

0.8   Johnson   NorthClean   0.65

0.35

FIGURE 2

Look again at transition matrix P for income-class changes.

$$\begin{array}{c} & \begin{array}{ccc} 1 & 2 & 3 \end{array} \\ \begin{array}{c} 1 \\ 2 \\ 3 \end{array} & \begin{bmatrix} 0.65 & 0.15 & 0.12 \\ 0.28 & 0.67 & 0.36 \\ 0.07 & 0.18 & 0.52 \end{bmatrix} = P \end{array}$$

This matrix shows the probability of change in income class from one generation to the next. Now let us investigate the probabilities for changes in income class over *two* generations, assuming that the transition probabilities remain the same. For example, if a parent is in state 3 (the upper-income class), what is the probability that a grandchild will be in state 2?

To find out, start with a tree diagram, as shown in Figure 3 on the next page. This diagram shows only the part of the tree that starts in state 3. The various probabilities come from transition matrix P.

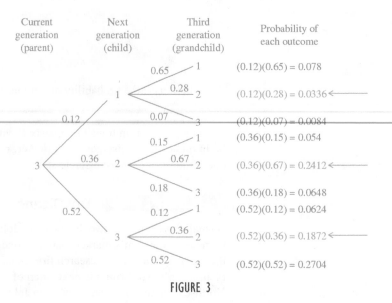

Current generation (parent)	Next generation (child)	Third generation (grandchild)	Probability of each outcome
		1	$(0.12)(0.65) = 0.078$
	1	2	$(0.12)(0.28) = 0.0336 \leftarrow$
0.12		3	$(0.12)(0.07) = 0.0084$
		1	$(0.36)(0.15) = 0.054$
3	0.36 2	2	$(0.36)(0.67) = 0.2412 \leftarrow$
		3	$(0.36)(0.18) = 0.0648$
	0.52	1	$(0.52)(0.12) = 0.0624$
	3	2	$(0.52)(0.36) = 0.1872 \leftarrow$
		3	$(0.52)(0.52) = 0.2704$

FIGURE 3

FOR REVIEW

Multiplication of matrices was covered in an earlier chapter. To get the entry in row i, column j of a product, multiply row i of the first matrix times column j of the second matrix and add up the products. For example, to get the element in row 1, column 1 of P^2, where

$$P = \begin{bmatrix} 0.65 & 0.15 & 0.12 \\ 0.28 & 0.67 & 0.36 \\ 0.07 & 0.18 & 0.52 \end{bmatrix},$$

we calculate $(0.65)(0.65) + (0.15)(0.28) + (0.12)(0.07) = 0.4729 \approx 0.47$. To get row 3, column 2, the computation is $(0.07)(0.15) + (0.18)(0.67) + (0.52)(0.18) = 0.2247$. You should review matrix multiplication by working out the rest of P^2 and verifying that it agrees with the result given in Example 2.

The arrows point to the outcomes "grandchild in state 2"; the grandchild can get to state 2 after having had parents in either state 1, state 2, or state 3. The probability that a parent in state 3 will have a grandchild in state 2 is given by the sum of the probabilities indicated with arrows, or

$$0.0336 + 0.2412 + 0.1872 = 0.4620.$$

We used p_{ij} to represent the probability of changing from state j to state i in one generation. This notation can be used to write the probability that a parent in state 3 will have a grandchild in state 2:

$$p_{21} \cdot p_{13} + p_{22} \cdot p_{23} + p_{23} \cdot p_{33}.$$

This sum of products of probabilities should remind you of matrix multiplication—it is nothing more than one step in the process of multiplying matrix P by itself. In particular, it is row 2 of P times column 3 of P. If P^2 represents the matrix product $P \cdot P$, then P^2 gives the probabilities of a transition from one state to another in *two* repetitions of an experiment.

Similarly, to find the probabilities for three repetitions of an experiment, multiply P^2, the probability for two repetitions, by P to get $P^2 \cdot P$, which we denote as P^3. We could also have multiplied P by P^2 to get $P \cdot P^2$, which should also equal P^3. Because of the associate property of matrix multiplication, $A \cdot (A \cdot A) = (A \cdot A) \cdot A$, so the order of multiplication doesn't matter here. This is fortunate, because it means that P^n, representing P multiplied by itself n times, is unambiguous; we get the same answer regardless of whether we start by multiplying on the right or on the left.

P^n **gives the probabilities of a transition from one state to another in** n **repetitions of an experiment, provided the transition probabilities remain constant from one repetition to the next.**

EXAMPLE 2   Income-class Changes

Use the transition matrix P for income-class changes to find the following.

(a) Find the probability that the grandchild of an upper-class parent is middle-class. Also, find the probability that the grandchild is lower-class.

APPLY IT

SOLUTION   To find the probability that the grandchild is middle- or lower-class, we calculate P^2 using matrix multiplication.

$$P^2 = \begin{bmatrix} 0.65 & 0.15 & 0.12 \\ 0.28 & 0.67 & 0.36 \\ 0.07 & 0.18 & 0.52 \end{bmatrix} \begin{bmatrix} 0.65 & 0.15 & 0.12 \\ 0.28 & 0.67 & 0.36 \\ 0.07 & 0.18 & 0.52 \end{bmatrix} = \begin{bmatrix} 0.4729 & 0.2196 & 0.1944 \\ 0.3948 & 0.5557 & 0.4620 \\ 0.1323 & 0.2247 & 0.3436 \end{bmatrix}$$

The entry in row 2, column 3 of P^2 gives the probability that a person in state 3 will have a grandchild in state 2; that is, that an upper-class person will have a middle-class grandchild. This number, 0.4620, is the same result found through using the tree diagram.

Row 1, column 3 of P^2 gives the number 0.1944, the probability that a person in state 3 will have a grandchild in state 1; that is, that an upper-class person will have a lower-class grandchild.

(b) Find the probability that the great-grandchild of an upper-class parent is middle-class. Also, find the probability that the great-grandchild is lower-class.

SOLUTION In the same way that matrix P^2 gives the probability of income-class changes after *two* generations, the matrix $P^3 = P \cdot P^2$ gives the probabilities after *three* generations.

For matrix P,

$$P^3 = P \cdot P^2 = \begin{bmatrix} 0.65 & 0.15 & 0.12 \\ 0.28 & 0.67 & 0.36 \\ 0.07 & 0.18 & 0.52 \end{bmatrix} \begin{bmatrix} 0.4729 & 0.2196 & 0.1944 \\ 0.3948 & 0.5557 & 0.4620 \\ 0.1323 & 0.2247 & 0.3436 \end{bmatrix}$$

$$\approx \begin{bmatrix} 0.3825 & 0.2531 & 0.2369 \\ 0.4446 & 0.5147 & 0.4877 \\ 0.1730 & 0.2322 & 0.2754 \end{bmatrix}.$$

YOUR TURN 2 In Example 2, find the probability that a lower-class person will have an upper-class great-grandchild.

Matrix P^3 gives a probability of 0.4877 that a person in state 3 will have a great-grandchild in state 2. The probability is 0.2369 that a person in state 3 will have a great-grandchild in state 1. **TRY YOUR TURN 2**

TECHNOLOGY NOTE

A graphing calculator with matrix capability is useful for finding powers of a matrix. If you enter matrix A, then multiply by A, then multiply the product by A again, you get each new power in turn. You can also raise a matrix to a power just as you do with a number. On a TI-84 Plus C, for example, P^3 to four decimal places is calculated as illustrated by Figure 4, where P was entered into the matrix $[A]$ on the calculator.

```
round([A]³, 4)
[.3825   .2531   .2369]
[.4446   .5147   .4877]
[.173    .2322   .2754]
■
```

FIGURE 4

EXAMPLE 3 **Dry Cleaners**

Use the transition matrix for the dry cleaners, found in Example 1, to calculate the following probabilities.

$$\begin{array}{c} \\ \textit{Second Batch} \end{array} \begin{array}{cc} & \textit{First Batch} \\ & \begin{array}{cc} \text{Johnson} & \text{NorthClean} \end{array} \\ \begin{array}{c} \text{Johnson} \\ \text{NorthClean} \end{array} & \begin{bmatrix} 0.8 & 0.35 \\ 0.2 & 0.65 \end{bmatrix} \end{array}$$

(a) Find the probability that a person bringing his first batch of dry cleaning to Johnson will also bring his third batch to Johnson.

SOLUTION To find the probabilities for the third batch, the second stage of this Markov chain, find the square of the transition matrix. If C represents the transition matrix, then

$$C^2 = C \cdot C = \begin{bmatrix} 0.8 & 0.35 \\ 0.2 & 0.65 \end{bmatrix} \begin{bmatrix} 0.8 & 0.35 \\ 0.2 & 0.65 \end{bmatrix} = \begin{bmatrix} 0.71 & 0.5075 \\ 0.29 & 0.4925 \end{bmatrix}.$$

From C^2 the probability that a person bringing his first batch of clothes to Johnson will also bring his third batch to Johnson is 0.71. Likewise, the probability that a person bringing his first batch to NorthClean will bring his third batch to NorthClean is 0.4925.

(b) Find the probability that a person bringing his first batch of dry cleaning to NorthClean will bring his fourth batch to Johnson.

SOLUTION The cube of matrix C gives the probabilities for the fourth batch, the third step in our experiment.

YOUR TURN 3 In Example 3, find the probability that a person bringing his first batch to Johnson will bring his fifth batch to NorthClean.

$$C^3 = C \cdot C^2 \approx \begin{bmatrix} 0.6695 & 0.5784 \\ 0.3305 & 0.4216 \end{bmatrix}$$

Row 1, column 2 gives the number 0.5784, the probability that a person bringing his first batch to NorthClean will bring his fourth batch to Johnson.   TRY YOUR TURN 3

Distribution of States

Look again at the transition matrix for income-class changes:

$$P = \begin{bmatrix} 0.65 & 0.15 & 0.12 \\ 0.28 & 0.67 & 0.36 \\ 0.07 & 0.18 & 0.52 \end{bmatrix}$$

Suppose the table on the left gives the initial distribution of people in the three income classes.

Initial Distribution		
Class	State	Proportion
Lower	1	21%
Middle	2	68%
Upper	3	11%

To see how these proportions would change after one generation, use the tree diagram in Figure 5 below. For example, to find the proportion of people in state 2 after one generation, add the numbers indicated with arrows.

$$0.0588 + 0.4556 + 0.0396 = 0.5540$$

In a similar way, the proportion of people in state 1 after one generation is

$$0.1365 + 0.1020 + 0.0132 = 0.2517,$$

and the proportion of people in state 3 after one generation is

$$0.0147 + 0.1224 + 0.0572 = 0.1943.$$

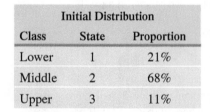

FIGURE 5

The initial distribution of states, 21%, 68%, and 11%, becomes, after one generation, 25.17% in state 1, 55.4% in state 2, and 19.43% in state 3. These distributions can be written as *probability vectors* (where the percents have been changed to decimals rounded to the nearest hundredth)

$$\begin{bmatrix} 0.21 \\ 0.68 \\ 0.11 \end{bmatrix} \text{ and } \begin{bmatrix} 0.25 \\ 0.55 \\ 0.19 \end{bmatrix},$$

respectively. A **probability vector** is a matrix of only one column, having nonnegative entries, with the sum of the entries equal to 1.

The work with the tree diagram to find the distribution of states after one generation is exactly the work required to multiply the transition matrix P and the initial probability vector $v_0 = \begin{bmatrix} 0.21 \\ 0.68 \\ 0.11 \end{bmatrix}$:

$$PV_0 = P \cdot V_0 = \begin{bmatrix} 0.65 & 0.15 & 0.12 \\ 0.28 & 0.67 & 0.36 \\ 0.07 & 0.18 & 0.52 \end{bmatrix} \begin{bmatrix} 0.21 \\ 0.68 \\ 0.11 \end{bmatrix} = \begin{bmatrix} 0.2517 \\ 0.5540 \\ 0.1943 \end{bmatrix}$$

EXAMPLE 4   Distribution of Income Classes

Find the distribution of income classes after two generations.

SOLUTION   To find the distribution of income classes after two generations, multiply the square of P (the matrix P^2) and the initial probability vector. Using P^2 from Example 2,

$$P^2 v_0 = \begin{bmatrix} 0.4729 & 0.2196 & 0.1944 \\ 0.3948 & 0.5557 & 0.4620 \\ 0.1323 & 0.2247 & 0.3436 \end{bmatrix} \begin{bmatrix} 0.21 \\ 0.68 \\ 0.11 \end{bmatrix} \approx \begin{bmatrix} 0.2700 \\ 0.5116 \\ 0.2184 \end{bmatrix}$$

We could have also calculated this result by taking Pv_0 and multiplying it on the left by P, since $P \cdot (P \cdot v_0) = P^2 \cdot v_0$ (See Exercise 25.)   **TRY YOUR TURN 4**

YOUR TURN 4 In Example 4, find the distribution of income classes after three generations.

In the next section we will develop a long-range prediction for the proportion of the population in each income class. The work in this section is summarized below.

Suppose a Markov chain has initial probability vector

$$v_0 = \begin{bmatrix} i_1 \\ i_2 \\ i_3 \\ \vdots \\ i_n \end{bmatrix}$$

and transition matrix P. The probability vector after n repetitions of the experiment is

$$P^n v_0 = P^n \cdot v_0.$$

15.1 WARMUP EXERCISES

Find the matrix product AB for each of the following pairs of matrices. (Sec. 2.4)

W1. $A = \begin{bmatrix} 4 & 6 \\ 5 & 7 \end{bmatrix}, B = \begin{bmatrix} 2 \\ 3 \end{bmatrix}$

W2. $A = \begin{bmatrix} 1 & 5 & 3 \\ 2 & 7 & 1 \\ 6 & 2 & 5 \end{bmatrix}, B = \begin{bmatrix} 4 \\ 5 \\ 3 \end{bmatrix}$

Find A^2 for each of the following matrices. (Sec. 2.4)

W3. $A = \begin{bmatrix} 3 & 2 \\ 5 & 7 \end{bmatrix}$

W4. $A = \begin{bmatrix} 3 & 1 & 6 \\ 2 & 8 & 5 \\ 1 & 4 & 5 \end{bmatrix}$

15.1 EXERCISES

Decide whether each matrix could be a probability vector.

1. $\begin{bmatrix} \frac{2}{3} \\ \frac{1}{3} \\ \frac{1}{2} \end{bmatrix}$

2. $\begin{bmatrix} \frac{1}{2} \\ 1 \end{bmatrix}$

3. $\begin{bmatrix} 0 \\ 1 \end{bmatrix}$

4. $\begin{bmatrix} 0.1 \\ 0.1 \end{bmatrix}$

5. $\begin{bmatrix} 0.4 \\ 0.2 \\ 0 \end{bmatrix}$

6. $\begin{bmatrix} \frac{1}{4} \\ \frac{1}{8} \\ \frac{5}{8} \end{bmatrix}$

7. $\begin{bmatrix} 0.07 \\ 0.04 \\ 0.37 \\ 0.52 \end{bmatrix}$

8. $\begin{bmatrix} 0 \\ -0.2 \\ 0.6 \\ 0.6 \end{bmatrix}$

Decide whether each matrix could be a transition matrix, by definition. Sketch a transition diagram for any transition matrices.

9. $\begin{bmatrix} 0.6 & 0 \\ 0 & 0.6 \end{bmatrix}$

10. $\begin{bmatrix} \frac{3}{4} & 1 \\ \frac{1}{4} & 0 \end{bmatrix}$

11. $\begin{bmatrix} \frac{1}{3} & \frac{1}{2} \\ \frac{2}{3} & \frac{1}{2} \end{bmatrix}$

12. $\begin{bmatrix} \frac{1}{4} & 2 \\ \frac{3}{4} & 0 \end{bmatrix}$

13. $\begin{bmatrix} \frac{1}{3} & 0 & \frac{1}{2} \\ \frac{1}{3} & 1 & 0 \\ \frac{1}{3} & 0 & \frac{1}{2} \end{bmatrix}$

14. $\begin{bmatrix} \frac{1}{3} & 0 & \frac{1}{2} \\ \frac{1}{2} & 1 & \frac{1}{2} \\ 1 & 0 & 1 \end{bmatrix}$

In Exercises 15 and 16, write each transition diagram as a transition matrix.

15.

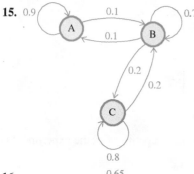

16.

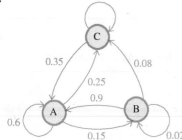

Find the first three powers of each transition matrix in Exercises 17–22 (for example, A, A^2 and A^3 in Exercise 17). For each transition matrix, find the probability that state 1 changes to state 2 after three repetitions of the experiment.

17. $A = \begin{bmatrix} 1 & 0.7 \\ 0 & 0.3 \end{bmatrix}$

18. $B = \begin{bmatrix} 0.8 & 0 \\ 0.2 & 1 \end{bmatrix}$

19. $C = \begin{bmatrix} 0 & 0.2 & 0.1 \\ 0 & 0.6 & 0.7 \\ 1 & 0.2 & 0.2 \end{bmatrix}$

20. $D = \begin{bmatrix} 0.3 & 0 & 0.6 \\ 0.2 & 0 & 0.1 \\ 0.5 & 1 & 0.3 \end{bmatrix}$

21. $E = \begin{bmatrix} 0.8 & 0.3 & 0 \\ 0.1 & 0.6 & 1 \\ 0.1 & 0.1 & 0 \end{bmatrix}$

22. $F = \begin{bmatrix} 0.01 & 0.72 & 0.34 \\ 0.9 & 0.1 & 0 \\ 0.09 & 0.18 & 0.66 \end{bmatrix}$

 For each transition matrix, find the first five powers of the matrix. Then find the probability that state 2 changes to state 4 after 5 repetitions of the experiment.

23. $\begin{bmatrix} 0.1 & 0.2 & 0.2 & 0.3 & 0.1 \\ 0.2 & 0.1 & 0.1 & 0.1 & 0.3 \\ 0.2 & 0.1 & 0.4 & 0.1 & 0.1 \\ 0.3 & 0.2 & 0.2 & 0.2 & 0.1 \\ 0.2 & 0.4 & 0.1 & 0.3 & 0.4 \end{bmatrix}$

24. $\begin{bmatrix} 0.3 & 0.4 & 0.1 & 0.2 & 0.1 \\ 0.2 & 0.2 & 0.3 & 0.1 & 0.1 \\ 0.3 & 0.1 & 0.2 & 0.3 & 0.4 \\ 0.1 & 0.2 & 0.2 & 0.2 & 0.2 \\ 0.1 & 0.1 & 0.2 & 0.2 & 0.2 \end{bmatrix}$

25. (a) Verify that $P^n \cdot v_0$ can be computed in two ways: (1) by first multiplying P by itself n times, then multiplying this result times v_0; and (2) by multiplying $P \cdot v_0$, multiplying P times this result, and continuing to multiply P times the result a total of n times

(b) Which of the two methods in part (a) is simpler? Explain your answer.

APPLICATIONS

Business and Economics

26. Dry Cleaning The dry cleaning example in the text used the following transition matrix:

$$\begin{array}{cc} & \begin{array}{cc} \text{Johnson} & \text{NorthClean} \end{array} \\ \begin{array}{c} \text{Johnson} \\ \text{NorthClean} \end{array} & \begin{bmatrix} 0.8 & 0.35 \\ 0.2 & 0.65 \end{bmatrix} \end{array}.$$

Suppose now that each customer brings in one batch of clothes per week. Use various powers of the transition matrix to find the probability that a customer initially bringing a batch of clothes to Johnson also brings a batch to Johnson after the following time periods.

(a) 1 week **(b)** 2 weeks **(c)** 3 weeks **(d)** 4 weeks

(e) What is the probability that a customer initially bringing a batch of clothes to NorthClean brings a batch to Johnson after 2 weeks?

27. Dry Cleaning Suppose Johnson has a 40% market share initially, with NorthClean having a 60% share. Use this information to write a probability vector; use this vector, along with the transition matrix from Exercise 26, to find the share of the market for each firm after each of the following time periods. (As in Exercise 26, assume that customers bring in one batch of dry cleaning per week.)

(a) 1 week **(b)** 2 weeks **(c)** 3 weeks **(d)** 4 weeks

28. Insurance An insurance company classifies its drivers into three groups: G_0 (no accidents), G_1 (one accident), and G_2 (more than one accident). The probability that a G_0 driver will remain a G_0 after 1 year is 0.75, that the driver will become a G_1 is 0.20, and that the driver will become a G_2 is 0.05. A G_1 driver cannot become a G_0 (this company has a long memory). There is a 0.70 probability that a G_1 driver will remain a G_1. A G_2 driver must remain a G_2.

(a) Write a transition matrix using this information.

(b) Suppose that the company accepts 50,000 new policyholders, all of whom are G_0 drivers. Find the number in each group after the following time periods.

    (i) 1 year **(ii)** 2 years **(iii)** 3 years **(iv)** 4 years

29. Insurance The difficulty with the mathematical model in Exercise 28 is that no "grace period" is provided; there should be a certain positive probability of moving from G_1 or G_2 back to G_0. A new system with this feature might produce the following transition matrix.

$$\begin{bmatrix} 0.75 & 0.10 & 0.10 \\ 0.20 & 0.70 & 0.30 \\ 0.05 & 0.20 & 0.60 \end{bmatrix}$$

Suppose that when this new policy is adopted, the company has 50,000 policyholders, all in G_0. Find the number in each group after the following time periods.

(a) 1 year **(b)** 2 years **(c)** 3 years

(d) Write the transition matrix for a 2-year period.

(e) Use your result from part (d) to find the probability that a driver in G_0 is still in G_0 two years later.

30. Marketing A marketing study was done in England to find the likelihood that a family would buy the following types of laundry soap: detergent only (D), soap powder only (P), both detergent and soap powder (B), and neither (N). The researchers found that purchases from week to week could be modeled by the following transition matrix.

	D	P	B	N
D	0.6724	0.0367	0.1235	0.1465
P	0.0857	0.7179	0.2407	0.2584
B	0.0229	0.0444	0.5123	0.0219
N	0.2190	0.2010	0.1235	0.5732

In the first week of the study, 22% of the families used detergent only, 44% used powder only, 9% used both, and 25% used neither. *Source: Journal of Marketing Research.*

(a) Find the probability vector for the second week.

(b) Find the probability vector for the third week.

(c) Find the transition matrix for a two-week period.

(d) Using your answer from part (c), find the probability that a family using detergent only is still using detergent only in two weeks.

31. Solar Energy A community has set a goal of reducing their carbon footprint in 10 years. As part of their "Green in Ten" campaign, they have offered homeowners incentives to convert to solar energy for home heating. Community leaders can convince 5% of those who use electric heat and 10% of those who use fossil fuels to convert to solar heat annually. Leaders also realize that some homeowners will not cooperate and that 5% of those who use electric heat will instead convert to fossil fuels while 15% of those who use fossil fuels will convert to electric heat. Of course, those who use solar energy will continue using solar energy.

(a) Write a transition matrix using this information, labeling the rows and columns e, f, and s for electric, fossil fuels, and solar, respectively.

At the beginning of the campaign, 35% of homeowners use electric heat, 60% use fossil fuels, and only 5% use solar heat. Find the number of homeowners using each type of heat after the following time periods.

(b) 1 year **(c)** 2 years **(d)** 3 years

(e) The goal of the community leaders is to have at least 50% of homeowners using solar energy for home heating in 10 years. If this trend continues, will they meet their goal? How many years will it take until they achieve this goal?

32. Land Use In one state, a Board of Realtors land use survey showed that 35% of all land was used for agricultural purposes, while 10% was urban. Ten years later, of the agricultural land, 15% had become urbanized and 80% had remained agricultural. (The remainder lay idle.) Of the idle land, 20% had become urbanized and 10% had been converted for agricultural use. Of the urban land, 90% remained urban and 10% was idle. Assume that these trends continue.

(a) Write a transition matrix using this information.

(b) Write a probability vector for the initial distribution of land.

Find the land use pattern after the following time periods.

(c) 10 years   **(d)** 20 years

 (e) Write the transition matrix for a 20-year period.

(f) Use your result from part (e) to find the probability that an idle plot of land is still idle 20 years later.

33. Business The change in the size of businesses in a certain Canadian city from one year to the next can be described by a Markov chain. The businesses are classified into three categories based on size: small (2–10 employees), medium (11–43 employees), and large (44 or more employees). The transition matrix for a 1-year period is given below.

	Small	Medium	Large
Small	0.9216	0.0460	0.0003
Medium	0.0780	0.8959	0.0301
Large	0.0004	0.0581	0.9696

Suppose that in 2015, there were 2094 small, 2363 medium, and 2378 large businesses. Based on this model, find the number of businesses of each type that would be expected in each of the following years. *Source: Applied Statistics.*

(a) 2016   **(b)** 2017

(c) Write the transition matrix for a 2-year period.

Based on your answer to part (c), what percent of medium businesses are in each of the following categories after 2 years?

(d) Small businesses   **(e)** Large businesses

34. Queuing Chain In the queuing chain, we assume that people are queuing up to be served by, say, a bank teller. For simplicity, let us assume that once two people are in line, no one else can enter the line. Let us further assume that one person is served every minute, as long as someone is in line. Assume further that in any minute, there is a probability of 1/2 that no one enters the line, a probability of 1/3 that exactly one person enters the line, and a probability of 1/6 that exactly two people enter the line, assuming there is room. If there is not enough room for two people, then the probability that one person enters the line is 1/2. Let the state be given by the number of people in line.

(a) Verify that the transition matrix is

$$
\begin{array}{c}
 \\
0 \\
1 \\
2
\end{array}
\begin{array}{ccc}
0 & 1 & 2
\end{array}
\left[
\begin{array}{ccc}
\frac{1}{2} & \frac{1}{2} & 0 \\
\frac{1}{3} & \frac{1}{3} & \frac{1}{2} \\
\frac{1}{6} & \frac{1}{6} & \frac{1}{2}
\end{array}
\right]
$$

(b) Find the transition matrix for a 2-minute period.

(c) Use your result from part (b) to find the probability that a queue with no one in line has two people in line 2 minutes later.

Life Sciences

35. Immune Response A study of immune response in rabbits classified the rabbits into four groups, according to the strength of the response. From one week to the next, the rabbits changed classification from one group to another, according to the following transition matrix. *Source: Journal of Theoretical Biology.*

$$
\begin{array}{c}
1 \\
2 \\
3 \\
4
\end{array}
\begin{array}{cccc}
1 & 2 & 3 & 4
\end{array}
\left[
\begin{array}{cccc}
\frac{5}{7} & 0 & 0 & 0 \\
\frac{2}{7} & \frac{1}{2} & 0 & 0 \\
0 & \frac{1}{3} & \frac{1}{2} & \frac{1}{4} \\
0 & \frac{1}{6} & \frac{1}{2} & \frac{3}{4}
\end{array}
\right]
$$

(a) Five weeks later, what proportion of the rabbits in group 1 were still in group 1?

(b) In the first week, there were 9 rabbits in the first group, 4 in the second, and none in the third or fourth groups. How many rabbits would you expect in each group after 4 weeks?

(c) By investigating the transition matrix raised to larger and larger powers, make a reasonable guess for the long-range probability that a rabbit in group 1 or 2 will still be in group 1 or 2 after an arbitrarily long time. Explain why this answer is reasonable.

Social Sciences

36. Housing Patterns In a survey investigating changes in housing patterns in one urban area, it was found that 75% of the population lived in single-family dwellings and 25% in multiple housing of some kind. Five years later, in a follow-up survey, of those who had been living in single-family dwellings, 90% still did so, but 10% had moved to multiple-family dwellings. Of those in multiple-family housing, 95% were still living in that type of housing, while 5% had moved to single-family dwellings. Assume that these trends continue.

(a) Write a transition matrix for this information.

(b) Write a probability vector for the initial distribution of housing.

What percent of the population can be expected in each category after the following time periods?

(c) 5 years   **(d)** 10 years

(e) Write the transition matrix for a 10-year period.

(f) Use your result from part (e) to find the probability that someone living in a single-family dwelling is still doing so 10 years later.

37. Migration A study found that the way people living in one type of neighborhood migrate to another could be described by a Markov chain. The study classified housing into five types:

I: Middle-class family households;

II: Upper-middle-class households;

III: Sound, rented, two-family dwelling units;

IV: Unsound, rented, multi-family dwelling units; and

V: Commercial.

The transition matrix for a 1-year period, based on data from Cedar Rapids, Iowa, is given below.

$$
\begin{array}{c}
\text{I} \\ \text{II} \\ \text{III} \\ \text{IV} \\ \text{V}
\end{array}
\begin{bmatrix}
0.71 & 0.52 & 0.40 & 0.34 & 0.21 \\
0.19 & 0.31 & 0.16 & 0.19 & 0.25 \\
0.03 & 0.04 & 0.22 & 0.09 & 0.13 \\
0.07 & 0.13 & 0.22 & 0.37 & 0.37 \\
0.00 & 0.00 & 0.00 & 0.01 & 0.04
\end{bmatrix}
$$

Suppose that in some year, 20% of the population lives in each type of housing. Determine the percent of the population that can be expected in each type of housing after the following times. *Source: Annals of the Association of American Geographers.*

(a) 1 year

(b) 2 years

(c) Write the transition matrix for a 2-year period.

Based on your answer to part (c), what percent of those living in a commercial area can be expected to be living in each of the following types of housing after 2 years?

(d) Middle-class family households

(e) Unsound, rented, multi-family dwelling units.

38. Voting Trends At the end of June in a presidential election year, 40% of the voters were registered as liberal, 45% as conservative, and 15% as independent. Over a 1-month period, the liberals retained 80% of their constituency, while 15% switched to conservative and 5% to independent. The conservatives retained 70% and lost 20% to the liberals. The independents retained 60% and lost 20% each to the conservatives and liberals. Assume that these trends continue.

(a) Write a transition matrix using this information.

(b) Write a probability vector for the initial distribution.

Find the percent of each type of voter at the end of each month.

(c) July   **(d)** August

(e) September   **(f)** October

(g) Write the transition matrix for a 2-month period.

General Interest

39. Cricket The results of cricket matches between England and Australia have been found to be modeled by a Markov chain. The probability that England wins, loses, or draws is based on the result of the previous game, with the following transition matrix. *Source: The Mathematical Gazette.*

	Wins	Loses	Draws
Wins	0.443	0.277	0.266
Loses	0.364	0.436	0.304
Draws	0.193	0.287	0.430

(a) Compute the transition matrix for the game after the next one, based on the result of the last game.

(b) Use your answer from part (a) to find the probability that, if England won the last game, England will win the game after the next one.

(c) Use your answer from part (a) to find the probability that, if Australia won the last game, England will win the game after the next one.

40. Professional Football There has been an ongoing debate as to how NFL overtime games should be carried out. In the system in place from 1974 to 2010, a coin was tossed and the winner of the toss got to decide whether to kickoff or to receive the ball. The first team to score won. Based on data from the 2008 season, 36% of any given possession resulted in the offense scoring, while 62% of the possessions resulted in a change of possession. The remaining 2% of the possessions resulted in the defense scoring (by way of a turnover returned for a touchdown or a safety). The following transition matrix gives the probability of going from each column state to each row state. The first column tells the probability of being in any given situation after one possession, assuming that team A starts with the ball. *Source: Mathematics in Sports.*

	Possession for A	Possession for B	A wins	B wins
Possession for A	0	0.62	0	0
Possession for B	0.62	0	0	0
A wins	0.36	0.02	1	0
B wins	0.02	0.36	0	1

(a) Suppose that team A starts with the ball. Determine the probabilities that after one possession (i) team A wins, (ii) team B wins, and (iii) the game continues.

(b) Determine the same probabilities after two possessions.

(c) Determine the same probabilities after three possessions.

(d) Which team has an advantage in this method of overtime?

YOUR TURN ANSWERS

1.
$$
\begin{array}{c} \text{J} \\ \text{N} \end{array}
\begin{bmatrix}
0.68 & 0.21 \\
0.32 & 0.79
\end{bmatrix}
$$

2. 0.1730 **3.** 0.3487 **4.**
$$
\begin{bmatrix}
0.2785 \\
0.4970 \\
0.2245
\end{bmatrix}
$$

15.2 Regular Markov Chains

APPLY IT   Given the transition probabilities for two dry cleaners, how can we predict the market share of each cleaner far into the future if we do not know the current proportions?

In Example 2 of this section, we will see how to answer this question.

If we start with a transition matrix P and an initial probability vector v_0, we can use the nth power of P to find the probability vector $P^n v_0$ for n repetitions of an experiment. In this section, we try to decide what happens to an initial probability vector in the long run—that is, as n gets larger and larger. Again, we assume that the transition probabilities remain constant from repetition to repetition.

EXAMPLE 1   **Long-Term Trend of Dry Cleaner**

The transition matrix from the dry cleaning example in the previous section is

$$P = \begin{bmatrix} 0.8 & 0.35 \\ 0.2 & 0.65 \end{bmatrix}.$$

(a) Suppose that the initial probability vector, which gives the market share for each firm at the beginning of the experiment, is $v_0 = \begin{bmatrix} 0.4 \\ 0.6 \end{bmatrix}$. Find the long-term market share for each firm.

SOLUTION   Multiplying v_0 by successively higher powers of the transition matrix P gives the following table of values. (See Exercise 27 in the previous section.)

	Market Share		
Weeks After Start	**Johnson**	**NorthClean**	
0	0.4000	0.6000	v_0
1	0.5300	0.4700	$P^1 v_0$
2	0.5885	0.4115	$P^2 v_0$
3	0.6148	0.3852	$P^3 v_0$
4	0.6267	0.3733	$P^4 v_0$
5	0.6320	0.3680	$P^5 v_0$
13	0.6364	0.3636	$P^{13} v_0$
14	0.6364	0.3636	$P^{14} v_0$

The numbers for the market share distribution seem to approach the numbers in the probability vector $\begin{bmatrix} 0.6364 \\ 0.3636 \end{bmatrix}$.

So, in the long term we expect that Johnson will have about 64% of the market share, while NorthClean will have about 36% of the market share.

(b) Now suppose instead that the initial probability vector is $v_0 = \begin{bmatrix} 0.75 \\ 0.25 \end{bmatrix}$. Find the long-term market share for each firm.

SOLUTION   The market shares shown in the following table were found by using powers of the transition matrix.

	Market Share		
Weeks After Start	**Johnson**	**NorthClean**	
0	0.7500	0.2500	v_0
1	0.6875	0.3125	$P^1 v_0$
2	0.6594	0.3406	$P^2 v_0$
3	0.6467	0.3533	$P^3 v_0$
4	0.6410	0.3590	$P^4 v_0$
5	0.6385	0.3615	$P^5 v_0$
13	0.6364	0.3636	$P^{13} v_0$
14	0.6364	0.3636	$P^{14} v_0$

Once again, the numbers seem to approach the numbers in the probability vector $\begin{bmatrix} 0.6364 \\ 0.3636 \end{bmatrix}$, which we also observed in part (a). In either case, the long-term trend is for a market share of about 64% for Johnson and 36% for NorthClean.

The example above suggests that this long-term trend does not depend upon the initial distribution of market shares. This means that if the initial market share for Johnson was less than 64%, the advertising campaign has paid off in terms of a greater long-term market share. If the initial share was more than 64%, the campaign did not pay off.

To better understand these apparently identical long-term behaviors, consider the following powers of the original transition matrix P from Example 1.

$$P^2 = \begin{bmatrix} 0.71 & 0.5075 \\ 0.29 & 0.4925 \end{bmatrix} \qquad P^3 = \begin{bmatrix} 0.6695 & 0.5784 \\ 0.3305 & 0.4216 \end{bmatrix} \qquad P^4 = \begin{bmatrix} 0.6513 & 0.6103 \\ 03487 & 0.3897 \end{bmatrix}$$

$$P^5 = \begin{bmatrix} 0.6431 & 0.6246 \\ 0.3569 & 0.3754 \end{bmatrix} \qquad P^{10} = \begin{bmatrix} 0.6365 & 0.6361 \\ 0.3635 & 0.3639 \end{bmatrix} \qquad P^{20} = \begin{bmatrix} 0.6364 & 0.6364 \\ 0.3636 & 0.3636 \end{bmatrix}$$

TECHNOLOGY NOTE

Figure 6 shows the result of taking P^{10} and P^{20} to four decimal places on a T1-84 Plus 1C, where the transition matrix P from the dry cleaning example was entered into the matrix [A] on the calculator.

round([A]^{10}, 4)
$\begin{bmatrix} .6365 & .6361 \\ .3635 & .3639 \end{bmatrix}$
round([A]^{20}, 4)
$\begin{bmatrix} .6364 & .6364 \\ .3636 & .3636 \end{bmatrix}$

FIGURE 6

It seems that

$$P^n \rightarrow \begin{bmatrix} 0.6364 & 0.6364 \\ 0.3636 & 0.3636 \end{bmatrix} \text{ as } n \text{ gets large.}$$

Note that the successively higher powers of P^n approach a matrix that has identical columns.

Recall from the previous section that the ij^{th} entry of P^n (i.e., $[P^n]_{ij}$) is the probability of moving from state j to state i after n steps. If v_0 is an initial distribution vector then

$$P^n v_0 = \text{expected distribution after } n \text{ steps}$$

If we take the initial probability vector to be $\begin{bmatrix} 0.4 \\ 0.6 \end{bmatrix}$ as in Example 1 (a), then

$$P^n v_0 = \begin{bmatrix} 0.6364 & 0.6364 \\ 0.3636 & 0.3636 \end{bmatrix} \begin{bmatrix} 0.4 \\ 0.6 \end{bmatrix} = \begin{bmatrix} 0.6364 \\ 0.3636 \end{bmatrix},$$

which is precisely one of the identical columns of P^n for large values of n. Let's now choose a very different initial distribution, say $v_0 = \begin{bmatrix} 0.9 \\ 0.1 \end{bmatrix}$. Then

$$P^n v_0 = \begin{bmatrix} 0.6364 & 0.6364 \\ 0.3636 & 0.3636 \end{bmatrix} \begin{bmatrix} 0.9 \\ 0.1 \end{bmatrix} = \begin{bmatrix} 0.6364 \\ 0.3636 \end{bmatrix} \text{ again!}$$

To get some sense of what's happening, let v_0 be *any* initial distribution, so $v_0 = \begin{bmatrix} p \\ 1 - p \end{bmatrix}$ where $0 \le p \le 1$, in which case

$$P^n v_0 = \begin{bmatrix} 0.6364 & 0.6364 \\ 0.3636 & 0.3636 \end{bmatrix} \begin{bmatrix} p \\ 1 - p \end{bmatrix} = \begin{bmatrix} 0.6364p + 0.6364(1 - p) \\ 0.3636p + 0.3636(1 - p) \end{bmatrix} = \begin{bmatrix} 0.6364 \\ 0.3636 \end{bmatrix} \text{ still!}$$

This final calculation confirms that the long-term market share for each dry cleaning firm does not depend on the initial distribution.

Regular Markov Chains

In our dry cleaning example, the initial distribution of market share did not affect the long-term distribution of market share. Regardless of the initial probability vector, the system will approach a fixed vector V. This unexpected and remarkable fact is the basic property of a class of Markov chains known as regular Markov chains. Such predictions are always possible with **regular transition matrices**. A transition matrix is *regular* if some power of the matrix contains all positive entries. A Markov chain is a **regular Markov chain** if its transition matrix is regular.

For the special case of regular Markov chains, it can be shown that the limiting distribution is always independent of the initial distribution. (It is not possible, however, to make long-term predictions with all transition matrices.)

EXAMPLE 2 Regular Transition Matrices

Decide whether the following transition matrices are regular.

(a) $A = \begin{bmatrix} 0.75 & 0 & 0.6 \\ 0.25 & 0.5 & 0.4 \\ 0 & 0.5 & 0 \end{bmatrix}$

SOLUTION Square A.

$$A^2 = \begin{bmatrix} 0.5625 & 0.3 & 0.45 \\ 0.3125 & 0.45 & 0.35 \\ 0.125 & 0.25 & 0.2 \end{bmatrix}$$

Since all entries in A^2 are positive, matrix A is regular.

(b) $B = \begin{bmatrix} 0.5 & 0 & 0 \\ 0 & 1 & 0 \\ 0.5 & 0 & 1 \end{bmatrix}$

YOUR TURN 1 Decide whether the following transition matrix is regular.

$$C = \begin{bmatrix} 0.2 & 0.3 & 0.2 \\ 0.1 & 0.7 & 0 \\ 0.7 & 0 & 0.8 \end{bmatrix}$$

SOLUTION Find various powers of B.

$$B^2 = \begin{bmatrix} 0.25 & 0 & 0 \\ 0 & 1 & 0 \\ 0.75 & 0 & 1 \end{bmatrix}; B^3 = \begin{bmatrix} 0.215 & 0 & 0 \\ 0 & 1 & 0 \\ 0.875 & 0 & 1 \end{bmatrix}; B^4 = \begin{bmatrix} 0.0625 & 0 & 0 \\ 0 & 1 & 0 \\ 0.9375 & 0 & 1 \end{bmatrix}$$

Further powers of B will still give the same zero entries, so no power of matrix B contains all positive entries. For this reason, B is not regular. **TRY YOUR TURN 1**

NOTE If a transition matrix P has some zero entries, and P^2 does as well, you may wonder how far you must compute P^n to be certain that the matrix is not regular. The answer is that if all zeros occur in the identical places in both P^n and P^{n+1} for any n, they will appear in those places for all higher powers of P, so P is not regular.

Suppose that v is any probability vector. It can be shown that for a regular Markov chain with a transition matrix P, there exists a single vector V that does not depend on v, such that $P^n v$ gets closer to V as n gets larger and larger.

Equilibrium Vector of a Markov Chain

If a Markov chain with transition matrix P is regular, then there is a unique vector V such that, for any probability vector v and for large values of n,

$$P^n v \approx V.$$

Vector V is called the **equilibrium vector** or the **fixed vector** of the Markov chain. (Because of the variety of applications of Markov chains, the equilibrium vector is also called the long-term probability vector, the stability distribution, and the steady-state matrix.)

In the example with Johnson Cleaners, the equilibrium vector V is approximately $\begin{bmatrix} 0.6364 \\ 0.3636 \end{bmatrix}$. Vector V can be determined by finding P^n for larger and larger values of n, and then looking for a vector that the product $P^n v$ approaches. Such an approach can be very tedious, however, and is prone to error. To find a better way, start with the fact that for a large value of n,

$$P^n v \approx V,$$

as mentioned above. From this result, $P \cdot P^n v \approx PV$, so that

$$P \cdot P^n v = P^{n+1} v \approx PV.$$

Since $P^n v \approx V$ for large values of n, it is also true that $P^{n+1} v \approx V$ for large values of n (the product $P^n v$ approaches V, so that $P^{n+1} v$ must also approach V). Thus, $P^{n+1} v \approx V$ and $P^{n+1} v \approx PV$, which suggests that

$$PV = V.$$

If a Markov chain with transition matrix P is regular, then there exists a probability vector V such that

$$PV = V.$$

Recall from Section 10.5 that the matrix equation $Ax = \lambda x$ determines eigenvalues λ and corresponding eigenvectors x for the matrix A. If we call our matrix P instead of A, and our vector V instead of x, then the matrix equation

$$PV = V = 1 \cdot V$$

turns out to be a special case of what we already did in Section 10.5. Specifically, solving $PV = V$ means finding the eigenvector V corresponding to eigenvalue $\lambda = 1$ for the Markov chain with coefficient matrix P.

We are interested in the long-term distribution, or proportion, of each category relative to the entire population, so divide the entries of V by the sum of its entries to get the *normalized* eigenvector $\hat{V}$.

When the eigenvalue/eigenvector concept was first introduced, the power and wide-ranging applications of it ware not likely to be apparent. Now, we have seen applications of eigenvalues and eigenvectors arise in differential equations and in Markov Chains.

The central results of our discussion of regular Markov chains can be summarized as follows.

Properties of a Regular Markov Chain

Suppose a regular chain has a transition matrix P.

1. The successive powers of P^n approach a matrix $\hat{P}$, called the **stability matrix** of the matrix P, as n gets larger. Specifically,

$$\lim_{n \to \infty} P^n = \hat{P}.$$

2. Given any initial distribution v_0, the product $P^n v_0$ approaches a unique vector V, called the equilibrium vector. That is,

$$\lim_{n \to \infty} P^n v_0 = \hat{P} v_0 = V.$$

3. The columns of the stability matrix $\hat{P}$ are all equal to the equilibrium vector V.

4. The equilibrium vector V has the property that $PV = V$. This means that V is the normalized eigenvector corresponding to the eigenvalue $\lambda = 1$ for the regular Markov matrix P.

5. Recall from an earlier chapter that eigenvectors associated with a particular eigenvalue are not unique, they are multiples of each other. Thus, to find V, we first solve the matrix equation $PX = X$ for X and normalize to get V. Equivalently, this means solving $(P - I)X = 0$ and normalizing.

EXAMPLE 3   Equilibrium Vector for Dry Cleaners

Use Property 5 to find the long-term trend for for the Markov chain in the dry cleaning example with transition matrix

$$P = \begin{bmatrix} 0.8 & 0.35 \\ 0.2 & 0.65 \end{bmatrix}$$

SOLUTION   To find the equilibrium vector, V, we will find an eigenvector $X = \begin{bmatrix} x_1 \\ x_2 \end{bmatrix}$ associated with the eigenvalue $\lambda = 1$ by solving the system $(P - I)X = 0$ and then normalize. Since

$$P - I = \begin{bmatrix} 0.8 & 0.35 \\ 0.2 & 0.65 \end{bmatrix} - \begin{bmatrix} 1 & 0 \\ 0 & 1 \end{bmatrix} = \begin{bmatrix} -0.2 & 0.35 \\ 0.2 & -0.35 \end{bmatrix},$$

our system of equations is

$$(P - I)X = \begin{bmatrix} -0.2 & 0.35 \\ 0.2 & -0.35 \end{bmatrix} \begin{bmatrix} x_1 \\ x_2 \end{bmatrix} = \begin{bmatrix} 0 \\ 0 \end{bmatrix}.$$

The corresponding augmented matrix is

$$\begin{bmatrix} -0.2 & 0.35 & | & 0 \\ 0.2 & -0.35 & | & 0 \end{bmatrix}.$$

Verify that using Gauss-Jordan elimination, we obtain

$$\begin{bmatrix} 1 & -7/4 & | & 0 \\ 0 & 0 & | & 0 \end{bmatrix}.$$

This system has an infinite number of solutions in the form of $x_1 = \frac{7}{4} x_2$.

Letting x_2 be any arbitrary real number, we obtain a specific solution. For example, if $x_2 = 4$, then $x_1 = 7$. To find V, we normalize the solution we found by simply dividing each component of the solution by the sum $7 + 4 = 11$. That is

$$V = \begin{bmatrix} x_1/11 \\ x_2/11 \end{bmatrix} = \begin{bmatrix} 7/11 \\ 4/11 \end{bmatrix} \approx \begin{bmatrix} 0.6364 \\ 0.3636 \end{bmatrix},$$

which is what we observed in Example 1.

EXAMPLE 4	**Equilibrium Vector**

Use Property 5 to find the equilibrium vector for the transition matrix

$$K = \begin{bmatrix} 0.2 & 0.1 & 0.3 \\ 0.6 & 0.1 & 0.3 \\ 0.2 & 0.8 & 0.4 \end{bmatrix}$$

SOLUTION To find the equilibrium vector V, we will find an eigenvector $X = \begin{bmatrix} x_1 \\ x_2 \\ x_3 \end{bmatrix}$

associated with the eigenvalue $\lambda = 1$ by solving the system $(K - I)X = 0$ and then normalize. Since

$$K - I = \begin{bmatrix} 0.2 & 0.1 & 0.3 \\ 0.6 & 0.1 & 0.3 \\ 0.2 & 0.8 & 0.4 \end{bmatrix} - \begin{bmatrix} 1 & 0 & 0 \\ 0 & 1 & 0 \\ 0 & 0 & 1 \end{bmatrix} = \begin{bmatrix} -0.8 & 0.1 & 0.3 \\ 0.6 & -0.9 & 0.3 \\ 0.2 & 0.8 & -0.6 \end{bmatrix},$$

our system of equations is

$$(K - I)X = \begin{bmatrix} -0.8 & 0.1 & 0.3 \\ 0.6 & -0.9 & 0.3 \\ 0.2 & 0.8 & -0.6 \end{bmatrix} \begin{bmatrix} x_1 \\ x_2 \\ x_3 \end{bmatrix} = \begin{bmatrix} 0 \\ 0 \\ 0 \end{bmatrix}.$$

The corresponding augmented matrix is

$$\begin{bmatrix} -0.8 & 0.1 & 0.3 & | & 0 \\ 0.6 & -0.9 & 0.3 & | & 0 \\ 0.2 & 0.8 & -0.6 & | & 0 \end{bmatrix}.$$

Verify that using Gauss-Jordan elimination, we obtain

$$\begin{bmatrix} 1 & 0 & -5/11 & | & 0 \\ 0 & 1 & -7/11 & | & 0 \\ 0 & 0 & 0 & | & 0 \end{bmatrix}.$$

This system has an infinite number of solutions in the form of $x_1 = \frac{5}{11}x_3$ and $x_2 = \frac{7}{11}x_3$.

YOUR TURN 3 Find the equilibrium vector for the transition matrix

$$K = \begin{bmatrix} 0.2 & 0.3 & 0.2 \\ 0.1 & 0.7 & 0 \\ 0.7 & 0 & 0.8 \end{bmatrix}$$

Letting x_3 be any arbitrary real number, we obtain a specific solution. For example, if $x_3 = 11$, then $x_1 = 5$ and $x_2 = 7$. To find V, we normalize the solution we found by simply dividing each component of the solution by the sum $11 + 5 + 7 = 23$. That is

$$V = \begin{bmatrix} x_1/23 \\ x_2/23 \\ x_3/23 \end{bmatrix} = \begin{bmatrix} 5/23 \\ 7/23 \\ 11/23 \end{bmatrix}.$$

TRY YOUR TURN 3

15.2 WARMUP EXERCISES

Solve each of the following linear system. (sec 2.2)

W1.
$$\begin{aligned} v_1 + v_2 + v_3 &= 1 \\ 2v_1 + 3v_2 + 4v_3 &= 3.3 \\ 3v_1 + v_2 - v_3 &= 0.4 \\ 5v_1 - v_2 + 2v_3 &= 1.7 \end{aligned}$$

W2.
$$\begin{aligned} v_1 + v_2 + v_3 &= 1 \\ 3v_1 + 3v_2 + 2v_3 &= 2.6 \\ 5v_1 - 2v_2 + 3v_3 &= 2.8 \\ -4v_1 + 6v_2 + 7v_3 &= 2.4 \end{aligned}$$

15.2 EXERCISES

Which of the following transition matrices are regular?

1. $\begin{bmatrix} 0.2 & 0.9 \\ 0.8 & 0.1 \end{bmatrix}$

2. $\begin{bmatrix} 0.28 & 0.47 \\ 0.72 & 0.53 \end{bmatrix}$

3. $\begin{bmatrix} 1 & 0.65 \\ 0 & 0.35 \end{bmatrix}$

4. $\begin{bmatrix} 0.55 & 0 \\ 0.45 & 1 \end{bmatrix}$

5. $\begin{bmatrix} 0 & 0.4 & 1 \\ 1 & 0.2 & 0 \\ 0 & 0.4 & 0 \end{bmatrix}$

6. $\begin{bmatrix} 0.3 & 1 & 0.5 \\ 0.5 & 0 & 0.1 \\ 0.2 & 0 & 0.4 \end{bmatrix}$

Find the equilibrium vector for each transition matrix.

7. $\begin{bmatrix} \frac{1}{4} & \frac{1}{2} \\ \frac{3}{4} & \frac{1}{2} \end{bmatrix}$

8. $\begin{bmatrix} \frac{2}{3} & \frac{1}{8} \\ \frac{1}{3} & \frac{7}{8} \end{bmatrix}$

9. $\begin{bmatrix} 0.4 & 0.3 \\ 0.6 & 0.7 \end{bmatrix}$

10. $\begin{bmatrix} 0.1 & 0.8 \\ 0.9 & 0.2 \end{bmatrix}$

11. $\begin{bmatrix} 0.1 & 0.4 & 0.1 \\ 0.1 & 0.3 & 0.2 \\ 0.8 & 0.3 & 0.7 \end{bmatrix}$

12. $\begin{bmatrix} 0.5 & 0.1 & 0.3 \\ 0.2 & 0.4 & 0.1 \\ 0.3 & 0.5 & 0.6 \end{bmatrix}$

13. $\begin{bmatrix} 0.25 & 0.1 & 0.55 \\ 0.35 & 0.3 & 0.4 \\ 0.4 & 0.6 & 0.05 \end{bmatrix}$

14. $\begin{bmatrix} 0.16 & 0.43 & 0.86 \\ 0.28 & 0.12 & 0.05 \\ 0.56 & 0.45 & 0.09 \end{bmatrix}$

Find the equilibrium vector for each transition matrix in Exercises 15–20. These matrices were first used in the exercises for Section 15.1. (*Note*: Not all of these transition matrices are regular, but equilibrium vectors still exist. Why doesn't this contradict the work of this section?)

15. Modified insurance categories (15.1 Exercise 29)

$$\begin{bmatrix} 0.75 & 0.10 & 0.10 \\ 0.20 & 0.70 & 0.30 \\ 0.05 & 0.20 & 0.60 \end{bmatrix}$$

16. Insurance categories (15.1 Exercise 28)

$$\begin{bmatrix} 0.75 & 0 & 0 \\ 0.20 & 0.70 & 0 \\ 0.05 & 0.30 & 1 \end{bmatrix}$$

17. Home heating systems (15.1 Exercise 31)

$$\begin{bmatrix} 0.9 & 0.15 & 0 \\ 0.05 & 0.75 & 0 \\ 0.05 & 0.1 & 1 \end{bmatrix}$$

18. Land use (10.1 Exercise 32)

$$\begin{bmatrix} 0.80 & 0 & 0.10 \\ 0.15 & 0.90 & 0.20 \\ 0.05 & 0.10 & 0.70 \end{bmatrix}$$

19. Voter registration (10.1 Exercise 38)

$$\begin{bmatrix} 0.80 & 0.20 & 0.20 \\ 0.15 & 0.70 & 0.20 \\ 0.05 & 0.10 & 0.60 \end{bmatrix}$$

20. Housing patterns (10.1 Exercise 36)

$$\begin{bmatrix} 0.9 & 0.05 \\ 0.1 & 0.95 \end{bmatrix}$$

21. Find the equilibrium vector for the transition matrix

$$\begin{bmatrix} p & 1-q \\ 1-p & q \end{bmatrix}.$$

where $0 < p < 1$ and $0 < q < 1$. Under what conditions is this matrix regular?

22. Show that the transition matrix

$$K = \begin{bmatrix} \frac{1}{4} & 0 & 0 \\ 0 & 1 & 0 \\ \frac{3}{4} & 0 & 1 \end{bmatrix}$$

has more than one vector V such that $KV = V$. Why does this not violate the statements of this section?

23. Let $P = \begin{bmatrix} a_{11} & a_{12} \\ a_{21} & a_{22} \end{bmatrix}$

be a regular matrix having *rows* sums of 1. Show that the equilibrium vector for P is $\begin{bmatrix} \frac{1}{2} \\ \frac{1}{2} \end{bmatrix}$.

24. Notice in Example 3 that the system of equations $KV = V$, with the extra equation that the sum of the elements of V must equal 1, had exactly one solution. What can you say about the number of solutions to the system $KV = V$?

APPLICATIONS

Business and Economics

25. Quality Control The probability that a complex assembly line works correctly depends on whether the line worked correctly the last time it was used. There is a 0.9 chance that the line will work correctly if it worked correctly the time before, and a 0.8 chance that it will work correctly if it did *not* work correctly the time before. Set up a transition matrix with this information and find the long-range probability that the line will work correctly.

26. Quality Control Suppose improvements are made in the assembly line of Exercise 25, so that the transition matrix becomes

	Works	Doesn't Work
Works	$\begin{bmatrix} 0.95$	$0.85 \end{bmatrix}$
Doesn't Work	$\begin{bmatrix} 0.05$	$0.15 \end{bmatrix}$

Find the new long-range probability that the line will work properly.

27. (a) Dry Cleaning Using the initial probability vector $\begin{bmatrix} 0.4 \\ 0.6 \end{bmatrix}$, find the probability vector for the next 9 weeks in Example 1 (the dry cleaning example). Compute your answers to at least 6 decimal places.

(b) Using your results from part (a) find the difference between the equilibrium proportion of customers going to Johnson and the proportion going there for each of the first 10 weeks. Be sure to compute the equilibrium proportions to at least 6 decimal places.

(c) Find the ratio between each difference calculated in part (b) and the difference for the previous week.

(d) Using your results from part (c) explain how the probability vector approaches the equilibrium vector.

(e) Repeat parts (a)–(d) of this exercise using the initial probability vector $\begin{bmatrix} 0.75 \\ 0.25 \end{bmatrix}$.

28. Mortgage Refinancing In 2009, many homeowners refinanced their mortgages to take advantage of lower interest rates. Most of the mortgages could be classified into four groups: adjustable rate, 15-year fixed rate, 20-year fixed rate, and 30-year fixed rate. (For this exercise, the small number of loans that are not of those four types will be classified with the adjustable rate loans.) Sometimes when a homeowner refinanced, the new loan was the same type as the old loan, and sometimes it was different. The breakdown of the percent (in decimal form) in each category is shown in the following table. If these conversion rates were to persist, find the long-range trend for the percent of loans of each type. *Source: Freddie Mac.*

	Old Loan			
New Loan	Adjustable	15-Year Fixed	20-Year Fixed	30-Year Fixed
Adjustable	0.04	0	0.01	0
15-Year Fixed	0.22	0.7	0.545	0.145
20-Year Fixed	0.07	0.02	0.075	0.055
30-Year Fixed	0.67	0.28	0.37	0.80

29. Business As we saw in the last section, the change in the size of businesses in a certain Canadian city from one year to the next could be described by a Markov chain. The businesses were classified into three categories based on size: small (2–10 employees), medium (11–43 employees), and large (44 or more employees). The transition period for a 1-year period is given below.

$$\begin{array}{c} \\ \text{Small} \\ \text{Medium} \\ \text{Large} \end{array} \begin{array}{ccc} \text{Small} & \text{Medium} & \text{Large} \\ \begin{bmatrix} 0.9216 & 0.0460 & 0.0003 \\ 0.0780 & 0.8959 & 0.0301 \\ 0.0004 & 0.0581 & 0.9696 \end{bmatrix} \end{array}$$

If these trends continue, what percent of the business will be small, medium, or large in the long run? *Source: Applied Statistics.*

30. Marketing In Exercise 30 of the previous section, the following transition matrix described the transition of families from using detergents only (D), soap powder only (P), both detergent and soap powder (B), and neither (N).

$$\begin{array}{c} D \\ P \\ B \\ N \end{array} \begin{array}{cccc} D & P & B & N \\ \begin{bmatrix} 0.6724 & 0.0367 & 0.1235 & 0.1465 \\ 0.0857 & 0.7179 & 0.2407 & 0.2584 \\ 0.0229 & 0.0444 & 0.5123 & 0.0219 \\ 0.2190 & 0.2010 & 0.1235 & 0.5732 \end{bmatrix} \end{array}$$

Find the long-range probability of a family using each-type of laundry soap. *Source: Journal of Marketing Research.*

31. Real Estate Zoning A study of zoning changes in real estate categorized properties as exclusively single-family residential (R), exclusively "other" (O), and mixed single-family and "other" (M). The study found that, for property that had the characteristics of single-family residential, the transition from one type of zoning to the next over a 10-year period could be modelled by the following transition matrix. *Sources: Journal of Urban Economics.*

$$\begin{array}{c} R \\ O \\ M \end{array} \begin{array}{ccc} R & O & M \\ \begin{bmatrix} 0.995 & 0.047 & 0.005 \\ 0.000 & 0.810 & 0.018 \\ 0.005 & 0.143 & 0.977 \end{bmatrix} \end{array}$$

(a) Find the long-range prediction for the portion of real estate in each of the zoning categories.

(b) Raise the transition matrix to increasingly large powers, as in the Technology Note in this section, until the rows becomes identical or your calculator gives you an error message. What do you observe in this section? Sometimes the convergence toward the limiting distribution is very slow!

Life Sciences

32. Research with Mice A large group of mice is kept in a cage having connected compartments A, B, and C. Mice in compartment A move to B with probability 0.3 and to C with probability 0.4. Mice in B move to A or C with probabilities of 0.15 and 0.55, respectively. Mice in C move to A or B with probabilities of 0.3 and 0.6, respectively. Find the long-range prediction for the fraction of mice in each of the compartments.

Social Sciences

33. Family Structure Data from the National Longitudinal Survey of Youth (NLSY) were analyzed to derive the probabilities that children will repeat the child-raising choices of their parents. The living arrangements of a group of children at age 14 were recorded. The NLSY then tracked those same children and recorded the living arrangements for their children. Based on these data, the following transition matrix gives the probabilities of change in child-raising choices from one generation to the next. Find the long-term proportions of child-raising choices if this trend were to continue. *Source: Journal for Economic Educators.*

	First Generation Living Arrangements				
	Couple	Mother	Father	Relative	Other
Couple	0.566	0.392	0.391	0.307	0.337
Mother	0.309	0.453	0.354	0.558	0.320
Father	0.083	0.066	0.109	0.040	0.025
Relative	0.023	0.061	0.108	0.056	0.252
Other	0.019	0.028	0.038	0.039	0.066

34. Class Mobility The following transition matrix shows the probabilities of a person attaining different income classes based on the parents' income class. The income classes, based on total household income, are defined as poor (lowest quintile), middle class (middle quintiles), and upper class (highest quintile). Find the long-range percent of poor, middle class, and upper class if these trends were to continue. *Source: Center for American Progress.*

	Poor	Middle	Upper
Poor	0.415	0.175	0.061
Middle	0.526	0.655	0.520
Upper	0.059	0.170	0.419

35. Migration As we saw in the last section, a study found that the probability that people living in one type of neighborhood migrate to another could be described by a Markov chain.

The study classified housing into five types:

I: Middle-class family households;

II: Upper-middle-class households;

III: Sound, rented, two-family dwelling units;

IV: Unsound, rented, multi-family dwelling units; and

V: Commercial.

The transition matrix for a 1-year period is given below.

	I	II	III	IV	V
I	0.71	0.52	0.40	0.34	0.21
II	0.19	0.31	0.16	0.19	0.25
III	0.03	0.04	0.22	0.09	0.13
IV	0.07	0.13	0.22	0.37	0.37
V	0.00	0.00	0.00	0.01	0.04

If these trends continue, what are the long-term probabilities of people living in each type of housing? *Source: Annals of the Association of American Geographers.*

36. Criminology A study of male criminals in Philadelphia found that the probability that one type of offense is followed by another type can be described by the following transition matrix.* *Source: The British Journal of Criminology.*

	Nonindex	Injury	Theft	Damage	Combination
Nonindex	0.645	0.611	0.514	0.609	0.523
Injury	0.099	0.138	0.067	0.107	0.093
Theft	0.152	0.128	0.271	0.178	0.183
Damage	0.033	0.033	0.030	0.064	0.022
Combination	0.071	0.090	0.118	0.042	0.179

(a) For a criminal who commits theft, what is the probability that his next crime is also a theft?

(b) For a criminal who commits theft, what is the probability that his second crime after that is also a theft?

(c) If these trends continue, what are the long-term probabilities for each type of crime?

37. Education At one liberal arts college, students are classified as humanities majors, science majors, or undecided. There is a 20% chance that a humanities major will change to a science major from one year to the next and a 45% chance that a humanities major will change to undecided. A science major will change

*The rounding was changed slightly so the rows of the transition matrix sum to 1.

to humanities with probability 0.15 and to undecided with probability 0.35. An undecided will switch to humanities or science with probabilities of 0.5 and 0.3, respectively.

(a) Find the long-range prediction for the fraction of students in each of these three majors.

(b) Compare the result of part (a) with the result of Exercise 23. Make a conjecture, and describe how this conjecture, if true, would allow you to predict the answer to part (a) with very little computation.

38. Rumors The manager of the slot machines at a major casino makes a decision about whether or not to "loosen up" the slots so that the customers get a larger payback. The manager tells only one other person, a person whose word cannot be trusted. In fact, there is only a probability p, where $0 < p < 1$, that this person will tell the truth. Suppose this person tells several other people, each of whom tells several people, what the manager's decision is. Suppose there is always a probability p that the decision is passed on as heard. Find the long-range prediction for the fraction of the people who will hear the decision correctly. (*Hint:* Use a transition matrix; let the first column be $\begin{bmatrix} p \\ 1-p \end{bmatrix}$ and the second column be $\begin{bmatrix} 1-p \\ p \end{bmatrix}$.)

39. Education A study of students taking a 20-question chemistry exam tracked their progress from one testing period to the next. For simplicity, we have grouped students scoring from 0 to 5 in group 1, from 6 to 10 in group 2, from 11 to 15 in group 3, and from 15 to 20 in group 4. The result is the following transition matrix. *Source: National Forum of Teacher Education Journal.*

	1.	2	3	4
1	0.065	0.042	0.018	0
2	0.585	0.44	0.276	0.044
3	0.34	0.42	0.452	0.292
4	0.01	0.098	0.254	0.664

(a) Find the long-range prediction for the proportion of the students in each group.

(b) The authors of this study were interested in the number of testing periods required before a certain proportion of the students had mastered the material. Suppose that once a student reaches group 4, the student is said to have mastered the material and is no longer tested, so the student stays in that group forever. Initially, all of the students in the study were in group 1. Find the number of testing periods you would expect for at least 70% of the students to have mastered the material. (*Hint:* Try increasing values of n in $P^n v_0$.)

Physical Sciences

40. Weather The weather in a certain spot is classified as fair, cloudy without rain, or rainy. A fair day is followed by a fair day 60% of the time and by a cloudy day 25% of the time. A cloudy day is followed by a cloudy day 35% of the time and by a rainy day 25% of the time. A rainy day is followed by a cloudy day 40% of the time and by another rainy day 25% of the time. What proportion of days are expected to be fair, cloudy, and rainy over the long term?

General Interest

41. Ehrenfest Chain The model for the Ehrenfest chain consists of 2 boxes containing a total of n balls, where n is any integer greater than or equal to 2. In each turn, a ball is picked at random and moved from whatever box it is in to the other box. Let the state of the Markov process be the number of balls in the first box.

(a) Verify that the probability of going from state i to state j is given by the following.

$$p_{ji} = \begin{cases} \frac{j}{n} & \text{if } j \geq 1 \text{ and } i = j - 1 \\ 1 - \frac{j}{n} & \text{if } j \leq n - 1 \text{ and } i = j + 1 \\ 1 & \text{if } j = 0 \text{ and } i = 1 \text{ or } j = n \text{ and } i = n - 1 \\ 0 & \text{otherwise.} \end{cases}$$

(b) Verify that the transition matrix is given by

$$\begin{array}{c} 0 \\ 1 \\ 2 \\ 3 \\ \vdots \\ n \end{array} \begin{bmatrix} 0 & \frac{1}{n} & 0 & \cdots & 0 \\ 1 & 0 & \frac{2}{n} & \cdots & 0 \\ 0 & 1 - \frac{1}{n} & 0 & \cdots & 0 \\ 0 & 0 & 1 - \frac{2}{n} & \cdots & 0 \\ \vdots & \vdots & \vdots & & \vdots \\ 0 & 0 & 0 & \cdots & 0 \end{bmatrix}$$

(c) Write the transition matrix for the case $n = 2$.

(d) Determine whether the transition matrix in part (c) is a regular transition matrix.

(e) Determine an equilibrium vector for the matrix in part (c). Explain what the result means.

42. Language One of Markov's own applications was a 1913 study of how often a vowel is followed by another vowel or a consonant by another consonant in Russian text. A similar study of a passage of English text revealed the following transition matrix.

	Vowel	Consonant
Vowel	0.12	0.54
Consonant	0.88	0.46

Find the percent of letters in English text that are expected to be vowels.

43. Random Walk Many phenomena can be viewed as examples of a random walk. Consider the following simple example. A security guard can stand in front of any one of three doors 20 ft apart in front of a building, and every minute he decides whether to move to another door chosen at random. If he is at the middle door, he is equally likely to stay where he is, move to the door to the left, or to move to the door to the right. If he is at the door on either end, he is equally likely to stay where he is or move to the middle door.

(a) Verify that the transition matrix is given by

$$\begin{array}{cc} & \begin{array}{ccc} 1 & 2 & 3 \end{array} \\ \begin{array}{c} 1 \\ 2 \\ 3 \end{array} & \begin{bmatrix} \frac{1}{2} & \frac{1}{3} & 0 \\ \frac{1}{2} & \frac{1}{3} & \frac{1}{2} \\ 0 & \frac{1}{3} & \frac{1}{2} \end{bmatrix}. \end{array}$$

(b) Find the long-range trend for the fraction of time the guard spends in front of each door.

44. Music Markov chains have been used to study music. The relative frequency with which one note is followed by another in a particular song can be recorded in a transition matrix, which can then be used to generate random sequences of notes with the same frequency pattern. If the rhythms are also incorporated, new songs that, are in some way similar to the original song can be generated. *Source: Significance*.

(a) Consider the simple melody "Merrily We Roll Along," with the following sequences of notes in the key of G:

BAGABBB
AAABBB
BAGABBB
AABAG.

Suppose this song is played in a loop, so that the final G is followed by the initial B. Construct a transition matrix for this melody. For example, of the 12 occurrences of B, 5 are followed by A, so the entry in column B, row A, is 5/12

(b) Determine an equilibrium vector for the matrix in part (a). Then explain why, in retrospect, this result is obvious by looking at the frequency of notes in the original melody.

YOUR TURN ANSWERS

1. C is regular. **2.** $\begin{bmatrix} 0.4 \\ 0.6 \end{bmatrix}$ **3.** $\begin{bmatrix} 0.2069 \\ 0.0690 \\ 0.7241 \end{bmatrix}$

15.3 Absorbing Markov Chains

APPLY IT If a gambler gambles until she either goes broke or wins some predetermined amount of money, what is the probability that she will eventually go broke?

Using properties of absorbing Markov chains, we will answer this question in Example 2.

Suppose a Markov chain has transition matrix

$$
\begin{array}{c}
\\ 1 \\ 2 \\ 3
\end{array}
\begin{array}{ccc}
1 & 2 & 3
\end{array}
\\
\begin{bmatrix}
0.3 & 0 & 0.6 \\
0.6 & 1 & 0.2 \\
0.1 & 0 & 0.2
\end{bmatrix} = P.
$$

The matrix shows that p_{21}, the probability of going from state 1 to state 2, is 0.6, and that p_{22}, the probability of staying in state 2, is 1. Thus, once state 2 is entered, it is impossible to leave. For this reason, state 2 is called an *absorbing state*. Figure 7 shows a transition diagram for this matrix. The diagram shows that it is not possible to leave state 2.

Generalizing from this example leads to the following definition.

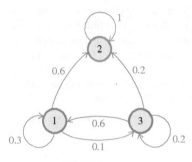

FIGURE 7

Absorbing State

State *i* of a Markov chain is an **absorbing state** if $p_{ii} = 1$.

Using the idea of an absorbing state, we can define an *absorbing Markov chain*.

Absorbing Markov Chain

A Markov chain is an **absorbing chain** if and only if the following two conditions are satisfied:

1. the chain has at least one absorbing state; and

2. it is possible to go from any nonabsorbing state to some absorbing state (perhaps in more than one step). That is, every non absorbing state must eventually proceed to an absorbing state.

Note that the second condition does not mean that it is possible to go from any nonabsorbing state to *any* absorbing state, but it is possible to go to *some* absorbing state.

EXAMPLE 1 **Absorbing Markov Chain**

Identify all absorbing states in the Markov chains having the following matrices. Decide whether the Markov chain is absorbing.

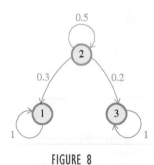

FIGURE 8

$$
\textbf{(a)} \quad
\begin{array}{c}
1 \\ 2 \\ 3
\end{array}
\begin{array}{ccc}
1 & 2 & 3
\end{array}
\\
\begin{bmatrix}
1 & 0.3 & 0 \\
0 & 0.5 & 0 \\
0 & 0.2 & 1
\end{bmatrix}
$$

SOLUTION Since $p_{11} = 1$ and $p_{33} = 1$, both state 1 and state 3 are absorbing states. (Once these states are reached, they cannot be left.) The only nonabsorbing state is state 2. There is a 0.3 probability of going from state 2 to the absorbing state 1, and a 0.2 probability of going from state 2 to state 3, so that it is possible to go from the nonabsorbing state to an absorbing state. This Markov chain is absorbing. The transition diagram is shown in Figure 8.

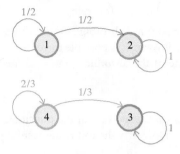

FIGURE 9

YOUR TURN 1 Identify all absorbing states in the following transition matrix. Decide whether the Markov chain is absorbing.

$$\begin{array}{c} \\ 1 \\ 2 \\ 3 \\ 4 \end{array}\begin{array}{cccc} 1 & 2 & 3 & 4 \end{array}\\ \begin{bmatrix} 1 & \frac{1}{5} & 0 & \frac{1}{4} \\ 0 & \frac{2}{5} & 0 & \frac{3}{4} \\ 0 & 0 & 1 & 0 \\ 0 & \frac{2}{5} & 0 & 0 \end{bmatrix}$$

(b)

$$\begin{array}{c} \\ 1 \\ 2 \\ 3 \\ 4 \end{array}\begin{array}{cccc} 1 & 2 & 3 & 4 \end{array}\\ \begin{bmatrix} \frac{1}{2} & 0 & 0 & 0 \\ \frac{1}{2} & 1 & 0 & 0 \\ 0 & 0 & 1 & \frac{1}{3} \\ 0 & 0 & 0 & \frac{2}{3} \end{bmatrix}$$

SOLUTION Since $p_{22} = 1$ and $p_{33} = 1$, both states 2 and 3 are absorbing. States 1 and 4 are nonabsorbing. As the transition diagram in Figure 9 shows, it is possible to go from state 1 to state 2 and from state 4 to state 3. Thus, it is possible to go from any nonabsorbing state to some absorbing state, so this Markov chain is absorbing.

(c)

$$\begin{array}{c} \\ 1 \\ 2 \\ 3 \\ 4 \end{array}\begin{array}{cccc} 1 & 2 & 3 & 4 \end{array}\\ \begin{bmatrix} 0.6 & 0 & 0.9 & 0 \\ 0 & 1 & 0 & 0 \\ 0.4 & 0 & 0.1 & 0 \\ 0 & 0 & 0 & 1 \end{bmatrix}$$

SOLUTION States 2 and 4 are absorbing, with states 1 and 3 nonabsorbing. From state 1, it is possible to go only to states 1 or 3; from state 3 it is possible to go only to states 1 or 3. As the transition diagram in Figure 10 shows, neither nonabsorbing state leads to an absorbing state, so that this Markov chain is nonabsorbing. **TRY YOUR TURN 1**

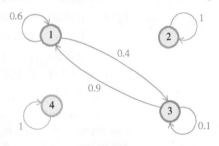

FIGURE 10

EXAMPLE 2 **Gambler's Ruin**

Suppose players A and B have a coin tossing game going on—a fair coin is tossed and the player predicting the toss correctly wins $1 from the other player. Suppose the players have a total of $6 between them and that the game goes on until one player has no money (is ruined).

(a) Write a transition matrix for this game.

SOLUTION Let us agree that the states of this system are the amounts of money held by player A. There are seven possible states: A can have 0, 1, 2, 3, 4, 5, or 6 dollars. When either state 0 or state 6 is reached, the game is over. In any other state, the amount of money held by player A will increase by $1, or decrease by $1, with each of these events having probability 1/2 (since we assume a fair coin). For example, in state 3 (A has $3), there is a 1/2 chance of changing to state 2 and a 1/2 chance of changing to state 4. Thus, $p_{23} = 1/2$ and $p_{43} = 1/2$. The probability of changing from state 3 to any other state is 0. Using this information gives the following 7×7 transition matrix.

$$\begin{array}{c} \\ 0 \\ 1 \\ 2 \\ 3 \\ 4 \\ 5 \\ 6 \end{array}\begin{array}{ccccccc} 0 & 1 & 2 & 3 & 4 & 5 & 6 \end{array}\\ \begin{bmatrix} 1 & \frac{1}{2} & 0 & 0 & 0 & 0 & 0 \\ 0 & 0 & \frac{1}{2} & 0 & 0 & 0 & 0 \\ 0 & \frac{1}{2} & 0 & \frac{1}{2} & 0 & 0 & 0 \\ 0 & 0 & \frac{1}{2} & 0 & \frac{1}{2} & 0 & 0 \\ 0 & 0 & 0 & \frac{1}{2} & 0 & \frac{1}{2} & 0 \\ 0 & 0 & 0 & 0 & \frac{1}{2} & 0 & 0 \\ 0 & 0 & 0 & 0 & 0 & \frac{1}{2} & 1 \end{bmatrix} = P$$

(b) Identify all absorbing states. Decide whether the Markov chain is absorbing.

SOLUTION   Based on the rules of the game, states 0 and 6 are absorbing—once these states are reached, they can never be left, and the game is over. It is possible to get from one of the nonabsorbing states, 1, 2, 3, 4, or 5, to one of the absorbing states, so the Markov chain is absorbing.

(c) Estimate the long-term trend of the game.

APPLY IT

SOLUTION   For the long-term trend of the game, find various powers of the transition matrix. A computer or a graphing calculator can be used to verify the following results.

$$P^{20} = \begin{bmatrix} 1.0000 & 0.8146 & 0.6385 & 0.4625 & 0.3052 & 0.1479 & 0.0000 \\ 0.0000 & 0.0094 & 0.0000 & 0.0188 & 0.0000 & 0.0094 & 0.0000 \\ 0.0000 & 0.0000 & 0.0282 & 0.0000 & 0.0282 & 0.0000 & 0.0000 \\ 0.0000 & 0.0188 & 0.0000 & 0.0375 & 0.0000 & 0.0188 & 0.0000 \\ 0.0000 & 0.0000 & 0.0282 & 0.0000 & 0.0282 & 0.0000 & 0.0000 \\ 0.0000 & 0.0094 & 0.0000 & 0.0188 & 0.0000 & 0.0094 & 0.0000 \\ 0.0000 & 0.1479 & 0.3052 & 0.4625 & 0.6385 & 0.8146 & 1.0000 \end{bmatrix}$$

$$P^{70} = \begin{bmatrix} 1.0000 & 0.8333 & 0.6667 & 0.5000 & 0.3333 & 0.1667 & 0.0000 \\ 0.0000 & 0.0000 & 0.0000 & 0.0000 & 0.0000 & 0.0000 & 0.0000 \\ 0.0000 & 0.0000 & 0.0000 & 0.0000 & 0.0000 & 0.0000 & 0.0000 \\ 0.0000 & 0.0000 & 0.0000 & 0.0000 & 0.0000 & 0.0000 & 0.0000 \\ 0.0000 & 0.0000 & 0.0000 & 0.0000 & 0.0000 & 0.0000 & 0.0000 \\ 0.0000 & 0.0000 & 0.0000 & 0.0000 & 0.0000 & 0.0000 & 0.0000 \\ 0.0000 & 0.1667 & 0.3333 & 0.5000 & 0.6667 & 0.8333 & 1.0000 \end{bmatrix}$$

As these results suggest, the system tends toward one of the absorbing states, so that the probability is 1 that one of the two gamblers will be wiped out. The probability that player A will end in state 0 (player A is ruined) depends on player A's initial state. For example, if player A starts with \$2 (state 2), there is a probability of 0.6667 (row 1, column 3 of P^{70}) of player A going broke (state 0), but if player A starts with \$5, there is only a probability of 0.1667 (row 1, column 6 of P^{70}) of player A going broke.

EXAMPLE 3   Long-term Trend

Estimate the long-term trend for the following transition matrix.

$$P = \begin{bmatrix} 0.2 & 0 & 0 \\ 0.3 & 1 & 0 \\ 0.5 & 0 & 1 \end{bmatrix}$$

SOLUTION   Both states 2 and 3 are absorbing, and since it is possible to go from nonabsorbing state 1 to an absorbing state, the chain will eventually enter either state 2 or state 3. To find the long-term trend, let us find various powers of P.

$$P^2 = \begin{bmatrix} 0.04 & 0 & 0 \\ 0.36 & 1 & 0 \\ 0.6 & 0 & 1 \end{bmatrix} \qquad P^4 = \begin{bmatrix} 0.0016 & 0 & 0 \\ 0.3744 & 1 & 0 \\ 0.624 & 0 & 1 \end{bmatrix}$$

$$P^8 = \begin{bmatrix} 0.000 & 0 & 0 \\ 0.375 & 1 & 0 \\ 0.625 & 0 & 1 \end{bmatrix} \qquad P^{16} = \begin{bmatrix} 0.000 & 0 & 0 \\ 0.375 & 1 & 0 \\ 0.625 & 0 & 1 \end{bmatrix}$$

Based on these powers, it appears that the transition matrix is getting closer and closer to the stability matrix

$$\hat{P} = \begin{bmatrix} 0.000 & 0 & 0 \\ 0.375 & 1 & 0 \\ 0.625 & 0 & 1 \end{bmatrix}.$$

If the system is originally in state 1, there is no chance it will end up in state 1, but a $0.375 = 3/8$ chance that it will end up in state 2 and a $0.625 = 5/8$ chance it will end up in state 3. If the system was originally in state 2, it will end up in state 2; a similar statement can be made for state 3.

The examples suggest the following properties of absorbing Markov chains, which can be verified using more advanced methods.

1. Regardless of the original state of an absorbing Markov chain, in a finite number of steps the chain will enter an absorbing state and then stay in that state.

2. As with regular matrices, the successive larger powers of P^n approximate the stability matrix $\hat{P}$ for P. Specifically, $\lim\limits_{n \to \infty} P^n = \hat{P}$.

3. The long-term trend depends on the initial state—changing the initial state can change the final result.

The third property distinguishes absorbing Markov chains from regular Markov chains, where the final result is independent of the initial state.

As in our treatment of regular matrices, we now would like a simple way of finding the stability matrix $\hat{P}$ for an absorbing matrix P without taking limits. Unlike regular matrices, however, the value of $\hat{P}$ depends on the specific initial condition, so clearly we need a different approach.

First rewrite P in **standard form**, namely by reorganizing rows and columns into non-absorbing and absorbing states as follows:

	0	6	1	2	3	4	5
0	1	0	$\frac{1}{2}$	0	0	0	0
6	0	1	0	0	0	0	$\frac{1}{2}$
1	0	0	0	$\frac{1}{2}$	0	0	0
2	0	0	$\frac{1}{2}$	0	$\frac{1}{2}$	0	0
3	0	0	0	$\frac{1}{2}$	0	$\frac{1}{2}$	0
4	0	0	0	0	$\frac{1}{2}$	0	$\frac{1}{2}$
5	0	0	0	0	0	$\frac{1}{2}$	0

Absorbing: rows 0, 6. Nonabsorbing: rows 1, 2, 3, 4, 5. $= P$

Teaching Tip: Illustrate the construction of P, the transition matrix for an absorbing Markov chain, very carefully. Make sure the students can identify I_{np}, Q, R, O, and the number of absorbing states.

Let I_2 represent the 2×2 identity matrix in the upper left corner; let O represent the matrix of zeros in the lower left; let R represent the matrix in the upper right, and let Q represent the matrix in the lower right. Using these symbols, P can be written as

$$P = \left[\begin{array}{c|c} I_2 & R \\ \hline O & Q \end{array}\right].$$

The **fundamental matrix** for an absorbing Markov chain is defined as matrix F, where

$$F = (I_n - Q)^{-1}.$$

Here I_n is the $n \times n$ identity matrix corresponding in size to matrix Q, so that the difference $I_n - Q$ exists.

For the gambler's ruin problem, using I_5 gives

$$F = \left(\begin{bmatrix} 1 & 0 & 0 & 0 & 0 \\ 0 & 1 & 0 & 0 & 0 \\ 0 & 0 & 1 & 0 & 0 \\ 0 & 0 & 0 & 1 & 0 \\ 0 & 0 & 0 & 0 & 1 \end{bmatrix} - \begin{bmatrix} 0 & \frac{1}{2} & 0 & 0 & 0 \\ \frac{1}{2} & 0 & \frac{1}{2} & 0 & 0 \\ 0 & \frac{1}{2} & 0 & \frac{1}{2} & 0 \\ 0 & 0 & \frac{1}{2} & 0 & \frac{1}{2} \\ 0 & 0 & 0 & \frac{1}{2} & 0 \end{bmatrix} \right)^{-1}$$

$$= \begin{bmatrix} 1 & -\frac{1}{2} & 0 & 0 & 0 \\ -\frac{1}{2} & 1 & -\frac{1}{2} & 0 & 0 \\ 0 & -\frac{1}{2} & 1 & -\frac{1}{2} & 0 \\ 0 & 0 & -\frac{1}{2} & 1 & -\frac{1}{2} \\ 0 & 0 & 0 & -\frac{1}{2} & 1 \end{bmatrix}^{-1}$$

$$= \begin{array}{c} \\ 1 \\ 2 \\ 3 \\ 4 \\ 5 \end{array} \begin{bmatrix} \frac{5}{3} & \frac{4}{3} & 1 & \frac{2}{3} & \frac{1}{3} \\ \frac{4}{3} & \frac{8}{3} & 2 & \frac{4}{3} & \frac{2}{3} \\ 1 & 2 & 3 & 2 & 1 \\ \frac{2}{3} & \frac{4}{3} & 2 & \frac{8}{3} & \frac{4}{3} \\ \frac{1}{3} & \frac{2}{3} & 1 & \frac{4}{3} & \frac{5}{3} \end{bmatrix}$$

The inverse was found using techniques from a previous chapter. Recall, we also discussed finding the inverse of a matrix with a graphing calculator there.

We have yet to find the stability matrix $\hat{P}$ for P, although if P is an absorbing Markov matrix, its fundamental matrix F is usually equally important. Specifically, the ij^{th} entry $[F]_{ij}$ can be interpreted as the average number of times a process that begins at non-absorbing state j can expect to be in state i before proceeding to one of its absorbing states. So, in this example, if player A currently has $2, then the second column of the fundamental matrix just computed says that she expects to have $1 an average of $1\frac{1}{3}$ times, and to have $3 twice, before quitting the game because she either runs out of money or wins $6. The total number of times that player A expects to have various amounts of money before quitting the game is the sum of entries in column 2 of F: $(4/3) + (8/3) + 2 + (4/3) + (2/3) = 8$. In other words, if player A currently has $2, she can expect to stay in the game 8 more turns before either she or player B goes broke.

To see why this is true, consider a Markov chain currently in state j. The expected number of times that the chain visits state i at this step is 1 for $i = j$ and 0 for all other states. The expected number of times that the chain visits state i at the next step is given by the element in row i, column j of the transition matrix Q. The expected number of times the chain visits state i two steps from now is given by the corresponding entry in the matrix Q^2. The expected number of visits in all steps is given by $I + Q + Q^2 + Q^3 + \cdots$. To find out whether this infinite sum is the same as $(I - Q)^{-1}$, multiply the sum by $(I - Q)$:

$$(I + Q + Q^2 + Q^3 + \cdots)(I - Q)$$
$$= I + Q + Q^2 + Q^3 + \cdots - Q - Q^2 - Q^3 + \cdots = I,$$

which verifies our result.

It can be shown that

$$P^k = \left[\begin{array}{c|c} I_m & R(I + Q + Q^2 + \ldots + Q^{k-1}) \\ \hline O & Q^k \end{array} \right]$$

where I_m is the $m \times m$ identity matrix. As k gets larger and larger (denoted by $k \rightarrow \infty$), Q^k approaches O_n (denoted by $Q^k \rightarrow O_n$), the $n \times n$ zero matrix, and

$$P^k \rightarrow \left[\begin{array}{c|c} I_m & RF \\ \hline O & O_n \end{array} \right],$$

so we see that RF gives the probabilities that if the system was originally in a nonabsorbing state, it ends up in one of the absorbing states.*

Finally, use the fundamental matrix F along with matrix R found above to get the product RF.

$$RF = \begin{bmatrix} \frac{1}{2} & 0 & 0 & 0 & 0 \\ 0 & 0 & 0 & 0 & \frac{1}{2} \end{bmatrix} \begin{bmatrix} \frac{5}{3} & \frac{4}{3} & 1 & \frac{2}{3} & \frac{1}{3} \\ \frac{4}{3} & \frac{8}{3} & 2 & \frac{4}{3} & \frac{2}{3} \\ 1 & 2 & 3 & 2 & 1 \\ \frac{2}{3} & \frac{4}{3} & 2 & \frac{8}{3} & \frac{4}{3} \\ \frac{1}{3} & \frac{2}{3} & 1 & \frac{4}{3} & \frac{5}{3} \end{bmatrix} = \begin{array}{c} \\ 0 \\ 6 \end{array} \begin{bmatrix} \overset{1}{\frac{5}{6}} & \overset{2}{\frac{2}{3}} & \overset{3}{\frac{1}{2}} & \overset{4}{\frac{1}{3}} & \overset{5}{\frac{1}{6}} \\ \frac{1}{6} & \frac{1}{3} & \frac{1}{2} & \frac{2}{3} & \frac{5}{6} \end{bmatrix}$$

The product matrix RF gives the probability that if the system was originally in a nonabsorbing state, it ended up in either of the two absorbing states. For example, the probability is $2/3$ that if the system was originally in state 2, it ended up in state 0; the probability is $5/6$ that if the system was originally in state 5 it ended up in state 6, and so on. Based on the original statement of the gambler's ruin problem, if player A starts with \$2 (state 2), there is a $2/3$ chance of ending in state 0 (player A is ruined); if player A starts with \$5 (state 5) there is a $1/6$ chance of player A being ruined, and so on. (Note that these results agree with the estimates found in Example 2.)

In the fundamental matrix F, the sum of the elements in column j gives the expected number of steps for the matrix to enter an absorbing state from the jth nonabsorbing state. Thus, for $j = 2$, $(4/3) + (8/3) + 2 + (4/3) + (2/3) = 8$ steps will be needed on the average for the system to go from state 2 to an absorbing state (0 or 6).

Let us summarize what we have learned about absorbing Markov chains.

Properties of an Absorbing Markov Chain

1. Regardless of the initial state, in a finite number of steps the chain will enter an absorbing state and then stay in that state.

2. The powers of the transition matrix get closer and closer to some particular matrix, $\hat{P}$. That is, $\lim\limits_{n \to \infty} P^n = \hat{P}$.

3. The long-term trend depends on the initial state.

4. Rearranging the rows and columns of a transition matrix P for an absorbing Markov chain so that the absorbing states come first gives the standard form

$$P = \left[\begin{array}{c|c} I_m & R \\ \hline O & Q \end{array} \right],$$

where I_m is an identity matrix, with m equal to the number of absorbing states, and O is a matrix of all zeros. The fundamental matrix is defined as

$$F = (I_n - Q)^{-1},$$

where I_n has the same size as Q. The element in row i, column j of the fundamental matrix gives the average number of times a process that begins at nonabsorbing state j can expect to be in state i before proceeding to one of its absorbing states.

5. The product RF gives the matrix of probabilities that a particular initial nonabsorbing state will lead to a particular absorbing state.

*We have omitted details in these steps that can be justified using advanced techniques.

EXAMPLE 4 Long-term Trend

Find the long-term trend for the transition matrix

$$\begin{bmatrix} 0.2 & 0 & 0 \\ 0.3 & 1 & 0 \\ 0.5 & 0 & 1 \end{bmatrix} = P$$

of Example 3.

SOLUTION Rewrite the matrix so that absorbing states 2 and 3 come first.

$$\begin{array}{c} \\ 2 \\ 3 \\ 1 \end{array} \begin{array}{ccc} 2 & 3 & 1 \\ \begin{bmatrix} 1 & 0 & 0.3 \\ 0 & 1 & 0.5 \\ 0 & 0 & 0.2 \end{bmatrix} \end{array}$$

Here $R = \begin{bmatrix} 0.3 \\ 0.5 \end{bmatrix}$ and $Q = [0.2]$. Find the fundamental matrix F.

$$F = (I_1 - Q)^{-1} = [1 - 0.2]^{-1} = [0.8]^{-1} = [1/0.8] = [10/8] = [5/4]$$

This tells us that the expected number of steps before ending up in an absorbing state is 5/4.

The product RF is

$$RF = \begin{bmatrix} 0.3 \\ 0.5 \end{bmatrix} [5/4] = \begin{bmatrix} 3/8 \\ 5/8 \end{bmatrix}$$

If the system starts in the nonabsorbing state 1, there is a 3/8 chance of ending up in the absorbing state 2 and a 5/8 chance of ending up in the absorbing state 3. **TRY YOUR TURN 2**

YOUR TURN 2 Find the long-term trend for the transition matrix

$$\begin{bmatrix} 1 & 0.1 & 0 \\ 0 & 0.6 & 0 \\ 0 & 0.3 & 1 \end{bmatrix}.$$

15.3 WARMUP EXERCISES

Find the inverse of each of the following matrices. (Sec. 2.5)

W1. $\begin{bmatrix} 4 & 2 \\ 8 & 7 \end{bmatrix}$ **W2.** $\begin{bmatrix} 3 & 5 \\ 1 & 7 \end{bmatrix}$

15.3 EXERCISES

Find all absorbing states for each transition matrix. Which are transition matrices for absorbing Markov chains?

1. $\begin{bmatrix} 0.25 & 0.35 & 0 \\ 0.05 & 0 & 0 \\ 0.7 & 0.65 & 1 \end{bmatrix}$

2. $\begin{bmatrix} 0.15 & 0 & 0.3 \\ 0.35 & 1 & 0.3 \\ 0.5 & 0 & 0.4 \end{bmatrix}$

3. $\begin{bmatrix} 1 & 0 & 0 \\ 0 & 0.25 & 0.85 \\ 0 & 0.75 & 0.15 \end{bmatrix}$

4. $\begin{bmatrix} 0.4 & 0 & 0.5 \\ 0 & 1 & 0 \\ 0.6 & 0 & 0.5 \end{bmatrix}$

5. $\begin{bmatrix} 0.2 & 0 & 0.9 & 0 \\ 0.5 & 1 & 0.02 & 0 \\ 0.1 & 0 & 0.04 & 0 \\ 0.2 & 0 & 0.04 & 1 \end{bmatrix}$

6. $\begin{bmatrix} 0.32 & 0.42 & 0 & 1 \\ 0.41 & 0.30 & 0 & 0 \\ 0.16 & 0 & 0 & 0 \\ 0.11 & 0.28 & 1 & 0 \end{bmatrix}$

Find the fundamental matrix F for the absorbing Markov chains with the matrices in Exercises 7–14. Also, find the product matrix RF.

7. $\begin{bmatrix} 1 & 0 & 0.15 \\ 0 & 1 & 0.35 \\ 0 & 0 & 0.5 \end{bmatrix}$

8. $\begin{bmatrix} 1 & 0.65 & 0 \\ 0 & 0.1 & 0 \\ 0 & 0.25 & 1 \end{bmatrix}$

9. $\begin{bmatrix} 1 & 0 & \frac{1}{2} \\ 0 & 1 & \frac{1}{6} \\ 0 & 0 & \frac{1}{3} \end{bmatrix}$

10. $\begin{bmatrix} 1 & \frac{5}{8} & 0 \\ 0 & \frac{1}{8} & 0 \\ 0 & \frac{1}{4} & 1 \end{bmatrix}$

11. $\begin{bmatrix} 1 & \frac{1}{3} & 0 & \frac{1}{4} \\ 0 & 0 & 0 & \frac{1}{4} \\ 0 & \frac{2}{3} & 1 & \frac{1}{4} \\ 0 & 0 & 0 & \frac{1}{4} \end{bmatrix}$

12. $\begin{bmatrix} \frac{1}{4} & 0 & 0 & \frac{1}{2} \\ \frac{1}{2} & 1 & 0 & 0 \\ 0 & 0 & 1 & 0 \\ \frac{1}{4} & 0 & 0 & \frac{1}{2} \end{bmatrix}$

13. $\begin{bmatrix} 1 & 0 & 0.1 & 0.3 & 0 \\ 0 & 1 & 0.2 & 0.5 & 0 \\ 0 & 0 & 0.3 & 0.1 & 0 \\ 0 & 0 & 0.2 & 0 & 0 \\ 0 & 0 & 0.2 & 0.1 & 1 \end{bmatrix}$

14. $\begin{bmatrix} 0.4 & 0 & 0 & 0.1 & 0 \\ 0.2 & 1 & 0 & 0.5 & 0 \\ 0.3 & 0 & 1 & 0.1 & 0 \\ 0 & 0 & 0 & 0.1 & 0 \\ 0.1 & 0 & 0 & 0.2 & 1 \end{bmatrix}$

15. (a) Write a transition matrix for a gambler's ruin problem when player A and player B start with a total of $4. (See Example 2.)

(b) Find matrix F for this transition matrix, and find the product matrix RF.

(c) Suppose player A starts with $1. What is the probability of ruin for A?

(d) Suppose player A starts with $3. What is the probability of ruin for A?

16. Suppose player B (Exercise 15) slips in a coin that is slightly "loaded"—such that the probability that B wins a particular toss changes from 1/2 to 3/5. Suppose that A and B start the game with a total of $5.

(a) If B starts with $3, find the probability that A will be ruined.

(b) If B starts with $1, find the probability that A will be ruined.

It can be shown that the probability of ruin for player A in a game such as the one described in this section is

$$x_a = \frac{b}{a+b} \text{ if } r = 1, \quad \text{and} \quad x_a = \frac{r^a - r^{a+b}}{1 - r^{a+b}} \text{ if } r \neq 1,$$

where a is the initial amount of money that player A has, b is the initial amount that player B has, $r = (1 - p)/p$, and p is the probability that player A will win on a given play.

17. Find the probability that A will be ruined if $a = 10$, $b = 30$, and $p = 0.49$.

18. Find the probability in Exercise 17 if p changes to 0.50.

19. Complete the following chart, assuming $a = 10$ and $b = 10$.

p	0.1	0.2	0.3	0.4	0.5	0.6	0.7	0.8	0.9
x_a									

20. How can we calculate the expected total number of times a Markov chain will visit state i before absorption, regardless of the current state?

21. Suppose an absorbing Markov chain has only one absorbing state. What is the product RF?

22. In the case with two absorbing states and one nonabsorbing state, as in Example 4, there is an easy way to find the probability of ending up in each of the absorbing states.

(a) Let states 1 and 2 be the absorbing states, and let state 3 be the nonabsorbing state. Suppose the probability of going from states 3 to state 1 is p, and to state 2 is q, where $p + q < 1$. Find the transition matrix for this Markov chain.

(b) Show that the probabilities of ending up in state 1 and state 2 are $p/(p + q)$ and $q/(p + q)$, respectively.

(c) Use the result from part (b) to quickly calculate the probabilities of ending up in states 2 and 3 in Example 4.

APPLICATIONS

Business and Economics

23. Solar Energy In Exercise 31 of the first section of this chapter, a community began a campaign to convince homeowners to convert their energy source for home heating to solar energy.

The leaders estimated the probability of homeowners changing their home heating energy source each year, giving the following transition matrix.

	electric	fossil	solar
electric	0.9	0.15	0
fossil	0.05	0.75	0
solar	0.05	0.1	1

(a) Find F and RF.

(b) Find the probability that a homeowner in this community will eventually use solar energy for home heating.

(c) Find the expected number of years until a homeowner who is presently using electric heat will convert to solar energy for a heating energy source.

24. Company Training Program A company with a new training program classified each worker into one of the following four categories: s_1, never in the program; s_2, currently in the program; s_3, discharged; s_4, completed the program. The transition matrix for this company is given below.

	s_1	s_2	s_3	s_4
s_1	0.4	0	0	0
s_2	0.2	0.45	0	0
s_3	0.05	0.05	1	0
s_4	0.35	0.5	0	1

(a) Find F and RF.

(b) Find the probability that a worker originally in the program is discharged.

(c) Find the probability that a worker not originally in the program goes on to complete the program.

Life Sciences

25. Contagion Under certain conditions, the probability that a person will get a particular contagious disease and die from it is 0.05, and the probability of getting the disease and surviving is 0.15. The probability that a survivor will infect another person who dies from it is also 0.05, that a survivor will infect another person who survives it is 0.15, and so on. A transition matrix using the following states is given on the next page. A person in state 1 is one who gets the disease and dies, a person in state 2 gets the disease and survives, and a person in state 3 does not get the disease. Consider a chain of people, each of whom interacts with the previous person and may catch the disease from that individual, and then may infect the next person.

(a) Verify that the transition matrix is as follows:

		First Person		
		1	2	3
	1	0.05	0.05	0
Second Person	2	0.15	0.15	0
	3	0.8	0.8	1

(b) Find F and RF.

(c) Find the probability that the disease eventually disappears.

(d) Given a person who has the disease and survives, find the expected number of people in the chain who will get the disease until a person who does not get the disease is reached.

26. Medical Prognosis A study using Markov chains to estimate a patient's prognosis for improving under various treatment plans gives the following transition matrix as an example. *Source: Medical Decision Making.*

$$
\begin{array}{c c}
 & \begin{array}{c c c} \text{Well} & \text{Ill} & \text{Dead} \end{array} \\
\begin{array}{c} \text{Well} \\ \text{Ill} \\ \text{Dead} \end{array} &
\left[\begin{array}{c c c}
0.3 & 0 & 0 \\
0.5 & 0.5 & 0 \\
0.2 & 0.5 & 1
\end{array} \right]
\end{array}
$$

(a) Estimate the probability that a well person will eventually end up dead.

(b) Verify your answer to part (a) using the matrix product RF

(c) Find the expected number of cycles that a well patient will continue to be well before dying and the expected number of cycles that a well patient will be before dying 10/3, 10/7.

Social Sciences

27. Transportation The city of Sacramento completed a new light rail system to bring commuters and shoppers into the downtown area and relieve freeway congestion. City planners estimate that each year, 15% of those who drive or ride in an automobile will change to the light rail system; 80% will continue to use automobiles; and the rest will no longer go to the downtown area. Of those who use light rail, 5% will go back to using an automobile, 80% will continue to use light rail, and the rest will stay out of the downtown area. Assume those who do not go downtown will continue to stay out of the downtown area.

(a) Write a transition matrix. Find F and RF.

(b) Find the probability that a person who commuted by automobile ends up avoiding the downtown area.

(c) Find the expected number of years until a person who commutes by automobile this year no longer enters the downtown area.

28. Student Retention At a particular two-year college, a student has a probability of 0.25 of flunking out during a given year, a 0.15 probability of having to repeat the year, and a 0.6 probability of finishing the year. Use the states below.

State	Meaning
1	Freshman
2	Sophomore
3	Has flunked out
4	Has graduated

(a) Write a transition matrix. Find F and RF.

(b) Find the probability that a freshman will graduate.

(c) Find the expected number of years that a freshman will be in college before graduating or flunking out.

29. Rat Maze A rat is placed at random in one of the compartments of the maze pictured. The probability that a rat in compartment 1 will move to compartment 2 is 0.3, to compartment 3 is 0.2,

and to compartment 4 is 0.1. A rat in compartment 2 will move to compartments 1, 4, or 5 with probabilities of 0.2, 0.6, and 0.1, respectively. A rat in compartment 3 cannot leave that compartment. A rat in compartment 4 will move to 1, 2, 3, or 5 with probabilities of 0.1, 0.1, 0.4, and 0.3, respectively. A rat in compartment 5 cannot leave that compartment.

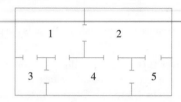

(a) Set up a transition matrix using this information. Find matrices F and RF.
Find the probability that a rat ends up in compartment 5 if it was originally in the given compartment.

(b) 1   **(c)** 2   **(d)** 3   **(e)** 4

(f) Find the expected number of times that a rat in compartment 1 will be in compartment 1 before ending up in compartment 3 or 5.

(g) Find the expected number of times that a rat in compartment 4 will be in compartment 4 before ending up in compartment 3 or 5.

30. Education Careers Data have been collected on the likelihood that a teacher, or a student with a declared interest in teaching, will continue on that career path the following year. We have simplified the classification of the original data to four groups: high school and college students, new teachers, continuing teachers, and those who have quit the profession. The transition probabilities are given in the following matrix. *Source: National Forum of Educational Administration and Supervision Journal.*

$$
\begin{array}{c c}
 & \begin{array}{c c c c} \text{Student} & \text{New} & \text{Continuing} & \text{Quit} \end{array} \\
\begin{array}{c} \text{Student} \\ \text{New} \\ \text{Continuing} \\ \text{Quit} \end{array} &
\left[\begin{array}{c c c c}
0.70 & 0 & 0 & 0 \\
0.11 & 0 & 0 & 0 \\
0 & 0.86 & 0.88 & 0 \\
0.19 & 0.14 & 0.12 & 1
\end{array} \right]
\end{array}
$$

(a) Find the expected number of years that a student with an interest in teaching will spend as a continuing teacher.

(b) Find the expected number of years that a new teacher will spend as a continuing teacher.

(c) Find the expected number of additional years that a continuing teacher will spend as a continuing teacher.

(d) Notice that the answer to part (b) is larger than the answer to part (a), and the answer to part (c) is even larger. Explain why this is to be expected.

(e) What other states might be added to this model to make it more realistic? Discuss how this would affect the transition matrix. (See the Extended Application for this chapter.)

General Interest

31. Gambler's Ruin

(a) Write a transition matrix for a gambler's ruin problem, where players A and B start with a total of $7. (See Example 2.)

(b) Find the probability of ruin for A if A starts with $4.

(c) Find the probability of ruin for A if A starts with $5.

32. Tennis Consider a game of tennis when each player has won at least two serves. After that, the first player to win two serves more than his opponent wins. There are five possibilities: Either the players are tied (deuce), the server is a point ahead (ad in), the other player is a point ahead (ad out), the server wins, or the server loses. If we assume that at each serve the server has a probability p of winning the next point, then the game can be modeled by a Markov chain. *Source: The Mathematics Teacher.*

(a) Verify that the transition matrix from the server's point of view is given by

$$
\begin{array}{c@{}c}
 & \begin{array}{ccccc} \text{Loss} & \text{Ad out} & \text{Deuce} & \text{Ad in} & \text{Win} \end{array} \\
\begin{array}{c} \text{Loss} \\ \text{Ad out} \\ \text{Deuce} \\ \text{Ad in} \\ \text{Win} \end{array} &
\left[\begin{array}{ccccc}
1 & 1-p & 0 & 0 & 0 \\
0 & 0 & 1-p & 0 & 0 \\
0 & p & 0 & 1-p & 0 \\
0 & 0 & p & 0 & 0 \\
0 & 0 & 0 & p & 1
\end{array}\right].
\end{array}
$$

(b) For the case in which $p = 0.6$, find the probability that the server will win when the score is ad out, deuce, and ad in.

33. Professional Football In Exercise 40 of the first section of this chapter, the method used by the NFL to determine the winner in an overtime game from 1974 to 2010 was analyzed. In this system, a coin was tossed and the winning team got to decide whether to kickoff or to receive the ball. The first team to score won. Based on data from the 2008 season, the following transition matrix was determined. The first column tells the probability of being in any given situation after one possession, assuming team A starts with the ball. *Source: Mathematics in Sports.*

	Possession for A	Possession for B	A wins	B wins
Possession for A	0	0.62	0	0
Possession for B	0.62	0	0	0
A wins	0.36	0.02	1	0
B wins	0.02	0.36	0	1

(a) Find F and RF.

(b) Find the probability that, if team A gets the ball first, team A wins.

(c) Find the probability that, if team B gets the ball first, team B wins.

(d) What is the expected number of possessions to determine a winner in overtime?

(e) Determine the strategy that each team should take. What does this imply about the winner of the coin toss (the one who gets to decide who gets the ball first)?

1. States 1 and 3 are absorbing states. The Markov chain is absorbing.

2. If the system starts in state 2, there is a 1/4 chance of ending up in state 1 and a 3/4 chance of ending up in state 3.

15 CHAPTER REVIEW

SUMMARY

Markov chains are useful for modeling a sequence of trials of an experiment in which the following conditions hold:

- the outcome of each experiment is one of a finite number of possible states;
- the outcome of each experiment depends only on the present state; and
- the probabilities of moving from one state to another state, known as transition probabilities, remain constant over time.

The matrix containing these probabilities is called the transition matrix P. A Markov chain can also be represented by a transition diagram, in which the states, represented by ovals, are connected by lines on which the transition probabilities are written. We saw in this chapter that to find the transition probabilities over n time periods, we raise the transition matrix to the nth power. Three other definitions presented in this chapter are the following:

- probability vector (a column matrix giving the probability of being in each state at a given time),
- regular Markov chain (some power of the transition matrix contains all positive entries), and
- absorbing Markov chain (one or more states, known as absorbing states, are impossible to leave and it is possible to go from any nonabsorbing state to some absorbing state).

A regular Markov chain has the following two properties:

- an equilibrium vector V can be found, which gives the long-range probability of being in each state;
- the powers of P^n approach a stability matrix $\hat{P}$ whose columns make up the entries of V.

The probability that a particular nonabsorbing state will lead to a particular absorbing state can be calculated by methods summarized below. The applications in this chapter show the usefulness of Markov chains, whether regular or absorbing.

Probability Vector   If v_0 is the initial probability vector and P is the transition matrix, then the probability vector after n repetitions of the experiment is

$$P^n v_0.$$

Equilibrium Vector   If a Markov chain with transition matrix P is regular, then the equilibrium vector V satisfies

$$PV = V.$$

This means that V is the normalized eigenvector corresponding to the eigenvalue $\lambda = 1$ for the regular Markov matrix P. To find V, we solve the system of equations $(P - I)X = 0$ for X and then normalize.

Absorbing Markov Chain   Rearrange the rows and columns of P so it can be written in standard form as

$$\left[\begin{array}{c|c} I_m & R \\ \hline O & Q \end{array}\right],$$

where I_m is an identity matrix, m is the number of absorbing states, and O is a matrix of all zeros.

Fundamental Matrix   The row i, column j element of the fundamental matrix

$$F = (I_n - Q)^{-1},$$

where I_n has the same size as Q, gives the expected number of visits to state i before absorption, given the current state j. The probabilities that a particular initial nonabsorbing state will lead to a particular absorbing state is given by the product

$$RF.$$

KEY TERMS

state	probability vector	stability matrix	fundamental matrix
15.1	**15.2**	**15.3**	
transition diagram	regular transition matrix	absorbing state	
transition matrix	regular Markov chain	absorbing chain	
Markov chain	equilibrium (or fixed) vector	standard form	

REVIEW EXERCISES

CONCEPT CHECK

Determine whether each of the following statements is true or false, and explain why.

1. In a Markov chain, the outcome of an experiment might depend not only on the present state but also on the state before that.

2. In a Markov chain, the transition probabilities might vary from one transition to the next.

3. A transition diagram contains the same information as a transition matrix.

4. To find the transition probabilities in k repetitions of an experiment, one should multiply the transition matrix P by k.

5. A regular transition matrix has no 0 elements.

6. A transition matrix can have more than one equilibrium vector.

7. For a regular Markov chain, the matrix equation $PV = V$ has only one solution.

8. For any transition matrix, the matrix P^n has no 0 elements if n is made large enough.

9. For any transition matrix, the matrix P^n approaches a limiting value as n is made larger and larger.

10. A transition matrix that is not regular can have an equilibrium vector.

11. A Markov chain can have more than one absorbing state.

12. An absorbing Markov chain will eventually reach an absorbing state with a probability of 1.

PRACTICE AND EXPLORATIONS

13. How can you tell by looking at a matrix whether it represents the transition matrix for a Markov chain?

14. Under what conditions is the existence of an equilibrium vector guaranteed?

Decide whether each matrix could be a transition matrix. Sketch a transition diagram for any transition matrices.

15. $\begin{bmatrix} -0.2 & 0.8 \\ 1.2 & 0.2 \end{bmatrix}$

16. $\begin{bmatrix} 0.4 & 1 \\ 0.6 & 0 \end{bmatrix}$

17. $\begin{bmatrix} 0.8 & 0 & 0.1 \\ 0.2 & 1 & 0.4 \\ 0 & 0 & 0.5 \end{bmatrix}$

18. $\begin{bmatrix} 0.6 & 0.1 & 0.3 \\ 0.2 & 0.5 & 0.3 \\ 0.3 & 0.4 & 0.4 \end{bmatrix}$

For each transition matrix, (a) find the first three powers; and (b) find the probability that state 2 changes to state 1 after three repetitions of the experiment.

19. $C = \begin{bmatrix} 0.7 & 1 \\ 0.3 & 0 \end{bmatrix}$

20. $D = \begin{bmatrix} 0.4 & 0.5 \\ 0.6 & 0.5 \end{bmatrix}$

21. $E = \begin{bmatrix} 0.2 & 0.3 & 0 \\ 0.5 & 0.4 & 1 \\ 0.3 & 0.3 & 0 \end{bmatrix}$

22. $F = \begin{bmatrix} 0.14 & 0.35 & 0.71 \\ 0.18 & 0.28 & 0.22 \\ 0.68 & 0.37 & 0.07 \end{bmatrix}$

In Exercises 23–26, use the transition matrix P, along with the given initial distribution D, to find the distribution after two repetitions of the experiment. Also, predict the long-range distribution.

23. $D = \begin{bmatrix} 0.3 \\ 0.7 \end{bmatrix}$; $P = \begin{bmatrix} 0.2 & 0.5 \\ 0.8 & 0.5 \end{bmatrix}$

24. $D = \begin{bmatrix} 0.8 \\ 0.2 \end{bmatrix}$; $P = \begin{bmatrix} 0.9 & 0.2 \\ 0.1 & 0.8 \end{bmatrix}$

25. $D = \begin{bmatrix} 0.2 \\ 0.4 \\ 0.4 \end{bmatrix}$; $P = \begin{bmatrix} 0.7 & 0.3 & 0.4 \\ 0.1 & 0.3 & 0.5 \\ 0.2 & 0.4 & 0.1 \end{bmatrix}$

26. $D = \begin{bmatrix} 0.1 \\ 0.1 \\ 0.8 \end{bmatrix}$; $P = \begin{bmatrix} 0.2 & 0.1 & 0.5 \\ 0.1 & 0.1 & 0.1 \\ 0.7 & 0.8 & 0.4 \end{bmatrix}$

Decide whether each transition matrix is regular.

27. $\begin{bmatrix} 0 & 0.2 \\ 1 & 0.8 \end{bmatrix}$

28. $D = \begin{bmatrix} \frac{1}{3} & 1 \\ \frac{2}{3} & 0 \end{bmatrix}$

29. $\begin{bmatrix} 0.4 & 0 & 0.6 \\ 0.2 & 1 & 0.3 \\ 0.4 & 0 & 0.1 \end{bmatrix}$

30. $\begin{bmatrix} 1 & 0 & 0.3 \\ 0 & 1 & 0.5 \\ 0 & 0 & 0.2 \end{bmatrix}$

31. How can you tell from the transition matrix whether a Markov chain is regular or not?

32. How can you tell from the transition matrix whether a Markov chain is absorbing or not?

33. How can you tell from the transition matrix where the absorbing states are in an absorbing chain?

34. Can a Markov chain be both regular and absorbing? Explain.

Find all absorbing states for each matrix. Which are transition matrices for an absorbing Markov chain?

35. $\begin{bmatrix} 0 & 0.5 & 0 \\ 1 & 0.1 & 0 \\ 0 & 0.4 & 1 \end{bmatrix}$

36. $\begin{bmatrix} 0.2 & 0 & 0.7 \\ 0 & 1 & 0 \\ 0.8 & 0 & 0.3 \end{bmatrix}$

37. $\begin{bmatrix} 0.5 & 0 & 1 & 0.1 \\ 0.1 & 0 & 0 & 0.8 \\ 0.1 & 1 & 0 & 0.05 \\ 0.3 & 0 & 0 & 0.05 \end{bmatrix}$

38. $\begin{bmatrix} 0.2 & 0 & 0 & 0.3 \\ 0.3 & 1 & 0 & 0 \\ 0.4 & 0 & 0.2 & 0.6 \\ 0.1 & 0 & 0.8 & 0.1 \end{bmatrix}$

Find the fundamental matrix F for the absorbing Markov chains with matrices as follows. Also find the matrix RF.

39. $\begin{bmatrix} 0.2 & 0 & 0 \\ 0.45 & 1 & 0 \\ 0.35 & 0 & 1 \end{bmatrix}$

40. $\begin{bmatrix} 1 & 0 & 0.25 \\ 0 & 1 & 0.15 \\ 0 & 0 & 0.6 \end{bmatrix}$

41. $\begin{bmatrix} \frac{1}{5} & 0 & \frac{1}{2} & 0 \\ \frac{1}{5} & 1 & \frac{1}{4} & 0 \\ \frac{2}{5} & 0 & \frac{1}{8} & 0 \\ \frac{1}{5} & 0 & \frac{1}{8} & 1 \end{bmatrix}$

42. $\begin{bmatrix} 0.3 & 0.4 & 0 & 0 \\ 0.5 & 0.1 & 0 & 0 \\ 0.1 & 0.3 & 1 & 0 \\ 0.1 & 0.2 & 0 & 1 \end{bmatrix}$

APPLICATIONS

Business and Economics

Advertising Currently, 35% of all hot dogs sold in one area are made by Dogkins and 65% are made by Long Dog. Suppose that Dogkins starts a heavy advertising campaign, with the campaign producing the following transition matrix.

		Before Campaign	
		Dogkins	Long Dog
After	Dogkins	0.8	0.45
Campaign	Long Dog	0.2	0.55

43. Find the share of the market for each company

(a) after one campaign;

(b) after three such campaigns.

44. Predict the long-range market share for Dogkins.

Credit Cards A credit card company classifies its customers in a given month in three groups; nonusers, light users, and heavy users. The transition matrix for these states is

	Nonuser	Light	Heavy
Nonuser	0.8	0.25	0.04
Light	0.15	0.55	0.21
Heavy	0.05	0.2	0.75

Suppose the initial distribution for the three states is $\begin{bmatrix} 0.4 \\ 0.4 \\ 0.2 \end{bmatrix}$.

Find the distribution after each of the following periods.

45. 1 month **46.** 2 months **47.** 3 months

48. What is the long-range prediction for the distribution of users?

Life Sciences

49. Medical Prognosis A study of patients at the University of North Carolina Hospitals used a Markov chain model with three categories of patients: 0 (death), 1 (unfavorable status), and 2 (favorable status). The transition matrix for a cycle of 72 hours was as follows. *Source: Journal of Applied Statistics.*

$$
\begin{array}{c}
 \\
0 \\
1 \\
2
\end{array}
\begin{array}{ccc}
0 & 1 & 2 \\
\begin{bmatrix}
1 & 0.085 & 0.017 \\
0 & 0.779 & 0.017 \\
0 & 0.136 & 0.966
\end{bmatrix}
\end{array}
$$

(a) Find the fundamental matrix.

(b) For a patient with a favorable status, find the expected number of cycles that the patient will continue to have that status before dying.

(c) For a patient with an unfavorable status, find the expected number of cycles that the patient will have a favorable status before dying.

Medical Research A medical researcher is studying the risk of heart attack in men. She first divides men into three weight categories: thin, normal, and overweight. By studying the male ancestors, sons, and grandsons of these men, the researcher comes up with the following transition matrix.

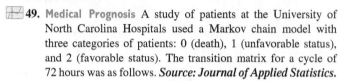

$$
\begin{array}{c}
\text{Thin} \\
\text{Normal} \\
\text{Overweight}
\end{array}
\begin{array}{ccc}
\text{Thin} & \text{Normal} & \text{Overweight} \\
\begin{bmatrix}
0.3 & 0.2 & 0.1 \\
0.5 & 0.6 & 0.5 \\
0.2 & 0.2 & 0.4
\end{bmatrix}
\end{array}
$$

Find the probabilities of the following for a man of normal weight.

50. Thin son

51. Thin grandson

52. Thin great-grandson

Find the probabilities of the following for an overweight man.

53. Overweight son

54. Overweight grandson

55. Overweight great-grandson

Suppose that the distribution of men by weight is initially given by $\begin{bmatrix} 0.2 \\ 0.55 \\ 0.25 \end{bmatrix}$. Find the following distributions.

56. After 1 generation

57. After 2 generations

58. After 3 generations

59. Find the long-range prediction for the distribution of weights.

Genetics Researchers sometimes study the problem of mating the offspring from the same two parents; two of these offspring are then mated and so on. Let A be a dominant gene for some trait, and a the recessive gene. The original offspring can carry genes AA, Aa, or aa. There are six possible ways that these offspring can mate.

State	Mating
1	AA and AA
2	AA and Aa
3	AA and aa
4	Aa and Aa
5	Aa and aa
6	aa and aa

60. Suppose that the offspring are randomly mated with each other. Verify that the transition matrix is given by the matrix below.

$$
\begin{array}{c}
1 \\ 2 \\ 3 \\ 4 \\ 5 \\ 6
\end{array}
\begin{array}{cccccc}
1 & 2 & 3 & 4 & 5 & 6 \\
\begin{bmatrix}
1 & \frac{1}{4} & 0 & \frac{1}{16} & 0 & 0 \\
0 & \frac{1}{2} & 0 & \frac{1}{4} & 0 & 0 \\
0 & 0 & 0 & \frac{1}{8} & 0 & 0 \\
0 & \frac{1}{4} & 1 & \frac{1}{4} & \frac{1}{4} & 0 \\
0 & 0 & 0 & \frac{1}{4} & \frac{1}{2} & 0 \\
0 & 0 & 0 & \frac{1}{16} & \frac{1}{4} & 1
\end{bmatrix}
\end{array}
$$

61. Identify the absorbing states.

62. Find matrix Q.

63. Find F and the product RF.

64. If two parents with the genes Aa are mated, find the number of pairs of offspring with these genes that can be expected before either the dominant or the recessive gene no longer appears.

65. If two parents with the genes Aa are mated, find the probability that the recessive gene will eventually disappear.

66. Genetics Suppose that a set of n genes includes m mutant genes. For the next generation, these genes are duplicated and a subset of n genes is selected from the $2n$ genes containing $2m$ mutant genes. Let the state be given by the number of mutant genes.

(a) Verify that the transition probability from state i to state j is given by

$$
p_{ji} = \frac{C(2i, j)\, C(2n - 2i, n - j)}{C(2n, n)}
$$

where i and j are the number of mutant genes in this generation and the next, and where $C(n, r)$ represents the number of combinations of n objects taken r at a time, discussed in Chapter 8. (*Hint*: Let $C(n, r) = 0$ when $n < r$. If the current generation has i mutant genes, it has $n - i$ nonmutant genes. When the genes are duplicated, this results in $2i$ mutant genes and $2(n - i)$ nonmutant genes.)

(b) What are the absorbing states in this chain?

(c) Calculate the transition matrix for the case $n = 3$.

(d) Find the fundamental matrix F and the product RF for $n = 3$.

(e) If a set of 3 genes has 1 mutant gene, what is the probability that the mutant gene will eventually disappear?

(f) If a set of 3 genes has 1 mutant gene, how many generations would be expected to have 1 mutant gene before either the mutant genes or the nonmutant genes disappear?

67. Class Mobility The following chart gives the probability that the child of a father in the bottom, second, middle, fourth, and top fifth of the U.S. population by income will end up in each of the five groups. *Source: The Institute for the Study of Labor.*

	Bottom	Second	Middle	Fourth	Top
Bottom	0.42	0.19	0.19	0.13	0.10
Second	0.25	0.28	0.19	0.18	0.12
Middle	0.15	0.21	0.26	0.20	0.19
Fourth	0.10	0.18	0.20	0.25	0.23
Top	0.08	0.14	0.16	0.24	0.36

(a) Find the probability that the grandson of someone in the bottom income group is in the top income group.

(b) Find the probability that the grandson of someone in the top income group is in the top income group.

(c) Find the long-range probability that a male is in each income group if the trends given by the transition matrix continue.

(d) Describe what the answers in part (c) tell you about the long-range distribution of income in the United States.

General Interest

68. Monopoly In an article on a Markov chain analysis of the game Monopoly, a simplified version of the game is presented. The board consists of the four squares shown.

POLICEMAN	COMMUNITY CHEST
JAIL	GO

Players move clockwise by flipping a coin and moving once for heads and twice for tails. If you land on the Policeman, you go directly to jail. Therefore, landing on the Policeman is equivalent to landing on Jail, so we need only consider three states in our Markov chain. If you land on the Community Chest, you pick a card that might give or take away money or might send you to Jail or to Go. The result is the following transition matrix. *Source: The College Mathematics Journal.*

$$
\begin{array}{c c}
 & \begin{array}{ccc} \text{Jail} & \text{CC} & \text{Go} \end{array} \\
\begin{array}{c} \text{Jail} \\ \text{CC} \\ \text{Go} \end{array} &
\begin{bmatrix} \frac{17}{32} & \frac{1}{2} & 1 \\ \frac{7}{16} & 0 & 0 \\ \frac{1}{32} & \frac{1}{2} & 0 \end{bmatrix}
\end{array}
$$

(a) Explain columns 2 and 3 of the transition matrix.

(b) There are 16 cards for the Community Chest. One sends you to Jail, one sends you to Go, and the others leave you on Community Chest. Use these facts to explain column 1 of the transition matrix.

(c) Find the long-term probabilities for being on Jail, the Community Chest, and Go.

69. Gambling Suppose a casino offers a gambling game involving a European roulette wheel, which has 37 slots numbered 0 through 36. The gambler's chance of winning depends on the number of chips he has when the wheel is spun. If the number of chips is a multiple of three, he wins one chip if the roulette wheel comes up 1, 2, or 3; otherwise he loses one chip. If the number of chips is not a multiple of 3, he wins one chip if the roulette wheel is any number between 1 and 28; otherwise he loses one chip. *Source: Math Horizons.*

(a) Find the average chance of winning if one assumes that the number of chips the gambler possesses is a multiple of three one-third of the time.

(b) In fact, the number of chips the gambler possesses is not a multiple of three one-third of the time. To see this, let the number of chips the player has be modeled by a Markov chain with states 0, 1, and 2, based on the remainder when the player's chips are divided by three. Find the transition matrix for this Markov chain.

(c) Find the probability of being in state 0, 1, and 2 in the long run.

(d) Based on the long run probabilities from part (c), find the gambler's average chance of winning.

EXTENDED APPLICATION

A MARKOV CHAIN MODEL FOR TEACHER RETENTION

In an article published in the *Review of Public Personnel Administration*, Michael Reid and Raymond Taylor used a Markov chain model to describe the employment patterns for public school teachers in a New England school district. They identified 8 possible states for teachers in the system: newly employed, continuing from the previous year, on leave without pay, on sabbatical, ill for at least 30 days during the year, resigned, retired, and deceased. Each teacher could transition to 1 of these 8 states in the following year, and the researchers recorded the transition for each teacher from year 1 of the study to year 2. The researchers also noted how each teacher in the system in year 2 transitioned to year 3. This gave them two sets of transition frequencies, which they combined in order to estimate the transition probabilities from each of the 8 possible states to each other state. The resulting transition matrix, arranged with the absorbing states in the upper-left portion of the array, is given below.

Note that there are 3 irreversible transitions: resigning, retiring, and dying, so the first 3 states listed are absorbing. Once you have entered the "resigned" state, you stay there forever (at least as far as the school system is concerned). The fourth row consists of zeros, since no one already in the system can transition into the state of being a new teacher. In the exercises you will look at some of the other transition probabilities, including some of the forbidden transitions, such as from being on sabbatical to being on sabbatical again the next year.

Following the procedure outlined in Section 15.3, we can compute the fundamental matrix F, which looks like this:

$$F = \begin{bmatrix} 1 & 0 & 0 & 0 & 0 \\ 10.405 & 12.988 & 3.252 & 12.988 & 11.078 \\ 0.322 & 0.402 & 1.507 & 0.402 & 0.343 \\ 0.073 & 0.091 & 0.023 & 1.091 & 0.078 \\ 0.222 & 0.234 & 0.058 & 0.234 & 1.257 \end{bmatrix}.$$

Recall that the rows and columns here represent the non absorbing states, in the same order in which they appear in the transition matrix. According to the properties of the fundamental matrix listed in Section 15.3, the entry in column A and row B represents the number of years during which a teacher currently in state A will be in state B before he or she exits the system into one of the absorbing states. For example, the 1 at the upper left indicates that a teacher who is new this year will spend exactly 1 year as a new teacher, which makes sense because you can only be new once. The entry 3.252 indicates that a teacher currently on leave without pay will, on the average, spend only about 3 years in the system, including the current year.

In the transition matrix, the matrix R sits under the identity matrix corresponding to the absorbing states. For the teacher transition matrix, R looks like this:

$$R = \begin{bmatrix} 0.194 & 0.04 & 0.533 & 0 & 0 \\ 0 & 0.016 & 0 & 0 & 0.139 \\ 0 & 0.002 & 0 & 0 & 0 \end{bmatrix}.$$

In the exercises you will compute the product RF, which gives information about the distribution of absorbing states for each possible nonabsorbing initial state. *Source: Review of Public Personnel Administration.*

| | Teacher Transition | | | | | | |
	Resigned	Retired	Deceased	New	Continuing	On Leave	On Sabbatical	Ill
Resigned	1	0	0	0.194	0.040	0.533	0	0
Retired	0	1	0	0	0.016	0	0	0.139
Deceased	0	0	1	0	0.002	0	0	0
New	0	0	0	0	0	0	0	0
Continuing	0	0	0	0.777	0.896	0.178	1	0.806
On Leave	0	0	0	0	0.022	0.289	0	0
On Sabbatical	0	0	0	0	0.007	0	0	0
Ill	0	0	0	0.033	0.017	0	0	0.055

EXERCISES

1. If a teacher is currently ill, what is the probability that he or she will retire during the following year? What is the probability that he or she will be ill again in the following year?

2. The entry in column 2 and row 2 of F is 12.988. What information does this give about teachers who are currently actively teaching?

3. Column 2 of F is nearly the same as column 1. Is this an accident? Can you explain the one difference?

4. What does the entry 0.091 in column 2 of the fundamental matrix tell you?

5. Compute the matrix RF and answer the following questions:

   (a) What is the probability that a teacher now on leave without pay will eventually resign? What is the probability that a teacher now on leave will resign the *following year*?

   (b) Who is more likely to leave the system by retirement, a new teacher or a teacher who is currently teaching but has at least 1 year in the system?

   (c) What is the probability that a new teacher will die on the job?

6. The study reported here collected two sets of transition data (year 1 to year 2 and year 2 to year 3). Why was this a good idea?

7. On the WolframAlpha.com website, the command $\{\{2, -1\}, \{1, -3\}\} . \{\{1, 2\}, \{0, 1\}\}$ gives the product of the matrices $\begin{bmatrix} 2 & -1 \\ 1 & -3 \end{bmatrix}$ and $\begin{bmatrix} 1 & 2 \\ 0 & 1 \end{bmatrix}$. Use this website and a similar command to determine RF in Exercise 5.

DIRECTIONS FOR GROUP PROJECT

Suppose your brother is president of a local school board and he has expressed concern about teacher retention at your former high school. Given that you are a college student and would like to make some money, you mention that you and your three friends are familiar with this problem and could lend some help to the school for a fee of $5000. His reply is that the School Board would have to agree to this. He invites you and your friends to the next School Board meeting to convince them that you can help them analyze their teacher retention issues. Prepare a presentation for the Board that describes the process of analyzing teacher retention, including the mathematics you will use for the analysis. Be sure to use Exercises 1–6 in making your presentation. Presentation software, such as Microsoft PowerPoint, should be used to present your case to the Board.

Exercises 15.1 Markov Chains

For exercises . . .	9–16, 28(a), 31(a), 32(a), 34(a), 36(a), 38(a)	17–24, 26, 29(a), (e), 30(c),(d), 32(e), (f), 33(c)–(e), 34(b), (c), 35(a), 36(e), (f), 37(c)–(e), 38(a), 39, 40	27, 28(b), 29(a)–(c), 30(a),(b), 31(b)–(e), 32(b)–(d), 33(a),(b), 35(b),(c), 36(b)–(d), 37(a), (b), 38(b)–(f)
Refer to example . . .	1	2,3	4

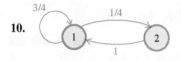

W1. $\begin{bmatrix} 26 \\ 31 \end{bmatrix}$ **W2.** $\begin{bmatrix} 38 \\ 46 \\ 49 \end{bmatrix}$ **W3.** $\begin{bmatrix} 19 & 20 \\ 50 & 59 \end{bmatrix}$ **W4.** $\begin{bmatrix} 17 & 35 & 53 \\ 27 & 86 & 77 \\ 16 & 53 & 51 \end{bmatrix}$

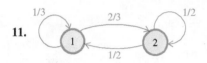

10.   **11.**   **12.**

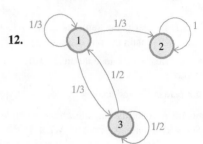

17. $A = \begin{bmatrix} 1 & 0.7 \\ 0 & 0.3 \end{bmatrix}$; $A^2 = \begin{bmatrix} 1 & 0.91 \\ 0 & 0.09 \end{bmatrix}$; $A^3 = \begin{bmatrix} 1 & 0.973 \\ 0 & 0.027 \end{bmatrix}$; 0

18. $B = \begin{bmatrix} 0.8 & 0 \\ 0.2 & 1 \end{bmatrix}$; $B^2 = \begin{bmatrix} 0.64 & 0 \\ 0.36 & 1 \end{bmatrix}$; $B^3 = \begin{bmatrix} 0.512 & 0 \\ 0.488 & 1 \end{bmatrix}$; 0.488

19. $C = \begin{bmatrix} 0 & 0.2 & 0.1 \\ 0 & 0.6 & 0.7 \\ 1 & 0.2 & 0.2 \end{bmatrix}$; $C^2 = \begin{bmatrix} 0.1 & 0.14 & 0.16 \\ 0.7 & 0.5 & 0.56 \\ 0.2 & 0.36 & 0.28 \end{bmatrix}$; $C^3 = \begin{bmatrix} 0.16 & 0.136 & 0.14 \\ 0.56 & 0.552 & 0.532 \\ 0.28 & 0.312 & 0.328 \end{bmatrix}$; 0.56

20. $D = \begin{bmatrix} 0.3 & 0 & 0.6 \\ 0.2 & 0 & 0.1 \\ 0.5 & 1 & 0.3 \end{bmatrix}$; $D^2 = \begin{bmatrix} 0.39 & 0.6 & 0.36 \\ 0.11 & 0.1 & 0.15 \\ 0.5 & 0.3 & 0.49 \end{bmatrix}$; $D^3 = \begin{bmatrix} 0.417 & 0.36 & 0.402 \\ 0.128 & 0.15 & 0.121 \\ 0.455 & 0.49 & 0.477 \end{bmatrix}$; 0.128

21. $E = \begin{bmatrix} 0.8 & 0.3 & 0 \\ 0.1 & 0.6 & 1 \\ 0.1 & 0.1 & 0 \end{bmatrix}$; $E^2 = \begin{bmatrix} 0.67 & 0.42 & 0.3 \\ 0.24 & 0.49 & 0.6 \\ 0.09 & 0.09 & 0.1 \end{bmatrix}$; $E^3 = \begin{bmatrix} 0.608 & 0.483 & 0.42 \\ 0.301 & 0.426 & 0.49 \\ 0.091 & 0.091 & 0.09 \end{bmatrix}$; 0.301

22. $F = \begin{bmatrix} 0.01 & 0.72 & 0.34 \\ 0.9 & 0.1 & 0 \\ 0.09 & 0.18 & 0.66 \end{bmatrix}$; $F^2 = \begin{bmatrix} 0.6787 & 0.1404 & 0.2278 \\ 0.099 & 0.658 & 0.306 \\ 0.2223 & 0.2016 & 0.4662 \end{bmatrix}$; $F^3 = \begin{bmatrix} 0.1536 & 0.5437 & 0.3811 \\ 0.6207 & 0.1922 & 0.2356 \\ 0.2256 & 0.2641 & 0.3833 \end{bmatrix}$; 0.6207

23. The first power is the given transition matrix; $\begin{bmatrix} 0.2 & 0.16 & 0.19 & 0.16 & 0.16 \\ 0.15 & 0.2 & 0.14 & 0.19 & 0.19 \\ 0.17 & 0.15 & 0.24 & 0.16 & 0.14 \\ 0.19 & 0.18 & 0.21 & 0.2 & 0.17 \\ 0.29 & 0.31 & 0.22 & 0.29 & 0.34 \end{bmatrix}$; $\begin{bmatrix} 0.17 & 0.171 & 0.18 & 0.175 & 0.167 \\ 0.178 & 0.178 & 0.163 & 0.174 & 0.184 \\ 0.171 & 0.161 & 0.191 & 0.164 & 0.158 \\ 0.191 & 0.185 & 0.197 & 0.187 & 0.182 \\ 0.29 & 0.305 & 0.269 & 0.3 & 0.309 \end{bmatrix}$;

$\begin{bmatrix} 0.1731 & 0.1709 & 0.1748 & 0.1712 & 0.1706 \\ 0.175 & 0.1781 & 0.1718 & 0.1775 & 0.1785 \\ 0.1683 & 0.1654 & 0.1753 & 0.1667 & 0.1641 \\ 0.188 & 0.1866 & 0.1911 & 0.1875 & 0.1858 \\ 0.2956 & 0.299 & 0.287 & 0.2971 & 0.301 \end{bmatrix}$;

$\begin{bmatrix} 0.1719 & 0.1717 & 0.1729 & 0.1719 & 0.1714 \\ 0.1764 & 0.1769 & 0.1749 & 0.1765 & 0.1773 \\ 0.1678 & 0.1667 & 0.1701 & 0.1671 & 0.1663 \\ 0.1878 & 0.1872 & 0.1888 & 0.1874 & 0.1870 \\ 0.2961 & 0.2975 & 0.2933 & 0.2970 & 0.2981 \end{bmatrix}$; 0.1872

24. The first power is the given transition matrix; $\begin{bmatrix} 0.23 & 0.26 & 0.23 & 0.19 & 0.17 \\ 0.21 & 0.18 & 0.18 & 0.19 & 0.20 \\ 0.24 & 0.26 & 0.24 & 0.27 & 0.26 \\ 0.17 & 0.16 & 0.19 & 0.18 & 0.19 \\ 0.15 & 0.14 & 0.16 & 0.17 & 0.18 \end{bmatrix}$; $\begin{bmatrix} 0.226 & 0.222 & 0.219 & 0.213 & 0.213 \\ 0.192 & 0.196 & 0.189 & 0.192 & 0.189 \\ 0.249 & 0.252 & 0.256 & 0.252 & 0.252 \\ 0.177 & 0.174 & 0.177 & 0.181 & 0.183 \\ 0.156 & 0.156 & 0.159 & 0.162 & 0.163 \end{bmatrix}$;

$$\begin{bmatrix} 0.2205 & 0.2206 & 0.2182 & 0.2183 & 0.2176 \\ 0.1916 & 0.1922 & 0.1920 & 0.1909 & 0.1906 \\ 0.2523 & 0.2512 & 0.2525 & 0.2526 & 0.2533 \\ 0.1774 & 0.1778 & 0.1781 & 0.1787 & 0.1787 \\ 0.1582 & 0.1582 & 0.1592 & 0.1595 & 0.1598 \end{bmatrix}; \begin{bmatrix} 0.2193 & 0.2196 & 0.2191 & 0.2188 & 0.2186 \\ 0.1917 & 0.1915 & 0.1915 & 0.1914 & 0.1915 \\ 0.2523 & 0.2523 & 0.2523 & 0.2525 & 0.2525 \\ 0.1780 & 0.1779 & 0.1782 & 0.1782 & 0.1782 \\ 0.1588 & 0.1587 & 0.1590 & 0.1591 & 0.1592 \end{bmatrix}; 0.1779$$

27. (a) 53% for Johnson and 47% for NorthClean **(b)** 58.85% for Johnson and 41.15% for NorthClean **(c)** 61.48% for Johnson and 38.52% for NorthClean **(d)** 62.67% for Johnson and 37.33% for Northclean

28. (a) $\begin{bmatrix} 0.75 & 0 & 0 \\ 0.20 & 0.70 & 0 \\ 0.05 & 0.30 & 1 \end{bmatrix}$ **(b) (i)** 37,500; 10,000; 2500 **(ii)** 28,125; 14,500; 7375 **(iii)** 21,094; 15,775; 13,131 **(iv)** 15,820; 15,261; 18,918 (rounded numbers do not sum to 50,000)

29. (a) 37,500 policyholders in G_0, 10,000 in G_1, and 2500 in G_2 **(b)** 29,375 policyholders in G_0, 15,250 in G_1, and 5375 in G_2
(c) 24,094 policyholders in G_0, 18,163 in G_1, and 7744 in G_2 (rounded number do not sum to 50,000)

(d) $\begin{bmatrix} 0.5875 & 0.165 & 0.165 \\ 0.305 & 0.57 & 0.41 \\ 0.1075 & 0.265 & 0.425 \end{bmatrix}$ **30. (a)** $\begin{bmatrix} 0.2118 \\ 0.4210 \\ 0.0762 \\ 0.2910 \end{bmatrix}$ **(b)** $\begin{bmatrix} 0.2099 \\ 0.4139 \\ 0.0689 \\ 0.3072 \end{bmatrix}$ **(c)** $\begin{array}{c} \\ D \\ P \\ B \\ N \end{array}\begin{bmatrix} D & P & B & N \\ 0.4902 & 0.0860 & 0.1732 & 0.1947 \\ 0.1813 & 0.5812 & 0.3386 & 0.3514 \\ 0.0357 & 0.0599 & 0.2787 & 0.0386 \\ 0.2928 & 0.2730 & 0.2095 & 0.4153 \end{bmatrix}$

31. (a) $\begin{array}{c} e \\ f \\ s \end{array}\begin{bmatrix} e & f & s \\ 0.9 & 0.15 & 0 \\ 0.05 & 0.75 & 0 \\ 0.05 & 0.1 & 1 \end{bmatrix}$ **(b)** $\begin{bmatrix} 0.405 \\ 0.4675 \\ 0.1275 \end{bmatrix}$ **(c)** $\begin{bmatrix} 0.4346 \\ 0.3709 \\ 0.1945 \end{bmatrix}$ **(d)** $\begin{bmatrix} 0.4468 \\ 0.2999 \\ 0.2533 \end{bmatrix}$ **32. (a)** $\begin{bmatrix} 0.80 & 0 & 0.10 \\ 0.15 & 0.90 & 0.20 \\ 0.05 & 0.10 & 0.70 \end{bmatrix}$ **(b)** $\begin{bmatrix} 0.645 & 0.01 & 0.15 \\ 0.265 & 0.83 & 0.335 \\ 0.09 & 0.16 & 0.515 \end{bmatrix}$

33. (a) 2039 small, 2352 medium, 2444 large **(b)** 1988 small, 2340 medium, 2507 large **(c)** $\begin{bmatrix} 0.8529 & 0.0836 & 0.0020 \\ 0.1418 & 0.8080 & 0.0562 \\ 0.0053 & 0.1084 & 0.9419 \end{bmatrix}$

34 (b) $\begin{bmatrix} 5/12 & 5/12 & 1/4 \\ 13/36 & 13/36 & 5/12 \\ 2/9 & 2/9 & 1/3 \end{bmatrix}$ **35. (b)** 2.34 rabbits in group 1, 2.62 rabbits group 2, 3.47 in group 3, and 4.56 in group 4.

36 (a) $\begin{array}{c} S \\ M \end{array}\begin{bmatrix} S & M \\ 0.90 & 0.05 \\ 0.10 & 0.95 \end{bmatrix}$ **(c)** 68.8% single-family and 31.3% multiple-family
(d) 63.4% single-family and 36.6% multiple-family **(e)** $\begin{bmatrix} 0.815 & 0.0925 \\ 0.185 & 0.9075 \end{bmatrix}$

37. $\begin{bmatrix} 0.6387 & 0.5906 & 0.53 & 0.5041 & 0.4653 \\ 0.2119 & 0.226 & 0.2026 & 0.2107 & 0.2185 \\ 0.0418 & 0.0485 & 0.0866 & 0.0722 & 0.0834 \\ 0.1069 & 0.1336 & 0.1786 & 0.2089 & 0.2275 \\ 0.0007 & 0.0013 & 0.0022 & 0.0041 & 0.0053 \end{bmatrix}$ **38. (a)** $\begin{bmatrix} 0.80 & 0.20 & 0.20 \\ 0.15 & 0.70 & 0.20 \\ 0.05 & 0.10 & 0.60 \end{bmatrix}$

(c) 44% liberals, 40.5% conservatives, and 15.5% independents
(d) 46.4% liberals, 38.05% conservatives, and 15.55% independents
(e) 47.84% liberals, 36.705% conservatives, and 15.455% independents **(g)** $\begin{bmatrix} 0.68 & 0.32 & 0.32 \\ 0.235 & 0.54 & 0.29 \\ 0.085 & 0.14 & 0.39 \end{bmatrix}$
(f) 48.704% liberals, 35.9605% conservatives, and 15.3355% independents

39 (a) $\begin{bmatrix} 0.3484 & 0.3198 & 0.3164 \\ 0.3786 & 0.3782 & 0.3601 \\ 0.2730 & 0.3020 & 0.3235 \end{bmatrix}$

Exercise 15.2

For exercises...	1–6	7–10,20,25–27	11–19,28–44
Refer to example...	2	3	4

14. $\begin{bmatrix} 7783/16{,}799 \\ 2828/16{,}799 \\ 6188/16{,}799 \end{bmatrix}$

25.

	Works	Doesn't Work
Works	0.9	0.8
Doesn't Work	0.1	0.2

$; 8/9$

27. (a) $\begin{bmatrix} 0.4 \\ 0.6 \end{bmatrix}; \begin{bmatrix} 0.53 \\ 0.47 \end{bmatrix}; \begin{bmatrix} 0.5885 \\ 0.4115 \end{bmatrix}; \begin{bmatrix} 0.614825 \\ 0.385175 \end{bmatrix}; \begin{bmatrix} 0.626671 \\ 0.373329 \end{bmatrix}; \begin{bmatrix} 0.632002 \\ 0.367998 \end{bmatrix}; \begin{bmatrix} 0.634401 \\ 0.365599 \end{bmatrix}; \begin{bmatrix} 0.635480 \\ 0.364520 \end{bmatrix}; \begin{bmatrix} 0.635966 \\ 0.364034 \end{bmatrix}; \begin{bmatrix} 0.636185 \\ 0.363815 \end{bmatrix}$

(b) 0.236364; 0.106364; 0.047864; 0.021539; 0.009693; 0.004362; 0.001963; 0.000884; 0.000398; 0.000179

(d) Each week, the difference between the probability vector and the equilibrium vector is slightly less than half of what it was the previous week.

(e) $\begin{bmatrix} 0.75 \\ 0.25 \end{bmatrix}; \begin{bmatrix} 0.6875 \\ 0.3125 \end{bmatrix}; \begin{bmatrix} 0.659375 \\ 0.340625 \end{bmatrix}; \begin{bmatrix} 0.646719 \\ 0.353281 \end{bmatrix}; \begin{bmatrix} 0.641023 \\ 0.358977 \end{bmatrix}; \begin{bmatrix} 0.638461 \\ 0.361539 \end{bmatrix}; \begin{bmatrix} 0.637307 \\ 0.362693 \end{bmatrix}; \begin{bmatrix} 0.636788 \\ 0.363212 \end{bmatrix}; \begin{bmatrix} 0.636555 \\ 0.363445 \end{bmatrix}; \begin{bmatrix} 0.636450 \\ 0.363550 \end{bmatrix};$
0.113636; 0.051136; 0.023011; 0.010355; 0.004659; 0.002097; 0.000943; 0.000424; 0.000191; 0.000086; roughly 0.45.

28. 0.04% adjustable, 36.47% 15-year fixed, 4.31% 20-year fixed, 59.18% 30-year fixed

31. (a) $\begin{bmatrix} 0.633 \\ 0.032 \\ 0.335 \end{bmatrix}$

36. (c) 0.607 for nonindex, 0.097 for injury, 0.174 for theft, 0.032 for damage, and 0.090 for combination

38. (a) 1.80% in group 1, 23.68% in group 2, 38.47% in group 3, and 36.04% in group 4

41. (c) $\begin{bmatrix} 0 & \frac{1}{2} & 0 \\ 1 & 0 & 1 \\ 0 & \frac{1}{2} & 0 \end{bmatrix}$

43. (b) The guard spends 3/7 of the time in front of the middle door and 2/7 of the time in front of each of the other door.

44. (a) $\begin{array}{c} \\ B \\ A \\ G \end{array} \begin{array}{ccc} B & A & G \\ \end{array}$ $\begin{bmatrix} \frac{7}{12} & \frac{4}{10} & \frac{1}{3} \\ \frac{5}{12} & \frac{3}{10} & \frac{2}{3} \\ 0 & \frac{3}{10} & 0 \end{bmatrix}$ **(b)** $\begin{bmatrix} 0.48 \\ 0.4 \\ 0.12 \end{bmatrix}$

Exercise 15.3

For exercises...	1–6	15,16,31	26(a)	7–14, 23–25, 26(b), (c), 27–30, 32, 33
Refer to example...	1	2	3	4

W1. $\begin{bmatrix} 7/12 & -1/6 \\ -2/3 & 1/3 \end{bmatrix}$ **W2.** $\begin{bmatrix} 7/16 & -5/6 \\ -1/16 & 3/16 \end{bmatrix}$

5. States 2 and 4 are absorbing; matrix is that of an absorbing Markov chain.

6. No states are absorbing; matrix is not that of an absorbing Markov chain.

7. $F = [2]; RF = \begin{bmatrix} 0,3 \\ 0,7 \end{bmatrix}$ **8.** $F = [10/9]; RF = \begin{bmatrix} 13/18 \\ 5/18 \end{bmatrix}$ **9.** $F = [3/2]; RF = \begin{bmatrix} 3/4 \\ 1/4 \end{bmatrix}$ **10.** $F = [8/7]; RF = \begin{bmatrix} 5/7 \\ 2/7 \end{bmatrix}$

11. $F = \begin{bmatrix} 1 & \frac{1}{3} \\ 0 & \frac{4}{3} \end{bmatrix}; RF = \begin{bmatrix} \frac{1}{3} & \frac{4}{9} \\ \frac{2}{3} & \frac{5}{9} \end{bmatrix}$ **12.** $F = \begin{bmatrix} 2 & 2 \\ 1 & 3 \end{bmatrix}; RF = \begin{bmatrix} 1 & 1 \\ 0 & 0 \end{bmatrix}$

13. $F = \begin{bmatrix} 25/17 & 5/34 \\ 5/17 & 35/34 \end{bmatrix}; RF = \begin{bmatrix} 4/17 & 11/34 \\ 15/34 & 37/68 \\ 11/34 & 9/68 \end{bmatrix}$

14. $F = \begin{bmatrix} 5/3 & 5/27 \\ 0 & 10/9 \end{bmatrix}; RF = \begin{bmatrix} 1/3 & 16/27 \\ 1/2 & 1/6 \\ 1/6 & 13/54 \end{bmatrix}$

15. (a)
$$\begin{bmatrix} 1 & \frac{1}{2} & 0 & 0 & 0 \\ 0 & 0 & \frac{1}{2} & 0 & 0 \\ 0 & \frac{1}{2} & 0 & \frac{1}{2} & 0 \\ 0 & 0 & \frac{1}{2} & 0 & 0 \\ 0 & 0 & 0 & \frac{1}{2} & 1 \end{bmatrix}$$

(b) $F = \begin{bmatrix} \frac{3}{2} & 1 & \frac{1}{2} \\ 1 & 2 & 1 \\ \frac{1}{2} & 1 & \frac{3}{2} \end{bmatrix}$; $RF = \begin{bmatrix} \frac{3}{4} & \frac{1}{2} & \frac{1}{4} \\ \frac{1}{4} & \frac{1}{2} & \frac{3}{4} \end{bmatrix}$

19.

p	0.1	0.2	0.3	0.4	0.5	0.6	0.7	0.8	0.9
x_a	0.9999999997	0.99999905	0.99979	0.98295	0.5	0.017046	0.000209	0.00000095	0.0000000003

22. (a)
$$\begin{matrix} & \begin{matrix} 1 & & 2 & & 3 \end{matrix} \\ \begin{matrix} 1 \\ 2 \\ 3 \end{matrix} & \begin{bmatrix} 1 & 0 & p \\ 0 & 1 & q \\ 0 & 0 & 1-p-q \end{bmatrix} \end{matrix}$$

23. (a) $F = \begin{bmatrix} 14.2857 & 8.5714 \\ 2.8571 & 5.7143 \end{bmatrix}$; $RF = \begin{bmatrix} 1 & 1 \end{bmatrix}$

24. (a) $F = \begin{bmatrix} 1.6667 & 0 \\ 0.6061 & 1.8182 \end{bmatrix}$; $RF = \begin{bmatrix} 0.1136 & 0.0909 \\ 0.8864 & 0.9091 \end{bmatrix}$

27. (a) $P = \begin{bmatrix} 0.80 & 0.05 & 0 \\ 0.15 & 0.80 & 0 \\ 0.05 & 0.15 & 1 \end{bmatrix}$; $F = \begin{bmatrix} 6.154 & 1.538 \\ 4.615 & 6.154 \end{bmatrix}$; $RF = \begin{bmatrix} 1.000 & 1.000 \end{bmatrix}$

28. (a) $P = \begin{bmatrix} 0.15 & 0 & 0 & 0 \\ 0.6 & 0.15 & 0 & 0 \\ 0.25 & 0.25 & 1 & 0 \\ 0 & 0.6 & 0 & 1 \end{bmatrix}$; $F = \begin{bmatrix} 20/17 & 0 \\ 240/289 & 20/17 \end{bmatrix}$; $RF = \begin{bmatrix} 145/289 & 5/17 \\ 144/289 & 12/17 \end{bmatrix}$

29. (a) $P = \begin{bmatrix} 0.4 & 0.2 & 0 & 0.1 & 0 \\ 0.3 & 0.1 & 0 & 0.1 & 0 \\ 0.2 & 0 & 1 & 0.4 & 0 \\ 0.1 & 0.6 & 0 & 0.1 & 0 \\ 0 & 0.1 & 0 & 0.3 & 1 \end{bmatrix}$; $F = \begin{bmatrix} 2.0436 & 0.6540 & 0.2997 \\ 0.7629 & 1.4441 & 0.2452 \\ 0.7357 & 1.0354 & 1.3079 \end{bmatrix}$; $RF = \begin{matrix} & \begin{matrix} 1 & & 2 & & 4 \end{matrix} \\ \begin{matrix} 3 \\ 5 \end{matrix} & \begin{bmatrix} 0.703 & 0.545 & 0.583 \\ 0.297 & 0.455 & 0.417 \end{bmatrix} \end{matrix}$

31. (a)
$$\begin{matrix} & \begin{matrix} 0 & 1 & 2 & 3 & 4 & 5 & 6 & 7 \end{matrix} \\ \begin{matrix} 0 \\ 1 \\ 2 \\ 3 \\ 4 \\ 5 \\ 6 \\ 7 \end{matrix} & \begin{bmatrix} 1 & \frac{1}{2} & 0 & 0 & 0 & 0 & 0 & 0 \\ 0 & 0 & \frac{1}{2} & 0 & 0 & 0 & 0 & 0 \\ 0 & \frac{1}{2} & 0 & \frac{1}{2} & 0 & 0 & 0 & 0 \\ 0 & 0 & \frac{1}{2} & 0 & \frac{1}{2} & 0 & 0 & 0 \\ 0 & 0 & 0 & \frac{1}{2} & 0 & \frac{1}{2} & 0 & 0 \\ 0 & 0 & 0 & 0 & \frac{1}{2} & 0 & \frac{1}{2} & 0 \\ 0 & 0 & 0 & 0 & 0 & \frac{1}{2} & 0 & 0 \\ 0 & 0 & 0 & 0 & 0 & 0 & \frac{1}{2} & 1 \end{bmatrix} \end{matrix}$$

33. (a) $F = \begin{bmatrix} 1.6244 & 1.0071 \\ 1.0071 & 1.6244 \end{bmatrix}$; $RF = \begin{bmatrix} 0.6049 & 0.3951 \\ 0.3951 & 0.6049 \end{bmatrix}$

(e) The team that wins the coin toss has an advantage. The team that chooses to take possession of the ball first wins 60.49% of the time.

Chapter 14 Review Exercise

For exercises...	1–4, 13, 15–26, 43, 45–57, 49(a), 50–58, 60, 67 (a)(b)	5–10, 14, 27–31, 44, 48, 59, 67(c), 68, 69	4–12, 32–38, 49(b) (c), 61–65, 66
Refer to example...	1	2	3

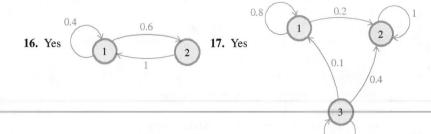

16. Yes   **17.** Yes

19. (a) $C = \begin{bmatrix} 0.7 & 1 \\ 0.3 & 0 \end{bmatrix}$; $C^2 = \begin{bmatrix} 0.79 & 0.7 \\ 0.21 & 0.3 \end{bmatrix}$; $C^3 = \begin{bmatrix} 0.763 & 0.79 \\ 0.237 & 0.21 \end{bmatrix}$ **(b)** 0.79

20. (a) $D = \begin{bmatrix} 0.4 & 0.5 \\ 0.6 & 0.5 \end{bmatrix}$; $D^2 = \begin{bmatrix} 0.46 & 0.45 \\ 0.54 & 0.55 \end{bmatrix}$; $D^3 = \begin{bmatrix} 0.454 & 0.455 \\ 0.546 & 0.545 \end{bmatrix}$ **(b)** 0.455

21. (a) $E = \begin{bmatrix} 0.2 & 0.3 & 0 \\ 0.5 & 0.4 & 1 \\ 0.3 & 0.3 & 0 \end{bmatrix}$; $E^2 = \begin{bmatrix} 0.19 & 0.18 & 0.3 \\ 0.6 & 0.61 & 0.4 \\ 0.21 & 0.21 & 0.3 \end{bmatrix}$; $E^3 = \begin{bmatrix} 0.218 & 0.219 & 0.18 \\ 0.545 & 0.544 & 0.61 \\ 0.237 & 0.237 & 0.21 \end{bmatrix}$ **(b)** 0.219

22. (a) $F = \begin{bmatrix} 0.14 & 0.35 & 0.71 \\ 0.18 & 0.28 & 0.22 \\ 0.68 & 0.37 & 0.07 \end{bmatrix}$; $F^2 = \begin{bmatrix} 0.5654 & 0.4097 & 0.2261 \\ 0.2252 & 0.2228 & 0.2048 \\ 0.2094 & 0.3675 & 0.5691 \end{bmatrix}$; $F^3 = \begin{bmatrix} 0.3067 & 0.3963 & 0.5074 \\ 0.2109 & 0.2170 & 0.2232 \\ 0.4825 & 0.3868 & 0.2694 \end{bmatrix}$ **(b)** 0.3963

35. State 3 is absorbing; matrix is that of an absorbing Markov chain.

36. Matrix is not that of an absorbing Markov chain; state 2 is absorbing.

37. No absorbing states; hence, matrix is not that of an absorbing Markov chain.

38. State 2 is absorbing; matrix is that of an absorbing Markov chain.

39. $F = [54]$; $RF = \begin{bmatrix} 9/16 \\ 7/6 \end{bmatrix}$

40. $F = [5/2]$; $RF = \begin{bmatrix} 5/8 \\ 3/8 \end{bmatrix}$

41. $F = \begin{bmatrix} 7/4 & 1 \\ 4/5 & 8/5 \end{bmatrix}$; $RF = \begin{bmatrix} 0.55 & 0.6 \\ 0.45 & 0.4 \end{bmatrix}$

42. $F = \begin{bmatrix} 2.0930 & 0.9302 \\ 1.1628 & 1.6279 \end{bmatrix}$; $RF = \begin{bmatrix} 0.5581 & 0.5814 \\ 0.4419 & 0.4186 \end{bmatrix}$

49. (a) $\begin{bmatrix} 6.536 & 3.268 \\ 26.144 & 42.484 \end{bmatrix}$

62. $Q = \begin{bmatrix} \frac{1}{2} & 0 & \frac{1}{4} & 0 \\ 0 & 0 & \frac{1}{8} & 0 \\ \frac{1}{4} & 1 & \frac{1}{4} & \frac{1}{4} \\ 0 & 0 & \frac{1}{4} & \frac{1}{2} \end{bmatrix}$

63. $F = \begin{bmatrix} 8/3 & 4/3 & 4/3 & 2/3 \\ 1/6 & 4/3 & 1/3 & 1/6 \\ 4/3 & 8/3 & 8/3 & 4/3 \\ 2/3 & 4/3 & 4/3 & 8/3 \end{bmatrix}$; $RF = \begin{bmatrix} 3/4 & 1/2 & 1/2 & 1/4 \\ 1/4 & 1/2 & 1/2 & 3/4 \end{bmatrix}$

66. (c) $\begin{array}{c} 0 \\ 1 \\ 2 \\ 3 \end{array} \begin{array}{cccc} 0 & 1 & 2 & 3 \end{array} \begin{bmatrix} 1 & 1/5 & 0 & 0 \\ 0 & 3/5 & 1/5 & 0 \\ 0 & 1/5 & 3/5 & 0 \\ 0 & 0 & 1/5 & 1 \end{bmatrix}$ **(d)** $F = \begin{bmatrix} 10/3 & 5/3 \\ 5/3 & 10/3 \end{bmatrix}$; $RF = \begin{bmatrix} 2/3 & 1/3 \\ 1/3 & 2/3 \end{bmatrix}$

69. (b) $\begin{array}{c} 0 \\ 1 \\ 2 \end{array} \begin{array}{ccc} 0 & 1 & 2 \end{array} \begin{bmatrix} 0 & 9/37 & 28/37 \\ 3/37 & 0 & 9/37 \\ 34/37 & 28/37 & 0 \end{bmatrix}$

EXTENDED APPLICATION

5. $RF =$

	New	Continuing	OnLeave	On Sabbatical	Ill
Resigned	0.785	0.734	0.933	0.734	0.626
Retired	0.198	0.240	0.060	0.240	0.352
Deceased	0.021	0.026	0.007	0.026	0.022

(a) 0.933; 0.533

(b) The teacher with a least one year in the system (probability 0.24 versus 0.197 for the new teacher).

(c) 0.021

Chapter 15 Markov Chains

Exercise 15.1

For exercises . . .	9–16, 28(a), 31(a), 32(a), 34(a), 36(a), 38(a)	17–24, 26, 29(d),(e), 30(c),(d), 32(e), (f), 33(c)–(e), 34(b),(c), 35(a), 36(e),(f), 37(c)–(e), 38(a), 39, 40	27, 28(b), 29(a)–(c), 30(a),(b), 31(b)–(e), 32(b)–(d), 33(a),(b), 35(b),(c), 36(b)–(d), 37(a), (b), 38(b)–(f)
Refer to example. . .	1	2,3	4

W1. $\begin{bmatrix} 26 \\ 31 \end{bmatrix}$ **W2.** $\begin{bmatrix} 38 \\ 46 \\ 49 \end{bmatrix}$ **W3.** $\begin{bmatrix} 19 & 20 \\ 50 & 59 \end{bmatrix}$ **W4.** $\begin{bmatrix} 17 & 35 & 53 \\ 27 & 86 & 77 \\ 16 & 53 & 51 \end{bmatrix}$

1. No **3.** Yes **5.** No **7.** Yes **9.** No

11. Yes 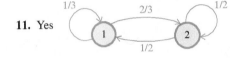 **13.** Yes 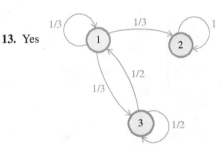 **15.** $\begin{bmatrix} 0.9 & 0.1 & 0 \\ 0.1 & 0.7 & 0.2 \\ 0 & 0.2 & 0.8 \end{bmatrix}$

17. $A = \begin{bmatrix} 1 & 0.7 \\ 0 & 0.3 \end{bmatrix}$; $A^2 = \begin{bmatrix} 1 & 0.91 \\ 0 & 0.09 \end{bmatrix}$; $A^3 = \begin{bmatrix} 1 & 0.973 \\ 0 & 0.027 \end{bmatrix}$; 0

19. $C = \begin{bmatrix} 0 & 0.2 & 0.1 \\ 0 & 0.6 & 0.7 \\ 1 & 0.2 & 0.2 \end{bmatrix}$; $C^2 = \begin{bmatrix} 0.1 & 0.14 & 0.16 \\ 0.7 & 0.5 & 0.56 \\ 0.2 & 0.36 & 0.28 \end{bmatrix}$; $C^3 = \begin{bmatrix} 0.16 & 0.136 & 0.14 \\ 0.56 & 0.552 & 0.532 \\ 0.28 & 0.312 & 0.328 \end{bmatrix}$; 0.56

21. $E = \begin{bmatrix} 0.8 & 0.3 & 0 \\ 0.1 & 0.6 & 1 \\ 0.1 & 0.1 & 0 \end{bmatrix}$; $E^2 = \begin{bmatrix} 0.67 & 0.42 & 0.3 \\ 0.24 & 0.49 & 0.6 \\ 0.09 & 0.09 & 0.1 \end{bmatrix}$; $E^3 = \begin{bmatrix} 0.608 & 0.483 & 0.42 \\ 0.301 & 0.426 & 0.49 \\ 0.091 & 0.091 & 0.09 \end{bmatrix}$; 0.301

23. The first power is the given transition matrix; $\begin{bmatrix} 0.2 & 0.16 & 0.19 & 0.16 & 0.16 \\ 0.15 & 0.2 & 0.14 & 0.19 & 0.19 \\ 0.17 & 0.15 & 0.24 & 0.16 & 0.14 \\ 0.19 & 0.18 & 0.21 & 0.2 & 0.17 \\ 0.29 & 0.31 & 0.22 & 0.29 & 0.34 \end{bmatrix}$; $\begin{bmatrix} 0.17 & 0.171 & 0.18 & 0.175 & 0.167 \\ 0.178 & 0.178 & 0.163 & 0.174 & 0.184 \\ 0.171 & 0.161 & 0.191 & 0.164 & 0.158 \\ 0.191 & 0.185 & 0.197 & 0.187 & 0.182 \\ 0.29 & 0.305 & 0.269 & 0.3 & 0.309 \end{bmatrix}$;

$\begin{bmatrix} 0.1731 & 0.1709 & 0.1748 & 0.1712 & 0.1706 \\ 0.175 & 0.1781 & 0.1718 & 0.1775 & 0.1785 \\ 0.1683 & 0.1654 & 0.1753 & 0.1667 & 0.1641 \\ 0.188 & 0.1866 & 0.1911 & 0.1875 & 0.1858 \\ 0.2956 & 0.299 & 0.287 & 0.2971 & 0.301 \end{bmatrix}$; $\begin{bmatrix} 0.1719 & 0.1717 & 0.1729 & 0.1719 & 0.1714 \\ 0.1764 & 0.1769 & 0.1749 & 0.1765 & 0.1773 \\ 0.1678 & 0.1667 & 0.1701 & 0.1671 & 0.1663 \\ 0.1878 & 0.1872 & 0.1888 & 0.1874 & 0.1870 \\ 0.2961 & 0.2975 & 0.2933 & 0.2970 & 0.2981 \end{bmatrix}$; 0.1872

27. (a) 53% for Johnson and 47% for NorthClean

(b) 58.85% for Johnson and 41.15% for NorthClean

(c) 61.48% for Johnson and 38.52% for NorthClean

(d) 62.67% for Johnson and 37.33% for Northclean

29. (a) 37,500 policyholders in G_0, 10,000 in G_1, and 2500 in G_2

(b) 29,375 policyholders in G_0, 15,250 in G_1, and 5375 in G_2

(c) 24,094 policyholders in G_0, 18,163 in G_1, and 7744 in G_2 (rounded number do not sum to 50,000)

(d) $\begin{bmatrix} 0.5875 & 0.165 & 0.165 \\ 0.305 & 0.57 & 0.41 \\ 0.1075 & 0.265 & 0.425 \end{bmatrix}$ **(e)** 0.5875

31. (a) $\begin{array}{c} \\ e \\ f \\ s \end{array}\begin{array}{c} e \quad\; f \quad\;\, s \\ \begin{bmatrix} 0.9 & 0.15 & 0 \\ 0.05 & 0.75 & 0 \\ 0.05 & 0.10 & 1 \end{bmatrix}\end{array}$ **(b)** $\begin{bmatrix} 0.405 \\ 0.4675 \\ 0.1275 \end{bmatrix}$ **(c)** $\begin{bmatrix} 0.4346 \\ 0.3709 \\ 0.1945 \end{bmatrix}$ **(d)** $\begin{bmatrix} 0.4468 \\ 0.2999 \\ 0.2533 \end{bmatrix}$ **(e)** Yes; 9 years

33. (a) 2039 small, 2352 medium, 2444 large

(b) 1988 small, 2340 medium, 2507 large

(c) $\begin{bmatrix} 0.8529 & 0.0836 & 0.0020 \\ 0.1418 & 0.8080 & 0.0562 \\ 0.0053 & 0.1084 & 0.9419 \end{bmatrix}$ **(d)** 8.36% **(e)** 10.84%

35. (a) 0.1859

(b) 2.34 rabbits in group 1, 2.62 rabbits in group 2, 3.47 in group 3, and 4.56 in group 4

(c) The long-range probability of rabbits in group 1 or 2 staying in group 1 or 2 is zero.

37. (a) 43.6%, 22%, 10.2%, 23.2%, 1%

(b) 54.57%, 21.39%, 6.65%, 17.11%, 0.27%

(c) $\begin{bmatrix} 0.6387 & 0.5906 & 0.53 & 0.5041 & 0.4653 \\ 0.2119 & 0.226 & 0.2026 & 0.2107 & 0.2185 \\ 0.0418 & 0.0485 & 0.0866 & 0.0722 & 0.0834 \\ 0.1069 & 0.1336 & 0.1786 & 0.2089 & 0.2275 \\ 0.0007 & 0.0013 & 0.0022 & 0.0041 & 0.0053 \end{bmatrix}$ **(d)** 46.53% **(e)** 22.75%

39. (a) $\begin{bmatrix} 0.3484 & 0.3198 & 0.3164 \\ 0.3786 & 0.3782 & 0.3601 \\ 0.2730 & 0.3020 & 0.3235 \end{bmatrix}$ **(b)** 0.3484 **(c)** 0.3198

Exercise 15.2

For exercise . . .	1–6	7–10, 20, 25–27	11–19, 28–44
Refer to example . . .	2	3	4

W1. (0.2,0.3,0.5)   **W2.** (0.4,0.2,0.4)

1. Regular

3. Not Regular

5. Regular

7. $\begin{bmatrix} 2/5 \\ 3/5 \end{bmatrix}$ **9.** $\begin{bmatrix} 1/3 \\ 2/3 \end{bmatrix}$ **11.** $\begin{bmatrix} 5/31 \\ 19/93 \\ 59/93 \end{bmatrix}$ **13.** $\begin{bmatrix} 170/563 \\ 197/563 \\ 196/563 \end{bmatrix}$ **15.** $\begin{bmatrix} 2/7 \\ 19/42 \\ 11/42 \end{bmatrix}$ **17.** $\begin{bmatrix} 0 \\ 0 \\ 1 \end{bmatrix}$

19. $\begin{bmatrix} 1/2 \\ 7/20 \\ 3/20 \end{bmatrix}$ **21.** $\begin{bmatrix} (1-q)/(2-p-q) \\ (1-p)/(2-p-q) \end{bmatrix}$

25. $\begin{array}{c} \\ \text{Works} \\ \text{Doesn't} \\ \text{Work} \end{array}\begin{array}{c} \quad\text{Works} \quad\; \begin{array}{c}\text{Doesn't}\\\text{Work}\end{array} \\ \begin{bmatrix} 0.9 & 0.8 \\ 0.1 & 0.2 \end{bmatrix}\end{array}$; 8/9

27. (a) $\begin{bmatrix} 0.4 \\ 0.6 \end{bmatrix}$; $\begin{bmatrix} 0.53 \\ 0.47 \end{bmatrix}$; $\begin{bmatrix} 0.5885 \\ 0.4115 \end{bmatrix}$; $\begin{bmatrix} 0.614825 \\ 0.385175 \end{bmatrix}$; $\begin{bmatrix} 0.626671 \\ 0.373329 \end{bmatrix}$; $\begin{bmatrix} 0.632002 \\ 0.367998 \end{bmatrix}$; $\begin{bmatrix} 0.634401 \\ 0.365599 \end{bmatrix}$; $\begin{bmatrix} 0.635480 \\ 0.364520 \end{bmatrix}$; $\begin{bmatrix} 0.635966 \\ 0.364034 \end{bmatrix}$; $\begin{bmatrix} 0.636185 \\ 0.363815 \end{bmatrix}$

(b) 0.236364; 0.106364; 0.047864; 0.021539; 0.009693; 0.004362; 0.001963; 0.000884; 0.000398; 0.000179

(c) Roughly 0.45

(d) Each week, the difference between the probability vector and the equilibrium vector is slightly less than half of what it was the previous week.

(e) $\begin{bmatrix} 0.75 \\ 0.25 \end{bmatrix}$; $\begin{bmatrix} 0.6875 \\ 0.3125 \end{bmatrix}$; $\begin{bmatrix} 0.659375 \\ 0.340625 \end{bmatrix}$; $\begin{bmatrix} 0.646719 \\ 0.353281 \end{bmatrix}$; $\begin{bmatrix} 0.641023 \\ 0.358977 \end{bmatrix}$; $\begin{bmatrix} 0.638461 \\ 0.361539 \end{bmatrix}$; $\begin{bmatrix} 0.637307 \\ 0.362693 \end{bmatrix}$; $\begin{bmatrix} 0.636788 \\ 0.363212 \end{bmatrix}$; $\begin{bmatrix} 0.636555 \\ 0.363445 \end{bmatrix}$; $\begin{bmatrix} 0.636450 \\ 0.363550 \end{bmatrix}$;

0.113636; 0.051136; 0.023011; 0.010355; 0.004659; 0.002097; 0.000943; 0.000424; 0.000191; 0.000086; roughly 0.45.

29. 16.91% small, 28.47% medium, 54.62% large

31. (a) $\begin{bmatrix} 0.633 \\ 0.032 \\ 0.335 \end{bmatrix}$

33. Couples 0.4675; mother 0.3802; father 0.0748; relative 0.0515; other 0.0261

35. 0.6053 in type I, 0.2143 in type II, 0.0494 in type III, 0.1295 in type IV, 0.0013 in type V

37. $\begin{bmatrix} 1/3 \\ 1/3 \\ 1/3 \end{bmatrix}$

39. (a) 1.80% in group 1, 23.68% in group 2, 38.47% in group 3, and 36.04% in group 4

(b) 8

41. (c) $\begin{bmatrix} 0 & \frac{1}{2} & 0 \\ 1 & 0 & 1 \\ 0 & \frac{1}{2} & 0 \end{bmatrix}$ **(d)** Not a regular matrix   **(e)** $\begin{bmatrix} 1/4 \\ 1/2 \\ 1/4 \end{bmatrix}$

43. (b) The guard spends 3/7 of the time in front of the middle door and 2/7 of the time in front of each of the other doors.

Exercise 15.3

For exercises . . .	1–6	15, 16, 31	26(a)	7–14, 23–25, 26(b),(c), 27–30, 32, 33
Refer to example . . .	1	2	3	4

W1. $\begin{bmatrix} 7/12 & -1/6 \\ -2/3 & 1/3 \end{bmatrix}$ **W2.** $\begin{bmatrix} 7/16 & -5/16 \\ -1/16 & 3/16 \end{bmatrix}$

1. State 3 is absorbing; matrix is that of an absorbing Markov chain.

3. State 1 is absorbing; matrix is not that of an absorbing Markov chain.

5. States 2 and 4 are absorbing; matrix is that of an absorbing Markov chain.

7. $F = [2]$; $RF = \begin{bmatrix} 0.3 \\ 0.7 \end{bmatrix}$

9. $F = [3/2]$; $RF = \begin{bmatrix} 3/4 \\ 1/4 \end{bmatrix}$

11. $F = \begin{bmatrix} 1 & 1/3 \\ 0 & 4/3 \end{bmatrix}$; $RF = \begin{bmatrix} 1/3 & 4/9 \\ 2/3 & 5/9 \end{bmatrix}$

13. $F = \begin{bmatrix} 25/17 & 5/34 \\ 5/17 & 35/34 \end{bmatrix}$; $RF = \begin{bmatrix} 4/17 & 11/34 \\ 15/34 & 37/68 \\ 11/34 & 9/68 \end{bmatrix}$

15. (a) $\begin{bmatrix} 1 & \frac{1}{2} & 0 & 0 & 0 \\ 0 & 0 & \frac{1}{2} & 0 & 0 \\ 0 & \frac{1}{2} & 0 & \frac{1}{2} & 0 \\ 0 & 0 & \frac{1}{2} & 0 & 0 \\ 0 & 0 & 0 & \frac{1}{2} & 1 \end{bmatrix}$ **(b)** $F = \begin{bmatrix} \frac{3}{2} & 1 & \frac{1}{2} \\ 1 & 2 & 1 \\ \frac{1}{2} & 1 & \frac{3}{2} \end{bmatrix}$; $RF = \begin{bmatrix} \frac{3}{4} & \frac{1}{2} & \frac{1}{4} \\ \frac{1}{4} & \frac{1}{2} & \frac{3}{4} \end{bmatrix}$ **(c)** 3/4   **(d)** 1/4

17. 0.8756

19.

p	0.1	0.2	0.3	0.4	0.5	0.6	0.7	0.8	0.9
x_a	0.9999999997	0.99999905	0.99979	0.98295	0.5	0.017046	0.000209	0.00000095	0.0000000003

21. A column matrix of all 1's

23. (a) $F = \begin{bmatrix} 14.2857 & 8.5714 \\ 2.8571 & 5.7143 \end{bmatrix}$; $RF = \begin{bmatrix} 1 & 1 \end{bmatrix}$ **(b)** 1   **(c)** 17.14 years

25. (b) $F = \begin{bmatrix} 1.0625 & 0.0625 \\ 0.1875 & 1.1875 \end{bmatrix}$; $RF = \begin{bmatrix} 1 & 1 \end{bmatrix}$ **(c)** 1   **(d)** 1.25

27. (a) $\begin{bmatrix} 0.80 & 0.05 & 0 \\ 0.15 & 0.80 & 0 \\ 0.05 & 0.15 & 1 \end{bmatrix}$; $F = \begin{bmatrix} 6.154 & 1.538 \\ 4.615 & 6.154 \end{bmatrix}$; $RF = \begin{bmatrix} 1.000 & 1.000 \end{bmatrix}$ **(b)** 1   **(c)** 10.77 yr

29. (a) $\begin{bmatrix} 0.4 & 0.2 & 0 & 0.1 & 0 \\ 0.3 & 0.1 & 0 & 0.1 & 0 \\ 0.2 & 0 & 1 & 0.4 & 0 \\ 0.1 & 0.6 & 0 & 0.1 & 0 \\ 0 & 0.1 & 0 & 0.3 & 1 \end{bmatrix}$; $F = \begin{bmatrix} 2.0436 & 0.6540 & 0.2997 \\ 0.7629 & 1.4441 & 0.2452 \\ 0.7357 & 1.0354 & 1.3079 \end{bmatrix}$; $RF = \begin{array}{c} 3 \\ 5 \end{array}\begin{array}{ccc} 1 & 2 & 4 \\ \begin{bmatrix} 0.703 & 0.545 & 0.583 \\ 0.297 & 0.455 & 0.417 \end{bmatrix} \end{array}$

    (b) 0.297   **(c)** 0.455   **(d)** 0   **(e)** 0.417   **(f)** 2.04   **(g)** 1.31

31. (a)

	0	1	2	3	4	5	6	7
0	1	$\frac{1}{2}$	0	0	0	0	0	0
1	0	0	$\frac{1}{2}$	0	0	0	0	0
2	0	$\frac{1}{2}$	0	$\frac{1}{2}$	0	0	0	0
3	0	0	$\frac{1}{2}$	0	$\frac{1}{2}$	0	0	0
4	0	0	0	$\frac{1}{2}$	0	$\frac{1}{2}$	0	0
5	0	0	0	0	$\frac{1}{2}$	0	$\frac{1}{2}$	0
6	0	0	0	0	0	$\frac{1}{2}$	0	0
7	0	0	0	0	0	0	$\frac{1}{2}$	1

33. (a) $F = \begin{bmatrix} 1.6244 & 1.0071 \\ 1.0071 & 1.6244 \end{bmatrix}$; $RF = \begin{bmatrix} 0.6049 & 0.3951 \\ 0.3951 & 0.6049 \end{bmatrix}$ **(b)** 0.6049   **(c)** 0.6049

    (d) About three possessions

    (e) The team that wins the coin toss has an advantage. The team that chooses to take possession of the ball first wins 60.49% of the time.

Chapter 14 Review Exercises

For exercises . . .	1–4,13,15–26,43,45–57,49(a),50–58,60,67(a),(b)	5–10,14,27–31,44,48,59,67(b),68,69	4–12,32–38,49(b),(c) 61–65,66
Refer to section . . .	1	2	3

1. False **2.** False **3.** True **4.** False **5.** False **6.** True **7.** False **8.** False **9.** False **10.** True **11.** True **12.** True **15.** No **17.** Yes

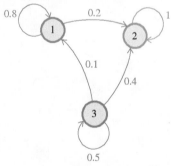

19. (a) $C = \begin{bmatrix} 0.7 & 1 \\ 0.3 & 0 \end{bmatrix}$; $C^2 = \begin{bmatrix} 0.79 & 0.7 \\ 0.21 & 0.3 \end{bmatrix}$; $C^3 = \begin{bmatrix} 0.763 & 0.79 \\ 0.237 & 0.21 \end{bmatrix}$; 0.79

21. (a) $E = \begin{bmatrix} 0.2 & 0.3 & 0 \\ 0.5 & 0.4 & 1 \\ 0.3 & 0.3 & 0 \end{bmatrix}$; $E^2 = \begin{bmatrix} 0.19 & 0.18 & 0.3 \\ 0.6 & 0.61 & 0.4 \\ 0.21 & 0.21 & 0.3 \end{bmatrix}$; $E^3 = \begin{bmatrix} 0.218 & 0.219 & 0.18 \\ 0.545 & 0.544 & 0.61 \\ 0.237 & 0.237 & 0.21 \end{bmatrix}$ **(b)** 0.219

23. $\begin{bmatrix} 0.377 \\ 0.623 \end{bmatrix}$; $\begin{bmatrix} 5/13 \\ 8/13 \end{bmatrix}$ **25.** $\begin{bmatrix} 0.492 \\ 0.264 \\ 0.244 \end{bmatrix}$; $\begin{bmatrix} 43/80 \\ 19/80 \\ 9/40 \end{bmatrix}$

27. Regular   **29.** Not regular

35. State 3 is absorbing; matrix is that of an absorbing Markov chain.

37. No absorbing states; hence, matrix is not that of an absorbing Markov chain.

39. $F = [5/4]$; $RF = \begin{bmatrix} 9/16 \\ 7/16 \end{bmatrix}$

41. $F = \begin{bmatrix} 7/4 & 1 \\ 4/5 & 8/5 \end{bmatrix}$; $RF = \begin{bmatrix} 0.55 & 0.6 \\ 0.45 & 0.4 \end{bmatrix}$

43. (a) $\begin{bmatrix} 0.5725 \\ 0.4275 \end{bmatrix}$ (b) $\begin{bmatrix} 0.6776 \\ 0.3224 \end{bmatrix}$

45. $\begin{bmatrix} 0.428 \\ 0.322 \\ 0.25 \end{bmatrix}$ **47.** $\begin{bmatrix} 0.4307 \\ 0.2839 \\ 0.2854 \end{bmatrix}$

49. (a) $\begin{bmatrix} 6.536 & 3.268 \\ 26.144 & 42.484 \end{bmatrix}$ (b) 42.484   (c) 26.144

51. 0.2   **53.** 0.4   **55.** 0.256

57. $\begin{bmatrix} 0.1945 \\ 0.5555 \\ 0.25 \end{bmatrix}$ **59.** $\begin{bmatrix} 7/36 \\ 5/9 \\ 1/4 \end{bmatrix}$

61. States 1 and 6

63. $F = \begin{bmatrix} 8/3 & 4/3 & 4/3 & 2/3 \\ 1/6 & 4/3 & 1/3 & 1/6 \\ 4/3 & 8/3 & 8/3 & 4/3 \\ 2/3 & 4/3 & 4/3 & 8/3 \end{bmatrix}$; $RF = \begin{bmatrix} 3/4 & 1/2 & 1/2 & 1/4 \\ 1/4 & 1/2 & 1/2 & 3/4 \end{bmatrix}$ **65.** 1/2

67. (a) 0.1454   (b) 0.2400   (c) 0.2094, 0.2057, 0.2018, 0.1903, 0.1929

69. (a) 59/111   (b) $\begin{array}{c} \\ 0 \\ 1 \\ 2 \end{array} \begin{array}{ccc} 0 & 1 & 2 \\ \begin{bmatrix} 0 & 9/37 & 28/37 \\ 3/37 & 0 & 9/37 \\ 34/37 & 28/37 & 0 \end{bmatrix} \end{array}$ (c) 301/775, 97/669, 7/15   (d) 0.494